The Rules of the Game

Mark A. Boyer, Series Editor

International Studies Intensives (ISI) is a book series that springs from the desire to keep students engaged in the world around them. ISI books pack a lot of information into a small space—they are meant to offer an intensive introduction to subjects often left out of the curriculum. ISI books are relatively short, visually attractive, and affordably priced.

Titles in the Series

The Rules of the Game: A Primer on International Relations,
by Mark R. Amstutz

A Tale of Two Quagmires: Iraq, Vietnam, and the Hard Lessons of War,
by Kenneth J. Campbell

Celebrity Diplomacy, by Andrew F. Cooper

People Count! Networked Individuals in Global Politics, by James N. Rosenau

Paradoxes of Power: U.S. Foreign Policy in a Changing World,
edited by David Skidmore

Global Democracy and the World Social Forums, by Jackie Smith et al.

Forthcoming

Development Wars: The Alter-Globalization Movement Meets Market Fundamentalism, by Robin Broad and John Cavanagh

Spirits Talking: Six Conversations on Right and Wrong in the Affairs of States, by Stephen D. Wrage

The Rules of the Game

A Primer on International Relations

Mark R. Amstutz

Paradigm Publishers
Boulder • London

For

Tate, Ellie, Elsa, and Brendan

green press INITIATIVE

Paradigm Publishers is committed to preserving ancient forests and natural resources. We elected to print *The Rules Of The Game* on 50% post consumer recycled paper, processed chlorine free. As a result, for this printing, we have saved:

9 Trees (40' tall and 6-8" diameter)
3,915 Gallons of Wastewater
1,574 Kilowatt Hours of Electricity
432 Pounds of Solid Waste
848 Pounds of Greenhouse Gases

Paradigm Publishers made this paper choice because our printer, Thomson-Shore, Inc., is a member of Green Press Initiative, a nonprofit program dedicated to supporting authors, publishers, and suppliers in their efforts to reduce their use of fiber obtained from endangered forests.

For more information, visit www.greenpressinitiative.org

Published in the United States by Paradigm Publishers, 3360 Mitchell Lane Suite E, Boulder, CO 80301 USA.

Paradigm Publishers is the trade name of Birkenkamp & Company, LLC, Dean Birkenkamp, President and Publisher.

Library of Congress Cataloging-in-Publication Data
Amstutz, Mark R.
The rules of the game : a primer on international relations / Mark R. Amstutz.
p. cm. — (International studies intensives)
Includes bibliographical references and index.
ISBN 978-1-59451-336-7 (hc) — ISBN 978-1-59451-337-4 (pbk)
1. International relations. 2. Game theory. I. Title.
JZ1308.A48 2008
327.101'5193—dc22
2007029905

Printed and bound in the United States of America on acid-free paper that meets the standards of the American National Standard for Permanence of Paper for Printed Library Materials.

DESIGNED AND TYPESET BY JANE RAESE

07 08 09 10 11 ❷ 5 4 3 2 1

Contents

PART III
Prospects for a New IR Game

List of IR Principles (P) and Rules (R)

Chapter 2: The Nature of the IR Game

P 2.1—Viable States Are Sovereign

P 2.2—States Must Respect the Autonomy of Other States

P 2.3—The Security and Prosperity of States Depend on
Their Own Resources

P 2.4—States Are Formally Equal

P 2.5—A State's Territory Is Inviolable

P 2.6—The Role of Coercive Force in Interstate Relations Is Declining

P 2.7—The Role of Nonstate Actors Is Expanding

P 2.8—The Influence of Global Governance Is Increasing

P 2.9—The Influence of Transnational Issues Is Rising

Chapter 3: The Players of the IR Game

P 3.1—States Are the Principal Players in the IR Game

P 3.2—States Are Unequal Because Their Capabilities Differ

P 3.3—People Have a Right to Self-Determination

P 3.4—Peoples That Succeed in Establishing a State Can Play the
IR Game

P 3.5—States Must Be Recognized by Other States before They Can
Play the IR Game

P 3.6—Prospective States Must Be Based on Former Territorial
Boundaries

P 3.7—Nonstate Actors Can Also Play the IR Game

Chapter 4: Goals and Strategies for Playing the IR Game

P 4.1—Foreign Policy Is the Means by Which States Pursue Interests in Global Society

P 4.2—The National Interest Represents the Fundamental Wants of a Nation

P 4.3—The Global Interest Represents the Common Concerns of the International Community

P 4.4—Power Is the Currency Used to Pursue Foreign Policy Goals

P 4.5—Diplomacy Can Facilitate the Peaceful Resolution of International Disputes

P 4.6—States Can Influence Other States through Economic Sanctions

P 4.7—States Can Influence Other States through Military Threats

P 4.8—States Can Compel Other States with Force

Chapter 5: Political Rules of the IR Game

R 5.1—Make the Safety of Your Country a Top Priority

R.5.2—Take Care of Your Nation First, Then Worry about Others

R 5.3—Resolve Disputes Peacefully

R 5.4—Do What Is Necessary to Protect Vital Interests

R 5.5—Keep Your Powder Dry

R 5.6—Mind Your Own Business

R 5.7—Build Coalitions and Alliances to Advance Foreign Policy Interests Multilaterally

R 5.8—Support International Institutions, but Do Not Rely on Them for Your Nation's Prosperity or Security

R 5.9—Protect Human Rights in Other Nations When Feasible

R 5.10—Promote and Protect Global Public Goods

Chapter 6: Economic Rules of the IR Game

P 6.1—Markets Are Economically Desirable

P 6.2—Governments Can Help Markets Work

Preface

THIS SHORT BOOK INTRODUCES International Relations (IR) using the metaphor of game. It uses the metaphor to highlight the nature or logic of IR and to illuminate the most important principles and rules governing international affairs among states. Since IR requires multifaceted knowledge of history, politics, economics, and law, most introductory texts of this field are long and comprehensive. Whereas comprehensive texts are an excellent source of conceptual, theoretical, and empirical information, they also can overwhelm the beginning student.

This book offers a different way to introduce IR. Rather than covering most of the key themes of the field, it focuses on the fundamental ideas, concepts, and principles. To ensure accessibility and coherence, international politics is presented through the metaphor of game. As I note in Chapter 1, the metaphor is used as an organizing principle for a number of reasons. First, since a game is a competitive, interactive activity, it emphasizes the dynamic nature of international politics. Second, the metaphor provides a means by which to introduce IR in a concise, coherent way. And third, the game metaphor offers a structure by which to highlight key elements of the IR field—namely, the nature and goals of the game, the rules of the game, and strategies for playing.

The book is divided into three parts. In Chapter 1, I describe the nature and value of the game metaphor and then explain the nature and role of principles and rules in structuring the IR game. In Part I (Chapters 2–4), I present foundational principles governing the IR game, focusing on the nature of the IR game, the actors that are entitled to play the game, and the principal strategies used by states in playing the IR game. In Chapter 2, I set forth the major features of the traditional Westphalian game. I then review some important revisions in this system, noting in particular the impact of the Cold War and globalization on the contemporary world. In Chapter 3, I describe the nature and role of major players of the IR game as well as the principles used to decide which political communities can become full players. Although sovereign states remain the primary players of IR, the postmodern world has resulted in a growing number of weak or failed states as well as a rise in nonstate actors that influence world politics. The growth in weak states is partly the result of increased civil strife in existing states, as ethnonationalistic groups demand greater political autonomy from governing authorities. The dramatic expansion in the number and influence of nonstate actors is partly the result of globalization and more particularly the increase in functional cooperation in areas of transnational concern, such as human rights, global warming, and health care. In Chapter 4, I describe how states play the IR game, focusing on the nature and role of foreign policy and some of the different ways that states seek to advance their vital interests in global society.

Part II (Chapters 5–8) sets forth the most important political, economic, legal, and moral rules structuring the IR game. Although this section focuses on rules, it also discusses core principles not covered earlier in Part I. As a result, Chapters 6, 7, and 8 present economic, legal, and moral principles that influence the IR game. Because many IR scholars view power as the decisive element in structuring global politics, Chapter 5, on political rules, might be considered the most important. Here I present the most influential rules that govern contemporary IR. Chapter 6 examines the most important principles and rules governing international economic relations. Because of the extraordinary success of market-based economies, the global economy has become increasingly influenced by institutions and rules based on a liberal political economic worldview. Chapter 7 examines some of the major principles and rules governing the international legal order. Although law plays a much more limited role in global relations than in domestic society, international legal principles and rules are nevertheless important in structuring the behavior of states. What is remarkable about international law is that states comply with norms even in the absence of an authoritative enforcement agency. Finally, I examine the role of international political morality in Chapter 8. Despite global cultural diversity, states share a common political morality that helps to structure international affairs. These shared moral norms provide a basis for action in such areas as human rights, the use of force, humanitarian relief, and environmental protection.

In Part III (Chapter 9), I conclude by exploring the future evolution of the IR game. I first examine the contemporary dynamics between globalization and political fragmentation along with the current tension between state sovereignty and globalism. Based on these contemporary challenges, I sketch three potential futures. These three models are based on the two dominant IR paradigms, realism and idealism/institutionalism, along with the emerging postmodern perspective arising from increased transnational governance and global integration. Although states are the major players in both the realist and idealist models, the postmodern world involves the growing influence of nonstate actors and a diminishing role for states. In effect, the postmodern model represents a significant departure from the classical system based on state sovereignty.

In preparing this book I have benefited from the encouragement, support, and research assistance of numerous people. First, I thank my students in IR 175 at Wheaton College for providing enthusiastic support for many of the ideas presented here and, in particular, for their encouragement in using the game metaphor to introduce IR. Second, I thank Jennifer Knerr, vice president at Paradigm Publishers, who saw the merits of using the game metaphor to present the essential elements and logic of IR. Third, I greatly appreciate the invaluable research and editorial assistance from my two teaching assistants, Natalie Murray and Anne Snyder. Fourth, I am grateful to the external reviewers whose comments and suggestions helped to improve the arguments of this book. Finally, I thank my wife, Donna, for her continuing love and support of my role as a teacher and scholar. This book is dedicated to my four grandchildren—Tate, Ellie, Elsa, and Brendan—in the hope that their world will be more peaceful, humane, prosperous, and just.

Mark R. Amstutz

ONE

International Relations
as a Game

In JUNE AND JULY 2006, Germany hosted the World Cup soccer championship. Soccer, the world's most popular sport, is a simple yet exciting game. It is simple because, unlike more complex games like rugby or American football, the rules of the game are few and accessible. The drama and excitement of the game arises out of the hope for success based on the skills of individual players and the effectiveness of team strategies in both defending the goal and attacking the opposing team. Although the superior skills of top players were evident throughout the 2006 World Cup, the play that perhaps best captured the extraordinary abilities of some of the best players was a goal by David Beckham, a British midfielder in the Ecuador–United Kingdom match. Beckham's goal was extraordinary because he took a free kick from about thirty-five yards from the goal, curving the ball over a defensive wall of Ecuadorian players and eluding the reach of the goalkeeper.

The importance of rules was also evident in the World Cup's final match between Italy and France. With the score tied 1–1 after ninety minutes of regulation time, the match was extended to two fifteen-minute overtime periods. In the second overtime, French captain Zinedine Zidane and Italian defender Marco Materazzi were walking down the field, when Zidane, angered by an ethnic slur from Materazzi, lowered his head and rammed it into Materazzi's chest. In response, the referee ejected Zidane for unsportsmanlike conduct. Although France managed to hold off Italy in the second overtime, in the subsequent shoot-out Italy prevailed 5–3. Later the French coach noted that the ejection had "changed everything." This incident, like Beckham's goal, illustrates the importance of competition within a structure of rules. Indeed, athletic events are exciting precisely because they are governed by the rules of the game.

The Metaphor of Game

This book uses the metaphor of an interactive game to introduce the subject of international relations. It does so for several reasons. First, the game metaphor provides a useful organizing principle to highlight the dynamic, interactive nature of IR. International affairs are continually changing as states shift priorities, maximize political power, compete for scarce economic resources, pursue shared global interests, devise new multilateral initiatives, and establish new institutions to foster greater international peace and prosperity. Despite the continuing political and economic changes in the world, however, the fundamental principles and institutions of global society have remained largely constant. Thus, the second reason for using the game metaphor is to highlight the foundational architecture of the IR game—the institutions, rules, and principles that structure international affairs.

Third, the game metaphor is used to highlight the coherent and cohesive nature of the IR field. IR is frequently introduced as a collection of different areas of knowledge—national security, foreign policy, international political economy, arms control, international law and organization, diplomacy, and global resource management—with little emphasis given to the underlying rules and principles that unify the IR field. This book therefore focuses on the essential logic of IR by describing and analyzing the foundational ideas and structures of global politics.

Fourth, the game metaphor is an appropriate pedagogical device because games have played an important role in both the study and practice of international affairs. For example, scholars have used games to model IR in wartime (war games), to highlight the gains from economic cooperation (positive-sum games), and to illuminate the competitive nature of international political relations (zero-sum games). Additionally, scholars have applied game theory to illuminate the logic of decision making in different environmental contexts such as cooperation on national security affairs (arms control) or the challenge of responding to serious security threats (deterrence).

Finally, games have contributed importantly to global cooperation (such as the World Olympics or World Cup soccer), to symbolic victories (such as when American Bobby Fischer defeated Russian Boris Spassky in the 1972 World Chess Championship in Reykjavik, Iceland), and to spearhead normalization of relations between two enemy states (such as the 1971 Ping Pong Diplomacy between the People's Republic of China and the United States).

It is important to stress that the game metaphor is not meant to trivialize international relations. IR is serious business, dealing with national welfare and at times with life and death. Because international peace and global prosperity are not automatic by-products of international relations, the conditions fostering global order and economic expansion must be created. How well states fulfill their responsibilities to their people and to the world at large therefore will profoundly affect the quality of life for many of the world's six billion inhabitants. The challenge in studying IR is to develop an understanding of the nature of IR, especially its foundational principles and institutions, and then acquire knowledge about the practices and policies most conducive to human dignity.

The logic of a game involves knowledge of three elements: first, the nature of the game and how victory is achieved; second, preconditions for players—that is, standards of eligibility for players of the game; and third, the rules of the game. In presenting the logic of the IR game, I describe the nature of the IR game, the eligibility of players, and the strategies for playing the game. I then examine the key principles and rules governing the IR game. I structure my analysis by focusing on political, economic, legal, and moral "rules of the game."

A major aim of international relations, a major subfield of political science, is to explain the public actions of states and other international persons in global society. Although international affairs involve social, cultural, religious, economic, and political transactions, IR is chiefly concerned with the political interactions of states. IR—which is essentially politics among nations—explores the quest for peace, security, and justice within the international society of nation-states. Fundamentally, its focus is on the public or society-wide dimensions of the international actions of states and other nonstate actors.

The aim here is to provide a roadmap to the field's key concepts and theories and to describe the principal norms governing the behavior of states in the IR game. The game metaphor is useful because it emphasizes the dynamic nature of IR over a static, institutional, or legal perspective. The metaphor is also helpful because it calls attention to distinctive features of the game, the eligibility of players, how the game is played, and alternative strategies for playing the game.

The IR game can be compared to chess, a complex game in which each player has sixteen pieces—a king and queen, two bishops, two knights, two rooks, and eight pawns. Like the varied chess pieces, each with a distinct role, IR players (states) also vary greatly in their resources and capabilities. Those with more wealth and power, like the queen and rooks in chess, have greater flexibility in determining the outcome of the game than less-influential players. This does not mean, however, that lesser players are unimportant. Indeed, although pawns have little flexibility and are the least valuable pieces, they play a crucial role in chess, because the loss or misplacement of one pawn can significantly affect the outcome of the game. Similarly, developments among peripheral states can affect the course of major conflicts. For example, during the Cold War, the United States and the Soviet Union carried out their superpower ideological conflict through proxy wars in numerous Third World countries, including Afghanistan, Angola, Dominican Republic, El Salvador, Ethiopia, Guatemala, Korea, Nicaragua, and Vietnam. In addition, IR, like chess, is a competitive game whose outcome is determined by strategy—that is, by the rational calculation of short-term and long-term gains in light of the actions and responses of other players. IR strategy, like chess, is therefore a dynamic process whose evolution is dependent upon the interactions of players. Finally, chess and IR also share flexibility in how games are terminated. Although chess typically ends in either victory or loss, it can also lead to a draw or loss by forfeiture. Although many IR conflicts end in victory or defeat for political opponents, disputes can also result in a stalemate where players must learn to live with partition or unsettled claims. This is the case with the de facto partition of Cyprus and the failure to establish a permanent territorial settlement between Jews and Palestinians in the Holy Land.

Although IR is similar to a game, IR is not strictly comparable to an athletic contest like soccer or to a board game like chess. To begin with, whereas the rules of competitive games generally remain fixed, those in IR tend to be under continuous challenge and revision. Thus, the rules for dominoes, chess, or soccer have remained largely the same over time. For example, the size of a soccer ball or the dimensions of a football field have changed little in the past fifty years. The rules governing IR, however, are constantly being reformed—partly in response to emerging problems in global society and also in response to the changing nature of states' interests and actions in the world.

A second difference between conventional games and IR is that in the former the rules tend to be clear and unambiguous. Indeed, in most games the rules are so explicit and widely accepted that no third party is needed to oversee the application of the rules. Thus, in simple games like dominoes or checkers, the players themselves ensure fairness by the honest and faithful application of the game's rules. However, in more complex sporting events, such as football, rugby, and basketball, an umpire or referee might be necessary to ensure the impartial application of rules and to make authoritative judgments about players' actions. Unlike simple or complex competitive games, the norms and rules of IR are often uncertain, unclear, or contested. And even when rules are clear and widely accepted—as with the norms of state sovereignty and nonintervention—states can interpret them and apply them in widely different ways. Most importantly, because no central political authority exists in the international community of states, no authoritative third party exists to interpret and apply norms to international disputes.

A third distinction between conventional games and IR is found in the meaning of victory. In competitive games, a victor is one who achieves the largest gains relative to other players. In this context, the game produces a winner and one or more losers. In international affairs, by contrast, the notion of winning is ambiguous. This is so because the foreign policy goals tend to vary, depending in part on the values, interests, capabilities, and resources of states. To be sure, most states desire political independence, territorial security, international political influence, economic prosperity, and a stable, peaceful global order. But the relative priority of goals such as these will vary among states. A small country whose existence is threatened by larger neighboring states will devote far more resources, proportionately, to military defense than a large, powerful country that is not facing major external threats. Moreover, states whose security and political sovereignty are assured are likely to make social, economic, and scientific cooperation far more a priority than states facing serious domestic civil strife or international aggression.

A fourth difference between global politics and conventional games is that whereas the latter are typically played with two or more players in a predictable context, the IR game is played in a wide variety of ways, ranging from isolation to global engagement, from bilateral competition to multilateral cooperation. For example, Denmark and the Netherlands have historically pursued a vigorous global agenda. Even though these two countries are small, during the seventeenth and eighteenth centuries they pursued a global agenda by acquiring colonial territories, and in the modern era they have pursued a strategy of peaceful political and economic engagement with most countries. By contrast, during the Cold War era, Albania followed an isolationist, reclusive strategy, maintaining little contact with other countries. At times, major powers have intervened in neighboring states, preventing them from maintaining normal relations with other member states. This is illustrated by China's invasion of Tibet in 1950 and Indonesia's intervention in East Timor in 1975, after the Portuguese gave up colonial control of the territory.

Perhaps the most significant difference between competitive games and IR is the variety of different patterns found in global society. In the early nineteenth century, the IR game was structured multilaterally, with six or seven major European powers providing global order through a system known as "balance of power." During the Cold War years of 1950 to 1990, global order was maintained by a fundamental equilibrium between two superpowers, the Soviet Union and the United States. This bipolar system encouraged countries to become aligned with either of the two superpowers or affiliated with an intermediary group known as the Nonaligned Movement (NAM). The IR game is therefore played in a variety of ways, ranging from unilateralism to bilateralism or multilateralism, and from close cooperation to intense conflict. The drama in IR arises from the continually shifting nature in which the game is played, as players respond to domestic political changes and to international political and economic developments. Box 1.1 illustrates the historic shift in U.S.–China relations in 1972 as the two countries move from isolation toward engagement.

A final, related difference between competitive games and IR lies in the different outcomes of the two. Typically, sporting events result in win-lose outcomes. Such games are known as zero-sum games because the gain of one player or team must come at the expense of an opposing player or team. Some interstate relations fit into this win-lose framework, such as when one state defeats another in war. For example, when

♟   ♟   ♟

Box 1.1 The Changing IR Game:
China versus the United States

Throughout the 1950s and 1960s, China (formally known as the People's Republic of China, or PRC) and the United States did not maintain diplomatic relations. Although both states were involved in the global IR game, they refused to deal directly with each other. The absence of direct ties was a result of the emergence of Communist rule in China in 1949. After Communist guerrillas, led by Mao Tse-tung, defeated the Nationalists under Gen. Chiang Kai-shek, the Nationalist forces fled to the island of Taiwan and established a government there. Because the United States, along with other Western states, regarded the Nationalist regime as the legitimate government of China, it maintained diplomatic relations with Taiwan, maintaining no ties with the PRC.

In 1971, President Richard Nixon directed his national security advisor, Henry Kissinger, to begin exploring the possibility of moving toward political accommodation with Mao's Communist regime. Several developments prompted Nixon to explore this high-risk initiative. First, because of a growing breach in the 1960s between China and the Soviet Union, Nixon thought that China might be open to accommodation with the West. Second, the president thought that China might be helpful not only in containing the Soviet Union but also in helping to bring about an end to a bitter and costly war in Vietnam. Third, Nixon was also aware that, given China's size and strategic location, a majority of states would in time consider the Communist regime the legitimate government of China. As a result, China eventually would be admitted into the United Nations and gain Taiwan's seat in the General Assembly and Security Council. As Kissinger later explained, "We moved to China . . . to shape a global equilibrium."[1]

Mao was also interested in closer ties with the United States. His economic policies under the Great Leap Forward had been disastrous, and the explosion of ideological radicalism under the Cultural Revolution in the 1960s had devastated the country economically and politically. Additionally, the rift with the former USSR had left China politically isolated. China was therefore eager to become more engaged in global affairs and to enhance its international credibility by developing closer ties with the United States.

After long and intense preparations, Kissinger made a secret exploratory trip to Beijing in July 1971. As a result of successful talks with Chinese leaders, Kissinger announced that President Nixon had accepted China's invitation to visit China in order to facilitate the normalization of bilateral relations and exchange views on matters of mutual concern. For Mao and his premier, Chou En-lai, the primary concern was the issue of

Taiwan. Since Taiwan and China each had a government, China was eager for the reunification of the two communities under Communist control. Nixon's historic trip in February 1972 did not resolve the Taiwan issue,[2] but it did lay the foundation for further political accommodation that resulted in full diplomatic relations in 1979. Sensing that the "China opening" would alter the dynamics of global politics, Nixon declared at the end of his trip, "this was the week that changed the world."[3]

From the perspective of a game, the China opening illuminates a number of lessons. First, although IR often involves declarations, treaties, accords, threats, and overt conflict, the development of understanding and accommodation also relies on subtle gestures and symbols. Because of distrust and limited contact between the two societies, the move toward political accommodation and restoration of bilateral ties required secrecy, cross-cultural sensitivity, and time. Second, political accommodation often requires that the negotiations focus on small, less-significant issues. Had China demanded at the outset of the talks that the United States withdraw its military support and break diplomatic relations with Taiwan, no accommodation would have been possible. Third, accommodation with enemies is possible when actors focus on their shared, fundamental interests. In this account, it is clear that both Mao and Nixon were guided by the realist credo articulated by Lord Palmerston, the influential nineteenth-century British statesman: "We have no eternal allies, and we have no perpetual enemies. Our interests are eternal and perpetual."[4] Finally, IR is not a single game but a series of games played at different levels—local, regional, bilateral, and multilateral. The decision by China and the United States to resume playing the IR game with each other influenced not only their bilateral ties but also the global political chessboard, especially their strategic relations with their mutual opponent, the Soviet Union.

Notes

1. Quoted in Margaret Macmillan, *Nixon and Mao: The Week That Changed the World* (New York: Random House, 2007), 122.

2. The different perspectives on Taiwan are set forth in the so-called Shanghai Communiqué. Although both countries affirmed that China and Taiwan are one country, the Chinese declared that the PRC was the sole government of China, and the United States stated that the resolution of the dispute needed to be carried out peacefully and solely by the Chinese people.

3. Macmillan, *Nixon and Mao*, xxi.

4. Quoted in Macmillan, *Nixon and Mao*, 9.

NATO officials demanded that Yugoslavia military and police forces be removed from Kosovo in 1999, Slobodan Milošević, the president of Serbia, refused. But after more than two months of intensive bombing by NATO forces that resulted in widespread destruction of Serbian infrastructure, Milošević decided to accept NATO's demands. Hence, the contest was a victory for NATO and a loss for Serbia.

IR can also result in lose-lose outcomes, however, where both states suffer substantial economic and military losses as well as a decline in reputation. Some domestic and transnational conflicts, such as the ongoing intractable dispute between Nationalists and Loyalists in Northern Ireland and Palestinians and Israelis in the Holy Land, are of this sort. In the Arab–Israeli conflict, Israel has achieved substantial gains in that it has maintained and increased its territorial security, even when it has been forced to devote significant financial resources to military defense. Since Israel came into existence in 1948, it has fought five major interstate wars, and since the late 1980s it has faced three major Palestinian insurrections (intifadas) involving demonstrations, civil disturbances, and terrorism. Although Israeli armed forces have succeeded in repulsing armed action by radical Muslim groups (e.g., Islamic Jihad and Hamas), the conflict remains unresolved. Neither side has won, and because of the ongoing suffering of Palestinian peoples and the high level of resources that Israel must devote to defense, the conflict remains a lose-lose situation.

Occasionally, IR relations can result in win-win outcomes. These so-called positive-sum games maximize collective gains for all through peaceful and cooperative action in the pursuit of shared objectives. International trade illustrates well this win-win type of game, because a rise in trade can lead to mutual gains for both parties as each increases its productive efficiency and thereby expands the availability of goods and services for consumers. For example, China's economic growth has been fueled by a dramatic rise in its exports. The modernization of the Chinese economy has not only greatly improved living conditions in China, but it has also benefited consumers in developed countries who are able to purchase industrial products at a lower cost than would have been otherwise possible. Thus, as the example of China suggests, international trade can result in win-win outcomes for all trading parties concerned.

The Nature and Role
of Ideas, Principles, and Rules

Ideas

In seeking to explain international relations, scholars emphasize the role of ideas, rules (or norms), and institutions. *Ideas* are generally defined as beliefs or principles that establish acceptable state goals, behavior patterns, and methods of conflict resolution.[1] Ideas are important because they provide concepts that structure the behavior of state and nonstate actors and the intellectual and conceptual building blocks that guide the analysis of global politics. Ideas are like a map that inform and guide action. According to Daniel Philpott, an IR scholar, ideas influence IR in two important ways: First, they shape people's identities and thereby affect their wants, interests, and goals; and second, ideas influence individual and collective behavior and are therefore a form of social power.[2] As Philpott notes, "ideas do not freely remake the world in their own image, but they are inestimably effectual. Ideas are a form of power, and are often a partner to other forms of power—and this, in intricate ways."[3]

Because ideas establish the framework for governmental goal-setting, they help establish the foreign policy goals of states. These core goals, defined as a country's *national interest,* provide not only direction but also inspiration for a state's foreign policy. Typically, the national interest is concerned with the maintenance of political sovereignty, territorial security, and economic prosperity of a country. Ideas also provide the ideals for discerning the *global interest*—the common transnational wants and concerns of states. Whereas the national interest is concerned with advancing national goals, the global interest defines the shared ideals and vision of the international community.

These latter concerns—often expressed as *international public goods*—involve the establishment of conditions that are conducive to a more stable, humane, and prosperous global society. Collective or public goods are those shared conditions that are freely available to all members of society, regardless of who contributed to their development.[4] Domestic public goods include an effective criminal justice system, protection of property rights, a reliable highway system, clean air, and a law enforcement system. Examples of international collective goods include a fair and efficient international economic order, international peace, a clean atmosphere, protection of endangered species, and airline safety regulations. Just as the rule of law, a stable currency, and a modern highway system are important goods in domestic society, so, too, a peaceful and stable international political order and an efficient international economic system are necessary for the security and economic development of nations. But whereas government typically takes the lead in creating and sustaining domestic public goods, the task of building and maintaining international public goods is far more difficult in global society because of the absence of a central authority. As a result, the quest for global public goods is generally carried out by the collaborative action of states, international governmental organizations (IGOs), and nongovernmental organizations (NGOs). For example, the 1992 Earth Summit, a UN-sponsored conference on environmental protection and economic growth that brought together more than twenty thousand governmental officials and NGO representatives, resulted in the adoption of a number of initiatives to encourage sustainable economic development and environmental protection.

The role of ideas in global affairs is powerfully illustrated in Michael Mandelbaum's *Ideas That Conquered the World.* In that book, Mandelbaum, a leading scholar of IR, argues that the dominance of three ideas—that war is not an acceptable tool of foreign policy, that democracy is the most humane and peaceful governmental system, and that markets are the most effective institutions in fostering economic growth—has helped to promote peace, freedom, and prosperity in the world.[5] Although significant poverty, war, and instability still persist in the international system, Mandelbaum shows that the powerful influence of political liberalism (individual rights and democratic government) and economic liberalism (capitalism and free trade) has resulted in the expansion of democracy in the world, increased economic growth and reduction in poverty, and a decline in the use of war as a means of resolving international disputes.

Historically, IR scholars have sought to understand global politics by focusing on factors such as the nature and role of states, the nature and role of power, foreign policy interests, and the role of international institutions. The two dominant traditions in IR, realism and idealism (often referred to as liberalism or institutionalism), emphasize these material, objective conditions in the analysis of IR. As I note in Chapter 5, *realism* focuses on the behavior of states and in particular on their quest for security, whereas *idealism* emphasizes the promotion of peaceful interstate cooperation through the development of institutions. Because ideas also have a significant, independent role in IR, it is important to incorporate insights from *constructivism*—the relatively new IR tradition that emphasizes the role of ideas in global affairs.[6]

Principles and Rules

In this book I emphasize two types of ideas—Principles (P) and Rules (R). *International principles* are fundamental beliefs, values, or doctrines that structure knowledge and human action. Principles are general and conceptual. Unlike rules, they do not provide a specific guide to action. Rather, they establish concepts and assumptions that shape the beliefs, values, and individual and collective actions of humans in global society. Principles can range from descriptive, regulatory concepts to ideals or utopian goals. Descriptive principles are conceptual building blocks that define basic beliefs and assumptions about the functioning of the existing political world. Examples of descriptive principles include ideas such as human rights, balance of power, political self-determination (the claim that peoples have an inherent right to autonomous rule), and sovereignty (supreme authority within the boundaries of a state). Prescriptive (or normative) principles, by contrast, set forth ideas that are associated with a desirable behavioral outcome. They are considered prescriptive because they establish obligations, which if fulfilled, will lead to a more prosperous, humane, and just world order. Examples of such principles include nonintervention (the prohibition of interference in the internal affairs of other states), equality of states (the claim that members of the society of states are formally equal), nonproliferation of weapons of mass destruction (WMD), and peaceful settlement of disputes.

International rules are implicit or explicit guidelines that define rights and duties of states and other relevant actors. Because rules specify behavioral guidelines for participants in global society, they establish the basic structure of the IR game. Because rules define both desirable actions and undesirable behaviors, they are both proscriptive and prescriptive. Raymond Cohen, a political scientist, has written that rules "indicate the limits of permissible conduct, thereby permitting conflict to be contained, and act as guidelines for desirable behavior, thereby facilitating active cooperation."[7] Unlike principles, which are general concepts, international rules are specific standards of behavior derived from widely shared practices, informal accords, or formal treaties. Because no central governing authority exists in the international community, rules almost always emerge from the implicit or explicit cooperative actions of states. Whether the rules are tacit or explicit, formal or informal, they perform the vital task of fostering cooperation, inhibiting conflict, promoting global order, and facilitating conflict resolution. Examples of international rules include the responsibility to protect human rights, the duty to settle international disputes peacefully, the responsibility to respect the autonomy and political independence of other states, and the responsibility to protect the global environment.

Rules can also be distinguished in terms of their purpose.[8] *Constitutive rules* establish the principles for defining who can participate in the game of global politics. Such rules are constitutive because they establish the standards for becoming a participating member of global society. Examples of constitutive rules include the right of national political self-determination and the right of political equality once the right of self-rule has been established. *Regulative rules,* by contrast, establish the fundamental behavioral architecture of global society. They specify rights and obligations of member states, thereby fostering international order and facilitating transnational cooperation.

Because the establishment and maintenance of international society is essentially a political task, IR typically emphasizes the political dimensions of global politics. But IR is not simply structured by political power. Rather, it is a multidimensional task involving economic transactions, religious practices, legal principles, moral obligations, and other related elements. Accordingly, in this book I examine a variety of rules that influence the international behavior of states, focusing on four different types—political, economic, legal, and moral. These various regulative rules, coupled with the constitutive rules defining membership, provide the foundational rules of the IR game. As such they can collectively be regarded as the unwritten constitution of global society.

As noted previously, principles provide the primary building blocks for the field of IR. Because they set forth the major concepts by which the IR game is conceived, they structure how people perceive world politics and the international system itself. To be sure, principles are not self-validating. Rather, one's understanding of international affairs will be strongly conditioned by how core concepts are defined and applied.

Because core ideas and principles are structured in a variety of predetermined patterns, these alternative perspectives—also called *paradigms*—provide alternative worldviews of global politics. In competitive sports, these different perspectives are illustrated in the different strategies that teams use in playing the game. Some football teams, for example, concentrate their resources on defense, seeking to emphasize resources on stopping either a passing offense or a running game. Other football teams might concentrate their offense on running the ball and throwing relatively few passes. Still others might pursue a balanced game. The importance of overall strategy is also evident in other sports, such as soccer, basketball, and baseball, where professional teams become known for distinctive strategies built around the relative strength of key players.

In international politics, government officials, along with scholars who study IR, often hold widely different conceptions of the world and how to play the IR game. Although these different IR perspectives might share a common conceptual vocabulary, they give different priority to concepts and principles and make different assumptions on the nature of the IR game. For example, a feminist perspective of IR is likely to emphasize the development of human cooperation and to minimize power relationships, especially the role of coercive force. By contrast, an idealist perspective is likely to give primacy to institutions, especially international law and international governmental organizations, and to view the rising influence of functional transnational networks as a beneficial development. Finally, realists are likely to emphasize the danger inherent in a world society where every state is ultimately responsible for its own security and well-being.

Paradigms are not true or false but rather cognitive maps that structure our conception of global realities. Because a major aim in studying IR is to explain global politics, the usefulness of paradigms lies in their ability to explain the existing world and contribute to the development of a more peaceful and humane global society. Unlike principles, which are general and descriptive, rules establish specific behavioral expectations.

IR rules perform four important tasks in the international community. First, they are like "sticks"—inhibiting actions that are considered detrimental to the international community. Like highway rules, IR rules specify which actions are permissible and which ones are prohibited. The rule of nonintervention, for example, indicates that states may not interfere in the domestic affairs of another state.

Second, rules serve as "carrots," encouraging desirable, beneficial behavior. In effect, rules are teaching devices for fostering actions regarded as beneficial. The sovereignty norm, for example, encourages governments to focus on the security and economic and social well-being of their people. Similarly, the norm of peaceful settlement of disputes encourages member states to resolve conflicts without resorting to force.

Third, rules help to establish and maintain an international community. Because community is impossible without order, and order is impossible without standards of behavior, IR rules are the political and economic pillars of global society—the foundational architecture of the international community. States, like individuals, desire to maximize individual freedom, but the liberty that is desired is not a disordered, unpredictable, chaotic environment but rather an ordered liberty in the context of an international community. Thus, rules in the international community provide the guidelines for ensuring freedom within the structure of international society.

Finally, rules are important because they shape expectations. Just as law serves as a teacher in domestic society, international rules perform an educative task in structuring the goals of member states.

The Interrelationship of Principles and Rules

This book focuses on four types of rules governing global society: political, economic, legal, and moral. Although economic principles and rules tend to function apart from the others, political, legal, and moral rules are strongly connected. Indeed, they often represent different dimensions of a similar concept or value. Thus, the idea of international human rights is expressed in moral, legal, and political terms. More specifically, human rights are based partly on moral values, expressed through legal claims, and asserted and defended as part of the political dynamics of the contemporary international community. Similarly, the claim of state sovereignty is regarded as a basic political principle that has been developed into an international legal doctrine and justified in moral language because it legitimizes a community's freedom of action in global society. The notion of pacific settlement of international disputes also illustrates the complementary nature of rules: According to political rule 5.3, states must resolve conflicts without resorting to war, and this political responsibility is reinforced by the legal rule 7.4 that imposes a legal duty to resolve conflicts peacefully. Because rules emerge

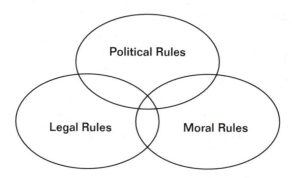

FIGURE 1.1 Interdependence of Political, Legal, and Moral Rules

from foundational principles, a close correspondence also exists between the two. For example, the sovereignty of states is a fundamental principle of global society (P 2.1) that is reinforced as a legal principle (P 7.1 and P 7.2) and a legal rule (R 7.2) and frequently as a moral entitlement (P 8.2). The close interrelationship of political, legal, and moral dimensions of rules is illustrated in Figure 1.1.

It is also important to stress that rules and principles are not necessarily complementary. Sometimes conflict arises between principles themselves. For example, although a fundamental principle of the IR game is the formal equality of states (P 2.4), in practice states differ in size, influence, and level of economic development. As a result, although the IR game is based on the idea of legal equality, IR players themselves vary greatly in their capabilities—a reality acknowledged in Principle 3.2, which states "states are unequal because their capabilities differ." A second type of conflict arises when a principle is undermined by a rule, or vice versa. For instance, a basic principle of the IR game is the obligation to not threaten or use force, but this norm is contradicted by states' legal and moral right of self-defense (R 8.2). Finally, rules might come into conflict with other rules. For example, a basic political rule of the IR game is the duty to respect the autonomy of other states. Rule 5.6 calls on states to "mind their own business," while Rule 7.3 seemingly violates this rule by suggesting that sovereignty may be violated in "exceptional circumstances," such as the halting of genocide or other egregious human rights abuses. In short, the complexity of the IR game derives from the inherent tension and inevitable conflict among rules and principles.

The International Community

Fundamentally, IR is concerned with the politics of global society. Because the major players of the IR game are states, the international com-

munity comprises distinct political actors, each with its own people, territorial configuration, history, culture, moral values, and political and economic institutions. How should this community of states be conceived?

Alternative Conceptions of the International Community

One way is to view the international community as a perfunctory system
that facilitates interaction among its players. When actors interact repeatedly, they develop shared patterns of action that result in common
principles and tacit or explicit rules. Such norms are important because
they structure and sustain interaction among the players and thereby
contribute to the institutionalization of a system of states. A *system of
states* is a natural by-product of states' international relations, because
their own national security and prosperity are dependent on each other's
capabilities and initiatives. And because states compete for power, scarce
material resources, and other goods, peace is not an automatic by-product of interstate relations. According to the system perspective, the world
is not a moral or political community of shared values and interests;
rather, it is a conglomeration of independent states, each seeking to maximize its own interests in a decentralized community where every member state is independent and free. But just as any club or association
needs to be guided by goals, principles, and rules if it is to be sustained,
so, too, the system of states requires "rules of the game" in order to
maintain the international community.

Another way of conceiving the international community is to view
the world as a *society of states*. Whereas a "system" is simply a means of
facilitating the interaction of players, a "society" represents a community
of actors that share values, interests, and a sense of belonging and that
are bound by certain commitments and ideals. Hedley Bull, one of the
first scholars to view the international community as an international society, suggests that "a society of states . . . exists when a group of states,
conscious of certain common interests and common values, forms a society in the sense that they conceive themselves to be bound by a common set of rules in their relations with one another, and share in the
working of common institutions."[9] Although a society of states presupposes a functioning international system based on interactions guided by
principles and rules, it goes beyond a system in that it presupposes a
community of shared interests and values. To be sure, although the social and cultural ties among states are frail, the reality of an international
society is evident by the fact that states share common interests, pursue
transnational concerns, undertake initiatives that transcend their own
national well-being, abide by accepted international rules, and fulfill obligations toward other member states.

This book assumes that the international community is a society of states. While acknowledging that the global community is a politically undeveloped society, it nevertheless assumes that the world is a rudimentary legal, political, economic, and moral community. The principles and rules that are set forth in Chapters 5–8 represent core norms that structure states' foreign relations. These norms not only establish rights and responsibilities for states and other actors but also establish institutions that create transnational values and global concerns. Evidence that an international society exists is found in the development of collective security measures (through the United Nations but also through regional organizations like the Organization of American States and NATO) to foster and maintain peace, the rise of international human rights law, and the many multinational declarations and conventions designed to protect the global environment. According to K. J. Holsti, states have "tamed themselves" by building institutions that constrain their freedom of action. But by voluntarily "taming" sovereignty, member states make possible a more peaceful and prosperous world.[10]

Three Views of the International Community

Scholars and public officials commonly refer to the world as an international community. This concept, however, often masks widely divergent conceptions of global solidarity. Three prominent perspectives of the international community are: realism, internationalism, and cosmopolitanism. *Realism,* which is based on the "system of states" perspective, holds that the international community is a fiction, because states, not international institutions, determine the IR game. Although international law and organizations can influence international affairs, realists believe that global politics is determined by the wants and actions of states, especially those with significant political and economic power. According to realists, national interests, not global interests, define world politics. U.S. Secretary of State Condoleezza Rice expressed this realist vision of the world in an influential article published while serving as foreign affairs advisor to the presidential candidate George W. Bush. In the article, Rice observed that foreign policy in a Republican administration would "proceed from the firm ground of national interest, not from the interests of an illusory international community."[11]

The second perspective, *internationalism,* is based on the "society of states" model. It assumes that both states and international institutions play an important role in the IR game. According to this perspective, the international community is a global society where states are the chief actors, but where their actions are constrained not only by their relative power but also by principles and binding rules. One of the first major expressions of the internationalist perspective was set forth in the seventeenth century by Hugo Grotius, a noted Dutch diplomat and scholar. In his great work *On the Law of War and Peace,* Grotius argued that states' international behavior is conditioned not only by resources and expediency but also by moral values. In his view, the legal and moral responsibilities of states, which are designed to uphold human dignity in all times and places, bind all persons in what Grotius calls "international society." The internationalist conception of the world is therefore a hybrid perspective—one that affirms the autonomy of states, but one that also affirms legal and moral norms that circumscribe that autonomy.

The third perspective is *cosmopolitanism.* According to this approach the international community is a unitary, moral society where human beings, not states, are the major actors. Cosmopolitans believe that the international community has progressed beyond a "society of states" to a world where persons are citizens of a global society, not of individual states. For them, the international community is not an ideal to be pursued but a reality that is expressed in the increasing role played by international institutions in structuring international relations. To be sure, the world remains a community of distinct states, but it regards the autonomy and boundaries of states as conditional on the fulfillment of moral responsibilities. This increasing acceptance of global responsibilities was evident at the 2005 UN World Summit, when member states affirmed the emerging norm of "responsibility to protect" (R2P). According to this principle state sovereignty is not simply the right to be free and independent but also the responsibility to care for people. Thus, when a state is unable or unwilling to protect human rights, the R2P norm imposes on the international community itself an obligation to protect people from gross human rights violations.

Global Governance

The concept of government is derived from the Greek verb *to govern,* which means to steer. Thus, to govern means to lead, direct, guide, and organize the affairs of a society. The responsibilities for governing a community are thus similar to those of a captain of a ship who must make decisions regarding the speed and direction of a vessel and who has ultimate responsibility for its cargo, passengers, and crew.

The international community is a society of states. The social, economic, and political life of each of these nation-states is ultimately in the hands of a *government*—the institutions in society that make, interpret, and enforce binding rules on their subjects.[12] Because states are *sovereign*—that is, have ultimate authority over public (society-wide) affairs—their governments have final decision-making authority within their territorial boundaries.[13] And because no world government exists that can override a state's authority, the state remains the fundamental actor in the international community of states.

Politics is the means by which societies decide who can make decisions (the government) and what those decisions should be. Fundamentally, it is the process for making society-wide decisions. Because conflict is a natural by-product of all social life, politics provides the means by which conflicts are contained, managed, and resolved. As one scholar has observed, the primordial task of politics is the "settling of disputes."[14] Because government is ultimately responsible for conflict resolution within domestic societies, a fundamental task of politics is to develop and sustain governmental decision making. In effect, politics provides the fuel (energy) for mobilizing and guiding governmental decision making, helping to enact rules that protect human rights, encourage economic prosperity, and foster peaceful cooperation.

In developed, well-functioning states, government normally plays a key role in resolving conflicts and promoting a society's economic and social welfare. In the international community, however, where no central governing authority exists, politics plays a far more decisive role than in domestic societies. Whereas governments within states have the authority to make, interpret, and enforce rules, in the international society of states, conflict resolution and the promotion of international cooperation are ultimately achieved through the voluntary actions of states.

Although there is no effective governing authority in the world, the international society of states is nonetheless a relatively stable, cooperative community. The order and stability of the world derive not from chance or from the domination of one or two powerful states but from the voluntary actions of states—actions that are taken in light of widely accepted values, procedures, behavioral patterns, and rules. When ideas, norms, and rules coalesce in areas of shared international concern, they result in what scholars call *institutions*. Because the development of institutions frequently results in the creation of international governmental organizations, some thinkers have used the terms *institution* and *organization* interchangeably. But this is incorrect, because an institution is a broader, more inclusive concept based on norms, tacit practices, formal rules, and governmental structures. Because institutions structure the behavior of state and nonstate actors in the international community, they are the foundation of the world's political architecture.

An example of an important international institution is the liberal international economic system. This system involves shared interests and values, rules governing international trade and global financial transactions, and formal organizations that facilitate trade (World Trade Organization [WTO]) and international financial transactions (International Monetary Fund [IMF]). This institution has been in the making for nearly two centuries, but it began to take shape after World War II with the creation of the World Bank (known as the International Bank for Reconstruction and Development) and the IMF and the establishment of procedures and principles designed to promote international trade. This arrangement, known as the General Agreement on Tariffs and Trade (GATT), served as the multilateral organization for reducing trade barriers for nearly four decades. In 1995, however, its tasks were taken over by the WTO, an organization with more authority to promote free and fair trade and to resolve trade disputes.

Although the world has no central government, it nevertheless has institutions (based on norms, rules, informal networks, and formal organizations) that foster cooperation, inhibit conflict, and promote shared ideals. Because these institutions structure states' international behavior, they are the foundation for the international community's *governance*. It is important not to confuse government with governance. Unlike government, which is the institution responsible for making society-wide decisions backed by a state's monopoly of force, global governance is not based on the authority to make and impose rules. Rather, the norms, rules, informal networks, and international governmental organizations that comprise governance help to regulate the behavior of states. Moreover, because international institutions have been expanding in both breadth and depth in recent years, the impact of global governance in the contemporary world has increased. The expanding breadth of governance has been greatly facilitated by the information revolution, which has resulted in a thick multilayer web of transnational information and action networks. Additionally, global governance has also increased its reach. This development has occurred partly in response to the increasing porosity of state borders and to expanding economic, social, and political globalization.

Even though there is no central governing authority in the world, member states find safety and prosperity by pursuing shared interests and values and by playing in accordance with established principles and rules of the IR game. Thus, global governance helps to foster common transnational interests, to facilitate negotiation, and to moderate conflict when peaceful accommodation is difficult, if not impossible. In effect, the drama of IR arises from the quest for national self-interest within the context of global society, just as the excitement of sporting events arises from competition within the rules of the game. Football and soccer are enjoyable games because they involve competition within established boundaries, following prescribed rules. If there were no norms, games would be meaningless.

The IR game is possible only because states' well-being is dependent on the condition of global society. If there were no shared ideals, common practices, or authoritative norms within the international community, peace, order, cooperation, and prosperity within the world would be impossible. Thus, when states respect the rights of other states and fulfill obligations to other communities, they help to sustain political order and make possible cooperation, without which the economic, social, and political well-being of individual states and global society are impossible.

Conclusion

Strictly speaking, IR is not like a competitive game, such as chess, football, or cricket. Nevertheless, the metaphor of game can be profitably used to analyze global politics and to highlight the foundational political and legal architecture of global society. To distill some of the distinctive features of the field of IR, I examine the nature of the international community and seek to uncover some of the major principles and rules that help to sustain that community. In effect, the aim of this study is to describe the nature of IR and set forth some of the major "rules of the game." Even though the international community has no central government, the institutionalization of "rules of the game" has resulted in legal, political, and economic institutions that structure IR.

RECOMMENDED READINGS

Bull, Hedley. *The Anarchical Society: A Study of Order in World Politics* (New York: Columbia University Press, 1977).

Carr, E. H. *The Twenty Years' Crises, 1919–1939: An Introduction to the Study of International Relations,* revised with a new introduction by Michael Cox (London: Palgrave, 2001).

Kennedy, Paul. *The Parliament of Man: The Past, Present, and Future of the United Nations* (New York: Random House, 2006).

Mandelbaum, Michael. *Ideas That Conquered the World: Peace, Democracy, and Free Markets in the Twenty-first Century* (New York: Public Affairs, 2002).

PART ONE

Foundations
of the IR Game

TWO

The Nature of the IR Game

THE MODERN GAME OF IR emerged in the mid-seventeenth century with the rise of the nation-state. The distinctive feature of this political organization was that rulers were sovereign—that is, had supreme authority within a given territory. Before the emergence of sovereign states, world politics was played with fewer, more diverse players. Some of these were large empires, others medium-sized feudal kingdoms, and still others were relatively small city-states. Additionally, some of the players were solely concerned with temporal affairs, whereas others (e.g., the Roman Catholic Church) were focused chiefly on religious affairs and to a lesser extent on questions of peace and justice.

Ever since sovereignty became the defining feature of the state with the Peace of Westphalia (1648), nation-states have served as the main IR players. Because wars in Europe in the early seventeenth century had been caused by religion, a major provision of the Westphalian accords was that decisions over the type and scope of religion within a country were to be in the hands of political leaders, not religious leaders. Religious conflicts were therefore to be settled by political rulers. Such an approach, it was hoped, would greatly reduce religiously motivated conflicts within and among political communities.

In the two centuries following Westphalia, the number of sovereign states grew to about thirty, and by the beginning of the twentieth century the number had grown to nearly fifty. Following World War II, as the principles of self-determination and human rights became more widespread, the number of states expanded dramatically. Once the notion of colonialism had become discredited in the 1950s, colonies began demanding political independence—in a very short time, more than fifty new states, mostly in Africa, and by the dawn of the twenty-first century, the international community had grown to nearly two hundred member states.

In this chapter I first describe some of the key features of the classical IR game that came into being in the mid-seventeenth century. In the second part I describe some of the important contemporary dynamics that are bringing about important changes in the traditional international order. This emerging postmodern system remains rooted in the Westphalian system but involves a number of important structural changes. In the chapter's third section I describe some of the key principles of the emerging postmodern order.

Although the essential character of athletic games generally remains the same, the rules of the game often change periodically. These changes can be made to increase the excitement of the game, alter defensive or offensive team strategies, ensure fairness of the game, protect players from injuries, or other related reasons. For example, in 1954 the U.S. National Basketball Association (NBA) introduced a "shot clock" to prevent stalling of the game. According to the rule, a team had twenty-four seconds to shoot the ball, otherwise the ball would be turned over to the other team. In the late 1970s, the NBA introduced the three-point basket—a ball shot from behind a circular line roughly twenty-two to twenty-three feet from the basket. And more recently the NBA established that a defensive player who is not closely guarding another player can remain in the center lane for only three consecutive seconds.

In a similar way, the IR game involves important developments in the character and context of the game. Although the game's fundamental logic has remained largely the same, the principles and practices of IR continue to evolve. This chapter therefore attempts to present not only the essential nature of the IR game but also to highlight some of the important shifts currently under way in how the game is being played.

The Traditional Game

The 1648 Peace Treaty of Westphalia is important because it marks the beginning of an international political order based on sovereign nation-states. Although the number and character of political actors have changed over time, the international community of states remains a state-centric order, in which each country is responsible for its own security and social and economic welfare. The classical system is based on five core principles: state sovereignty, nonintervention, self-help, formal equality, and territorial integrity.

☞ P 2.1 Viable States Are Sovereign

The idea of state *sovereignty* was first institutionalized with the Peace of Westphalia in 1648. In the sixteenth century Jean Bodin, a French political historian, coined the concept *sovereignty* to symbolize a ruler's unqualified power over persons within a defined territory. In Bodin's words, sovereignty was the "supreme power over citizens and subjects unrestrained by law."[1] Although Bodin identified sovereignty with the monarch, subsequent political theorists associated it with either the government or the people themselves. Sovereignty has two important dimensions—one domestic and the other international. Domestically, sovereignty means that government has legitimate, unqualified authority to make and enforce decisions and laws within specified territorial boundaries. Internationally, it means that a state is politically independent, not subject to the will of another state and is therefore the ultimate decision-making authority within global society.

The introduction and application of the idea of sovereignty in seventeenth-century Europe had a decisive impact on the nature of world politics.[2] No longer were empires, duchies, feudal kingdoms, churches, or religious institutions the ultimate actors in the international community. Because nation-states now had undisputed authority within a society, governmental institutions were responsible to maintain public order and promote the interests and well-being of their people. Additionally, since the international community of states did not have a central authority to resolve interstate conflicts and maintain peace, the task of promoting and maintaining international peace and global justice was in the hands of all member states. Indeed, each state was responsible for protecting itself from potential aggressors.

The Westphalian accord is important because it ended thirty years of religiously inspired wars in Europe. Even more significant is the fact that the peace treaty marks the beginning of the modern nation-state. The key norm emanating from the Westphalian peace accord was sovereignty—supreme or final authority within a specified territory. Under the Peace of Westphalia, this supreme authority was vested in a state's government, which now had the final responsibility over the type and scope of religion within its territory.

As state sovereignty became increasingly accepted and practiced by political communities, it became the foundational norm of global society. Thus, the first and most basic principle of the IR game is that only sovereign political communities can play. This means that a prerequisite to be a player in the international community is a polity's capacity to exert ultimate political control over its internal affairs and be able to defend and promote its people's interests in relation to other states. The first capacity—the ability of a government to make and enforce public decisions within its territorial boundaries—can be defined as domestic sovereignty; the second capacity—the ability to protect a people from other states and to promote their interests in the international community—can be defined as external sovereignty. Both dimensions are important to viable statehood.

🏛 P 2.2 States Must Respect the Autonomy of Other States

Although sovereignty is the most distinctive principle of the traditional system, the maintenance of a decentralized political system is sustainable only if states honor the independence of other states. Sovereignty therefore demands a reinforcing principle—*nonintervention*. This norm requires that states honor the sovereignty of other states by refraining from interfering in the internal affairs of other states. Without nonintervention it would be impossible to develop an international system of sovereign states. And without the willingness of states to honor the political independence of other states, there could be no Westphalian international system. Because the right of political autonomy can only be enjoyed if states honor the sovereignty of other states, sovereignty and nonintervention are different sides of the same coin. Thus, a key requirement for becoming a legitimate player of the IR game is that states must respect the sovereignty of other states by not intervening in their domestic affairs.

The obligation of nonintervention is a basic rule of the international legal order. The United Nations explicitly prohibits states from intervening in the domestic affairs of other states. In its founding charter (Art. 2.4), members agree to "refrain in their international relations from the use of force against the territorial integrity or political independence of any other state." And in 1965, the General Assembly expressed its condemnation of intervention in even more direct terms by declaring (in Res. 2131): "No State has the right to intervene, directly or indirectly, for any reason whatever, in the internal or external affairs of any other State." The resolution goes on to condemn military intervention and any other type of "interference or threats against the personality of the State."[3] The obligation of nonintervention requires that member states respect the political independence of other states and don't interfere in their domestic affairs. As a result, sending military forces into a foreign state without its knowledge is prohibited. Similarly, seeking to influence the political actions of the government of another state through covert measures is also contrary to the classical order. Indeed, the nonintervention norm is so basic to global order that even the United Nations itself is prohibited from interfering in the domestic affairs of member states (Art. 2.7). The only time that the UN can take military action against a state is when the Security Council regards actions by, or conditions in, a country as a threat to international peace.

⚔ P 2.3 The Security and Prosperity of States Depend on Their Own Resources

The well-being and security of each state depend, in the final analysis, on its own resources and capabilities. Although international organizations like the United Nations, the European Union, and the Association of Southeast Asian Nations can facilitate cooperation and promote coordination among its members, these organizations are not sovereign. They cannot ensure territorial security, protection of human rights, or economic prosperity, and they cannot compel states, except in exceptional circumstances.[4]

Because each state is sovereign, no authoritative international institution exists to resolve interstate disputes. Scholars define the absence of central authority as *anarchy*. This notion does not mean chaos and disorder. Rather, it connotes a lack of a central authority to make binding decisions concerning its members. The international community is like the "state of nature" in Thomas Hobbes and John Locke's social contract theory. In these theorists' views, the state of nature was prepolitical—without law or government. According to political theorist Roger Masters, the international community is similar to a primitive, stateless society. In his view, the international community is like a stateless society in three respects: First, it has no institutions to make rules; second, it has no institutions to enforce laws and shared obligations; and third, it has no formal government to judge and punish violators of the law.[5] Therefore, the international community is a *self-help system*, which IR theorist Kenneth Waltz has defined as "one in which those who do not help themselves, or who do so less effectively than others, will fail to prosper, will lay themselves open to dangers, will suffer."[6]

In sum, because the international community has no institutions to ensure peace and order, each member state is responsible for its own security and well-being. Ironically, such a decentralized system is surprisingly stable and orderly. The order does not derive from a central authority, as is the case in the state, but rather it derives from the voluntary actions and shared interests of member states.

♙ P 2.4 States Are Formally Equal

Once states are viable, they assume certain rights and responsibilities shared by all members of the society of states. One of these is the essential equality of all states comprising the international community, and the other is the inviolability of state autonomy.

Because states are free and independent and not subject to the control of other states, they are fundamentally equal. This norm specifies that states are entitled to be treated with respect, honoring their political independence and fundamental rights. Such respect is manifested through the norm of legal equality. Just as human dignity requires that persons honor the basic rights of others, so, too, does statehood demand that member states respect each other's autonomy.

Indeed, to sustain the Westphalian international system, the sovereignty norm has to be supplemented not only with the promise of nonintervention but also with respect for the legitimacy of other polities. As one legal scholar has observed, "there could be no Law of Nations with-

out a society of state units with formal equality."[7] The close correspondence between formal equality and state sovereignty is frequently expressed by the concept *sovereign equality*. This notion is well expressed in
the Final Act of the 1975 European Summit in Helsinki. In the act's
"Declaration of Principles," signatory states pledge to "respect each
other's sovereign equality and individuality as well as all the rights inherent in and encompassed by its sovereignty, including in particular the
right of every State to juridical equality, to territorial integrity and to
freedom and political independence."[8]

To be sure, states vary greatly in their size, wealth, military capabilities, and political influence. But whether rich or poor, large or small,
powerful or weak, sovereign states are legally entitled to equal rights
within the community of nations. This fundamental equality, expressed
by the right to territorial integrity and political independence, is represented in the United Nations, where every member state is entitled to
one vote in the General Assembly. Although the norm of juridical equality serves as a cornerstone of the contemporary international system, it
remains an unrealized ideal, because this legal norm does not translate
into equality of influence. Large, strong states like China and Russia will
enjoy far more influence in international affairs than fragile, weak states
like Haiti and Zimbabwe. Similarly, economically developed states like
Germany and Australia are likely to have far more impact on global politics than poor countries like Bolivia and Burma.

⌂ P 2.5 A State's Territory Is Inviolable

Finally, once states are viable their political autonomy and territorial integrity must be respected. Fundamentally, this means that member
states must accept each other's territorial boundaries as inviolable and
refrain from using force to alter them. It also means that states must respect the political independence of other member states and not seek to
threaten or use force to compromise their unity and autonomy. If disputes arise about borders or domestic political issues, such conflicts
must be settled in a pacific, nonviolent manner.

It needs to be stressed that the principles of equality and inviolability became increasingly a part of the traditional game only in the
twentieth century. When the *Westphalian system* began to emerge in the
mid-seventeenth century, only the first two principles—sovereignty and
self-help—governed interstate relations. But in response to the growing
destructiveness of war, political leaders sought to create institutions that
would inhibit international war and foster peaceful conflict resolution.
The most important of these was the establishment of the United Nations, an international association of states based on the autonomy and
territorial integrity of each of its members. Thus, the UN did not seek to

abolish the Westphalian order but rather to refine it by, among other things, formalizing the inclusion of the principles of nonintervention and equality.

As I will explain in later chapters, the extent of a state's independence in the international community (external sovereignty) is a matter of degree. One reason for the limitations on a state's freedom of action in the world is that a government's capabilities are themselves limited. Weak governments, for example, might have few resources to maintain domestic order or to control borders. But even strong states also have limited capabilities, especially when confronting widespread illegal or unacceptable behaviors. For example, although the United States is a strong state, its ability to regulate its territorial boundaries is not without limits. U.S. Border Patrol agents have great difficulty in halting illegal immigration, and customs officials struggle to completely stop the entry of illegal drugs. Clearly, a government's capacity to regulate its boundaries and to control the entry of foreign goods and persons will depend not only on the quality and authority of a state's institutions, but also on the number and persistence of people pursuing actions deemed undesirable by the host state.

A second limitation on a state's independence is the extent to which it is a part of the international community and more particularly the degree to which it is dependent on foreign resources. Japan, a country highly dependent on imported petroleum, is constrained in its foreign policy because it must maintain cordial relations with petroleum-exporting countries. Although every country is vulnerable to sudden and unexpected international political and economic developments, the degree of foreign vulnerability depends on a country's capacities and its dependence on external resources. Thus, when global investors lost confidence in South Asian economies in the late 1990s, they began to withdraw financial resources from countries like Indonesia, South Korea, and Thailand, leading to a dramatic fall in the region's economic well-being. And when radical Muslim terrorists successfully attacked New York City and Washington, D.C., on September 11, 2001, the effects were felt not only throughout North America but also in many other nations.

A state's political independence can also be constrained by international governmental organizations, international conventions and treaties, or bilateral agreements. Additionally, nongovernmental organizations (NGOs), especially transnational advocacy networks, can also exert significant influence on states as they transform global public opinion in such areas as global warming, environmental conservation, and human rights. When NGOs began demanding the banning of antipersonnel mines, for example, there were few governments supporting this action. But once NGOs established a global antimines movement, government officials responded by supporting a convention banning mines. This was similarly the case as human rights groups brought sig-

nificant pressure to bear on governments in calling for the creation of an
international court to prosecute human rights crimes. Although governments were ultimately responsible for the adoption of conventions banning antipersonnel mines and the creation of the International Criminal
Court, these treaties were a direct result of public policy advocacy by
NGO networks.

The Emerging Postmodern Game

In the past half century, the world has experienced dramatic changes in
economic and social life. As a result of the spread of modernization,
longevity has increased significantly in virtually every country, especially
in the low-income nations, and living conditions for many have also improved through better housing, education, and health care. Poverty, of
course, persists in many countries, especially African countries, but it is
undeniable that the standard of living for many people in developing nations has risen greatly. In addition to economic progress, the world has
experienced another significant development—*globalization.* This development, which began with increased internationalization of production,
has accelerated dramatically with two important developments—the rise
of instantaneous global communications through the Internet and the
increased speed and decreased cost of international transport and travel.
As a result of modernization and globalization, the international system
has become more functionally interdependent. And the result of greater
integration has been a decline in state autonomy.

Although the contemporary international system continues to be
based on the norms and rules of the Westphalian order, a new global order is emerging. I call this emerging system the *postmodern order,* and it
is characterized by several distinctive features. First, the increase in
functional interdependence has resulted in a more integrated global order where domestic and international politics are increasingly fused.
Whereas in the classical order boundaries were sharply differentiated, in
the emerging world order, sovereignty is less pronounced and independence is less important. Issues such as the shifting of jobs from high-
wage to low-wage countries (referred to as outsourcing), illegal
immigration, and environmental protection illustrate the merging of local and foreign contexts.

Second, the priorities of the postmodern order are focused on international collaboration to promote economic and social welfare, human
rights, and a safe environment. Whereas the classical game focuses on
security and political independence, the emerging order emphasizes the
creation of institutions to promote the well-being of nations and of
global society. Fundamentally, foreign policy in the postmodern world
seeks to integrate national and global interests.

Third, the emerging order has given way to a new type of actor—the postmodern state. Unlike modern states, which are based on political authority rooted in consent and backed by force, postmodern states are characterized by strong civil society (nongovernmental institutions), a tolerant political culture, pluralism, secularism, and belief that public policies can resolve society's fundamental problems. Although these states are limited in number now—and found chiefly in Western Europe—they are likely to become more prevalent as globalization expands its reach. According to political scientist Ronald Inglehart, the distinctive feature of the postmodern nation is that it is concerned chiefly with postmodernist values that seek to maximize individual well-being. Whereas modern states are primarily concerned with objective conditions that ensure survival and prosperity, the postmodern society is focused on subjective conditions that ensure a meaningful life.[9]

It is important to stress that the postmodern system is an emerging order. Postmodernism has not replaced the Westphalian system. Still, because the IR game is evolving, it is important to acknowledge changes in the traditional game, a topic that I explore next.

Sources of Transformation

A number of developments have begun to erode the architecture of the traditional IR system. Two important developments have contributed to the emergence of a more flexible, multilayered, and fluid international order: the end of the Cold War and the expansion of global interdependence, or simply globalization.

End of Cold War
During the Cold War era (1946 to 1990), two superpowers (the Soviet Union and the United States) dominated global politics, maintaining global stability through a fundamental equilibrium of power between them. When the Soviet empire began to disintegrate in 1989, the power and international influence of the USSR similarly declined. And when the Soviet Union ceased to exist in December 1991, only one superpower remained—the United States. Some thinkers had assumed that the end of the intense ideological competition between two nuclear powers would usher in an era of peace and tranquility. But rather than fostering peace and prosperity, the new world order increased civil strife within fragile, weak nations and produced some global instability as political groups competed for the right to establish new separate states.[10] Tribal and civil wars in Bosnia-Herzegovina, Congo, and Somalia, genocide in Rwanda, and ethnic cleansing in Bosnia, Kosovo, and Sudan left hundreds of thousands of persons dead, injured, or displaced. In response to growing civil strife, the United Nations established a growing

number of peacekeeping missions in order to prevent further suffering. By the mid-1990s, the number of UN peacekeeping missions had increased to more than fifteen, with nearly ninety thousand troops serving under UN auspices.

For the United States, the most significant event signaling the danger of the new world order was the terrorist attacks of September 11, 2001. On that day Muslim fanatics commandeered four jumbo jets and flew two of them into the World Trade Center in New York City and another into the Pentagon in Washington, D.C. More than three thousand died as a result of these airplane crashes, making it the single most destructive act of aggression against the territory of the United States. What made the 9/11 attacks significant, however, was not simply the magnitude of destruction, but rather the fact that the violence had been perpetrated by a gang, not a state. The terrorist attacks demonstrated that a small group of trained persons, representing a radical religious movement, could inflict significant harm on the most powerful state in the world.

In short, the end of the Cold War did not lead to a more coherent, peaceful world but to a potentially less stable order. One retired U.S. general has observed of the post–Cold War era: "Instead of global peace and prosperity, all the snakes came out, with consequences that are still unfolding."[11]

Globalization

The second development that has undermined the classical order is globalization. As a result of extraordinary innovations in science and technology, more pervasive and efficient global transportation and communications networks have been developed in recent decades. Journalist Thomas Friedman has written that globalization entails the integration of markets and states in a way that enables "individuals, corporations, and nation-states to reach around the world farther, faster, deeper and cheaper than ever before" and to enable "the world to reach into individuals, corporations and nation-states farther, faster, deeper, cheaper than ever before."[12] Although modern technology has greatly accelerated global transportation, the principal breakthrough in accelerating globalization was the rise of the Internet in the 1980s—a development that has resulted in the creation of low-cost global information networks. These networks have greatly accelerated global communications and facilitated more rapid and efficient global flows of capital and goods, information and ideas, and people. Although international interdependence has existed for many centuries, modern globalization is distinct in both its pervasive scope and its speed. Now globalization means that news is available instantaneously worldwide, and ideas and knowledge can be disseminated across state boundaries at virtually no cost. Because of the declining cost of international communication and transportation, the production of goods and services has become increasingly multinational, and international trade has greatly accelerated.

As a result of increased global networks, the world has become more integrated—between different states, between people and their own state, between states and governmental and nongovernmental organizations, and among people themselves—both within and among countries. Although governments continue to have supreme authority within their territorial boundaries, the growth of globalization has reduced the capacity of the state to regulate cross-border flows. States might be sovereign, but the application of modern science and technology to production, commerce, travel, and communications has decreased the capacity of states to control international flows of goods, services, and information. Unlike previous forms of global interaction, modern globalization is being carried out almost exclusively by individuals and small groups rather than by states or corporations. In this new world order, egalitarian, functional relationships among people and groups are replacing the traditional hierarchical relationships between rulers and people, leaders and workers. Hierarchies and geography are no longer decisive. Indeed, since education and training are the chief determinants of modern economic growth, journalist Thomas Friedman argues that the modern world is becoming "flat."[13]

Although globalization fosters increased transnational integration, it also encourages a contrary pattern—namely, political and social *fragmentation*. Friedman—who defines the tension between integration and fragmentation as a conflict between "The Lexus and the Olive Tree"—argues that although people desire the benefits of economic modernization, they also seek to preserve their group identities, which are rooted in the cultural, religious, and political traditions of their locality.[14] Indeed, since globalization celebrates the impersonal, universal benefits associated with the market and the polity, it reinforces the values of the tribe, clan, or nation. Friedman thinks that the forces of modernity and locality can be reconciled when societies are flexible and open to the beneficial aspects of globalization while seeking to preserve the distinctive features of their own cultures.[15]

In short, globalization is integrating the world along functional lines, but it is also creating new sources of division and fragmentation. As a result, the boundaries of the IR game are not as clearly defined as they once were, and the increasing prominence of nonstate actors is resulting in important changes in the game itself. I therefore highlight some of the important reforms under way in the international community and identify key rules of the emerging postmodern system.

Structural Changes in the International System

The emerging postmodern system also involves a number of important changes from the old order. These include 1) a decline in sovereignty, 2) a growth in the number of fragile, weak states, 3) a decline in the authority of central government, and 4) the decline in the role of military power in resolving interstate disputes. The first change—a direct by-product of globalization—involves the reduction in a state's capacity to control transnational movement of people, services, information, and behavior. Internal sovereignty implies the capacity to regulate people's behavior within the boundaries of a state and to control cross-border movement of people and products and international flows of information and capital. But because of the elusiveness of some global transactions, the rising speed and decreasing cost of transnational flows, and the growing multinational nature of production of goods and services, the regulation of domestic political and economic life is increasingly more difficult. To be sure, autocratic regimes that refuse to participate in the globalization of information and goods and services, such as Cuba or North Korea, can still maintain a high level of sovereign control of boundaries. But for most states that are seeking the benefits of economic modernization through globalization, state borders are increasingly porous. Not surprisingly, sovereignty for most states in the new millennium is under siege.

The second development associated with the postmodern system is a rise in the number of *fragile and failed states.* As I will explain in the next chapter, a stable international system requires strong, coherent states that are capable of carrying out their domestic responsibilities and international duties. To do so, states must have legitimate governmental institutions that can maintain domestic order, protect human rights, and initiate and implement responsible foreign policies. Weak, fragile states are not a new international phenomenon. Rather, what is new is the expansion of such regimes—a development that has been exacerbated by the loss of state sovereignty coupled with the growing demand of ethnic minorities for political independence, a rise in public corruption and the abuse of governmental authority, and the growth in human rights abuses among groups competing for political power. During the Cold War, superpowers intervened repeatedly in weak states to inhibit regional instability and prevent a change in a state's ideological alignment. But with the collapse of the bipolar world, the United States and other major powers had fewer political incentives to intervene in foreign states. Thus, when fragile countries collapsed altogether, creating major humanitarian crises, such as the famine in Somalia in 1991, ethnic cleansing in Bosnia in 1992, the Rwandan genocide in 1994, and the civil war in the late 1990s in the Congo Republic, the international community failed to intervene in a competent and timely manner to avoid widespread killing and human suffering.

The third feature of the emerging postmodern system is a decline in governmental authority—a development directly caused by the rise of fragile and failed states. Who is responsible for the widespread atrocities and regional chaos perpetrated by fragile or collapsed states? Must the rule of nonintervention, a norm I examine in Chapter 7, be honored even when states are unwilling or unable to fulfill their responsibilities? When a government is unable to maintain public order, what institutions are responsible for protecting human rights? During the 1990s, when ethnic, tribal, and political wars led to grave humanitarian crises in numerous countries, a growing number of observers and public officials began to question the sovereignty norm. In their view, when conflict arose between sovereignty and human rights, the former norm should not necessarily prevail over the latter. Sovereignty, they argued, was never designed to protect systemic atrocities, ethnic cleansing, and genocide. In accepting the Nobel Prize for Peace in 1991, UN Secretary-General Kofi Annan observed, "the sovereignty of States must no longer be used as a shield for gross violations of human rights."[16]

Finally, the emerging postmodern world is characterized by the decline in the legitimacy of force as a means of settling interstate disputes. Historically, war was the ultimate means of settling political conflicts among states. For statesmen and leaders of the traditional IR game, military force was a legitimate way of resolving international disputes, because no other instrument existed to ensure the defense of vital interests in the decentralized international community. In the nineteenth century, Prussian strategist Carl von Clausewitz set forth the classic description and defense of international war in his book *On War*. According to Clausewitz, war was like a wrestling match in which a player used physical force to compel an opponent. War was not an aimless activity, in his opinion, but purposeful action designed to advance national objectives— "a political instrument, a continuation of political activity by other means."[17] But as warfare became more destructive with the advent of modern weapons, the frequency of international war declined. Indeed, the historian John Lewis Gaddis attributes the "long peace" of the Cold War to the balance of thermonuclear terror between the United States and the Soviet Union.[18] John Mueller, a leading IR scholar, went so far as to predict the obsolescence of major war because of enormous destruction from a nuclear conflagration.[19]

The decrease in major war is also a result of the declining legitimacy of military force as an instrument of state policy. This loss of legitimacy has been associated with the rise of international law and international organizations that have sought to inhibit war. In the twentieth century, the world's major powers developed numerous bilateral and multilateral treaties to regulate war and reduce armed conflict. Additionally, they established two major international organizations to prevent war—the League of Nations (1919–1945) and the United Nations (1945 to present). These institutional developments have undoubtedly contributed to the declining role of force in international relations.

Ironically, the decline in wars among major states has not led to a more peaceful, stable international community. Instead, the post–Cold

War era has witnessed the rise of a new type of war fought chiefly within states and involving nonstate actors. Unlike classical wars, which are fought between states, the new wars involve conflicts between states and political groups or criminal gangs and conflicts among groups and gangs themselves. Moreover, whereas traditional wars generally follow widely accepted norms of warfare, postmodern wars are typically carried out domestically with few legal or political constraints. Additionally, such wars are often waged by ethnic, religious, or political groups in order to advance political objectives, such as altering government policies or demanding increased political autonomy. In some cases, group violence is perpetrated for monetary gain (e.g., the control of diamond mines in West Africa) or simply criminal reasons (e.g., the civil wars in Liberia and the Ivory Coast in the 1990s). Mary Kaldor, an IR scholar, argues that this new type of war is being facilitated by a variety of developments, including the loss of governmental authority, the growing privatization of military force, and the increasing influence of "identity politics."[20] Thus, although international wars are less frequent in the post–Cold War era, the international community continues to be a dangerous environment because of the expansion of violence within fragile states.

To illustrate the profound impact of globalization on global society, I explore briefly the effect of this process on soccer. In Box 2.1 I contrast a traditional game based on identity and a postmodern game based on performance. Whereas the first emphasizes the nationality of players, the postmodern game focuses only on the quality of teams and the skills of players.

Principles of the Emerging Postmodern System

The emerging postmodern system has resulted in political developments that have given rise to four principles: the decline of military power in interstate relations, the rise of nonstate actors as legitimate IR players, the growing role of international institutions, and the increasing sensitivity to global concerns. Although nonstate actors and global institutions are interrelated, I differentiate between them to highlight the participation of new transnational organizations and the expanding role of global governance structures.

⚜ P 2.6 The Role of Coercive Force in Interstate Relations Is Declining

As noted previously, international wars have become not only less frequent but also less acceptable. Although states' armed forces continue to consume a significant portion of governmental expenditures, the power to influence other states is increasingly dependent on economic, cultural, and moral resources. Indeed, the ability to play the IR game is as dependent on the ability to co-opt and entice others to do what you would like them to do as it is on the ability to threaten or compel others with military and economic resources. The first capability, known as *soft power*, refers to the ability to influence international affairs through co-optive strategies involving political ideals, cultural values, and economic and social norms. The second capability, *hard power*, is the ability to influence international behaviors through coercive threats or positive inducements.[21] The growing role of "soft power" in the post–Cold War era is illustrated by the widespread appeal of human rights, democracy, free trade and privatization, and environmental protection. The broad appeal of these ideals derives not only from the fact that the most powerful and prosperous states support them but also from the widespread belief that such norms are inherently conducive to a humane society.

Of course, military power and national economic prosperity continue to define the ability of a state to play the IR game. What has changed in the post–Cold War era is that the menu of resources has expanded. Nonmilitary and noneconomic resources are playing a more important role. In effect, the power of states is no longer dependent chiefly on armies, weapons, and wealth, but is being supplemented by ideas, culture, and religion as well as legal and moral considerations.

🐚 P 2.7 The Role of Nonstate Actors Is Expanding

In the traditional game, the sole players are states and formal intergovernmental organizations. In the emerging postmodern system, nonstate actors are increasingly important in defining and confronting global issues. The principal nonstate actors are typically NGOs—that is, private groups and associations from different countries that are pursuing a shared goal—and international advocacy networks. Some global NGOs focus on providing human services, such as job creation (Opportunity International), disaster relief (World Relief), and medical care (Doctors Without Borders); others are concerned with confronting global issues, such as corruption (Transparency International), human rights (Amnesty International), and environmental protection (Commission on Sustainable Development).

Unlike *international governmental organizations* (IGOs), which are directed and maintained by governments, NGOs are initiated, funded, and managed by citizen groups. Although most societies have numerous national NGOs that influence domestic affairs, here we are concerned only with those that represent and work in two or more countries. Whereas IGOs have increased modestly in size and influence, transnational NGOs have expanded dramatically in both number and impact—

♞ ♞ ♞

Box 2.1 Soccer as a Traditional Game and as a Postmodern Game

Soccer is the most global sport. It is played throughout the world and attracts more television viewers than any other athletic competition. It is estimated that about one in five persons (well over one billion persons) watched the championship match between Italy and France at the 2006 World Cup in Germany.

Soccer, internationally recognized as football, originated in England and spread to other continents in the second half of the nineteenth century through Britain's colonial ties and expansive international commercial ventures. In the early twentieth century, amateur soccer clubs were established in cities throughout Europe and Latin America. Although these clubs often were tied to the local community, many were based on trade union, political, or social affiliations. Poor English cities such as Coventry and Derby had their own soccer teams to foster communal solidarity. In Italy, the Agnelli family, owners of Fiat, purchased Juventus, a Turin-based soccer club, to provide weekend entertainment to workers. In the 1970s and 1980s, European soccer clubs increasingly became commercialized, leading to the growing dominance of a small group of rich teams such as AC Milan, Real Madrid, Chelsea, and Manchester United. The inequality in European club soccer became even more pronounced when teams began importing foreign players in the 1990s.

Up until 1995, soccer globalization had been held in check by limiting European professional teams to two foreign players. After the European Court of Justice (ECJ) ruled in 1995 that restricting soccer players' mobility was contrary to the Treaty of Rome, the founding treaty of the European Union (EU), and therefore unconstitutional, European clubs began importing a large number of top players from Africa and Latin America. Thus, just as globalization has modified the structure of international affairs, so too this process has resulted in important developments in soccer competition. To illuminate the impact of globalization on soccer, I contrast two different environments—the traditional game based on group and national identity and the postmodern game based on performance. Following is a brief description of their distinctive features.

The Traditional Game

This game is characterized by a deep team loyalty because of national, regional, political, or religious bonds. Take Glasgow for example. Its two major soccer teams—the Rangers and the Celtic Football Club—are associated with Protestantism and Catholicism, with the resulting competition symbolizing much more than a mere physical contest. As Franklin Foer notes, the Ranger-Celtic rivalry represents "an unfinished fight over the Protestant Reformation."[1]

The most important expression of the traditional game is the competition among national teams.[2] Because the Fédération Internationale de Football Association (FIFA), the agency that regulates international competition, prohibits players from switching national teams, the World Cup, the most important international competition, is essentially a defense of national identity—eliciting strong support from citizens, private associations, and even governments. Like the Olympics, the World Cup celebrates nationality with the displaying of flags and playing of national anthems, providing an outlet for "soft" nationalism. When Chile defeated the Soviet Union in the 1962 World Cup at home, Chileans rejoiced for weeks thereafter, interpreting the victory not only as a sporting contest but also as a symbol of the superiority of democratic politics over totalitarian communism. More recently, Ghana's national pride was bolstered when it qualified for the 2006 World Cup, a feat it had never achieved before. When the small Caribbean island of Trinidad and Tobago achieved the nearly impossible feat of a draw with Sweden in the 2006 World Cup, it caused astonishing jubilation for its one million inhabitants.

Historically, a small group of European and Latin American countries—including Argentina, Brazil, Germany, and Italy—have dominated international competition.[3] Although these countries continue to sponsor exceptionally strong teams, the expanded international interest in soccer coupled with the growing mobility of players has made World Cup competition more globally integrated and more competitive. To accommodate the rise in countries fielding national teams, FIFA has increased the number of national teams from sixteen to twenty-four in 1982 and to thirty-two in 1998.[4] More importantly, however, the increased international mobility of players has resulted in improved performance of Asian and African teams, leading one scholar to argue that globalization has contributed to a leveling of the international playing field.[5] Observers attribute the improved athletic skills of small Third World teams to the knowledge and experience their players gain by playing for European professional teams.

The Postmodern Game

Unlike the traditional game, which highlights affiliation based on nationality or some other source of identity, the postmodern game is cosmopolitan in character and concerned solely with team performance. As a result, it focuses on acquiring the best players in order to succeed in competition. Players' ethnicity or nationality is unimportant.

(continues)

BOX 2.1 continued

The emergence of the postmodern game is associated with the commercialization and globalization of soccer. Until the 1980s, European and Latin American professional soccer clubs were essentially local or national teams. Originally, European clubs—which are regulated by the Union of European Football Associations (UEFA)—were limited to two to three foreign players, but this gradually began to change in the 1990s. As noted earlier, the turning point occurred in 1995, when the ECJ ruled that such restrictions were unconstitutional. The court also ruled that the practice of limiting foreign players from other EU countries was also illegal. Although quotas remained in effect for non-EU players, the ECJ lifted these restrictions as well in 2005, thereby allowing complete international mobility of soccer players.

The internationalization of soccer, especially among European professional clubs, has greatly changed the composition of teams. Whereas the British Premier League had only eleven foreign players in 1992, by 2006 foreign players made up 46 percent of all league teams. Indeed, one London team (Arsenal) was composed entirely of foreigners, including a French coach. Although the growing role of foreign players has improved the quality of professional soccer in Europe and the United States, it has also created challenges for foreign players as they seek to coordinate their commitments to professional clubs as well as to their national teams. The extent to which national and professional obligations can conflict is evident in the growing percentage of national players who also play in foreign countries. In 1970, for example, the famous World Cup team from Brazil was made up entirely of players from local clubs. By contrast, most Brazilian players on the 2006 team were affiliated with European professional clubs.

In short, soccer—like the international community—is facing a time of dynamic transition where rules, loyalties, and practices are continually shifting. Just as national sovereignty is under pressure from growing functional interdependence, so the growing impact of the globalization of soccer is bringing about significant changes in the sport.

Notes

1 Franklin Foer, *How Soccer Explains the World: An (Unlikely) Theory of Globalization* (New York: HarperCollins, 2004), 36.

2 International competitions are carried out on a regional and global basis. Regional competitions are held in all the regions of the world every two, three, or four years, and the global competition, known as the World Cup, is held every four years. The most recent cup was in Germany in 2006, and South Africa will host the tournament in 2010.

3 Brazil has won the cup five times, Italy four times, Germany three times, and Argentina and Uruguay two times each.

4 The thirty-two teams are selected by regional competitions. In the 2006 cup,

Europe fielded thirteen teams, the Americas eight, Africa and Asia five each, and the Pacific one.

    5 Branco Milanovic, "Globalization and Goals: Does Soccer Show the Way?" *Review of International Political Economy* (December 2005): 844–45.

rising from fewer than five hundred at the end of World War II to more than 6,500 in 2005.

Although NGOs do not have the influence of major states, they can exert significant influence on the ideas and actions of states through their vast network of relationships that help mold public opinion. For example, NGOs have been increasingly influential in generating interest in and knowledge about global issues, such as sustainable development, AIDs, human rights, and global warming. Although international public policies are normally enacted by states through agreements or treaties, NGOs play a key preparatory role in initiating and developing strategies as well as in encouraging compliance. In effect, NGOs are the junior partners of states, providing them with expert opinion about issues and organizational structures to mobilize public opinion. For example, when twenty-five thousand representatives gathered in Rio de Janeiro in 1992 for the United Nations Conference on Environment and Development (dubbed the Earth Summit), nearly 70 percent of the delegates were associated with environmental NGOs. And once the conference had concluded, NGOs assumed a key role in promoting the ideas, declarations, and agreements that had been adopted at the summit.

♘ P 2.8 The Influence of Global Governance Is Increasing

A third development in the postmodern system is the expansion of networks that facilitate and structure functional interdependence among states. Because the international community has no central authority to resolve conflicts and coordinate international transactions, the responsibility for maintaining order and promoting international cooperation is in the hands of member states and the IGOs they have established. But the rapid expansion of international economic interdependence and the increased awareness of global problems have outpaced the capacity of existing governmental structures.

Because states are not able to provide the necessary structure to facilitate cooperation, improve coordination, and respond to global challenges, a number of new institutions have emerged in postmodern world institutions to address global concerns and facilitate international cooperation. Some of the most important of these emerging institutions include transnational governmental networks, NGOs, transnational nongovernmental networks, professional associations, religious movements, and other nongovernmental organizations. Although these institutions vary in purpose, size, and character, they all contribute in differing ways to the international management of global concerns. They do so, for example, by promoting international cooperation and coordination on the production and distribution of goods and services and the flow of knowledge, capital, and images. Additionally, advocacy networks are established periodically to confront perceived global problems. This was powerfully demonstrated by the creation in 1993 of an NGO network calling for the banning of landmines. Because this transnational network was able to mobilize significant international public opinion, an overwhelming number of states signed the Convention Banning Anti-Personnel Landmines in 1999.

Scholars refer to this growing composite of transnational governmental and nongovernmental organizations and processes, global networks, and public and private institutions as *global governance*. The Commission on Global Governance—an independent commission established to explore what structural reforms were needed to address global concerns more effectively—defines governance as "the sum of the many ways individuals and institutions, public and private, manage their common affairs. It is the continuing process through which conflicting or diverse interests may be accommodated and cooperative action may be taken."[22] Unlike government, which involves rule making and rule enforcement backed by the coercive authority of states, governance involves the pursuit of common goals that may or may not be based on formal legal authority. Because international governance involves public institutions but also informal, private organizations and associations, it is a broader, more encompassing regulative activity than formal government.

One of the most important developments associated with global governance is the rise of transnational governmental networks. Unlike the formal interactions of state officials from different countries, these governance networks focus on specific issues of shared concern—such as environmental protection and international trade, Third World development, human rights, and global warming—and are undertaken by officials with a high level of autonomy from the central government. Whereas traditional IR was conceived as formal interactions among unitary states, contemporary IR is facilitated by transnational governance structures and carried out by what Anne-Marie Slaughter has termed "disaggregated" states—that is, states where local and national governmental institutions interact with their foreign counterparts.[23] This means that when states confront global concerns, government officials, NGO specialists, and concerned civic leaders work together to develop a common understanding of problems and a shared strategy for addressing issues. The emergence of joint public-private transnational networks is not only transforming the way that states conduct foreign policy but it is also increasing the role of global governance. Thus, although the post-modern game remains state-centered, the way that states interact with other governmental and nongovernmental organizations is becoming more complex and multilayered.

It is important to stress that as the world has become more globalized through numerous and efficient networks of international interdependence, especially in communication and transportation, the ability of states to control domestic and international interactions has diminished. At the same time, the role of and need for international institutions has increased. IR scholar Robert Keohane has written that "globalization depends upon effective governance"—by which he means that the beneficial results of increased scientific, economic, and social interactions can only be sustained through global institutions that structure and manage international transactions.[24] The growing role of international institutions does not mean that state sovereignty is being eclipsed. Rather, continued globalization will continue to depend on the actions of sovereign states and on their ability to cooperate with others states in creating and sustaining institutions that facilitate effective and efficient global interdependence. Such governance should not be confused with government, however, which remains the sole prerogative of sovereign states.

♙ P 2.9 The Influence of Transnational Issues Is Rising

One of the important outcomes of increasing globalization and the revolution of global communications is the growing international awareness of world concerns, including issues such as human rights, global warming, and environmental protection. If global problems are to be addressed, however, leaders and the general public need knowledge about the major issues and a commitment to collectively address such concerns. The first challenge is essentially the responsibility of the media, academic and professional groups, and advocacy networks. The second is chiefly a responsibility of government leaders and public policy groups. The tasks of defining and reporting global issues and of developing global public support are greatly facilitated by modern telecommunications.

Modern technology allows computer networks to disseminate data instantaneously throughout the world, and satellite communications can transmit images from remote areas in faraway lands to modern metropolitan centers. As a result, knowledge of foreign affairs—wars, earth-quakes, human rights abuses, genocide, bombings, and natural catastro-phes—is distributed efficiently and instantaneously through official media and informally through global information networks. When well-coordinated terrorist bombings on the main commuter rail line in Mum-bai (formerly Bombay), India, killed 180 persons and left hundreds gravely injured in mid-July 2006, media networks reported destruction immediately throughout the world. And when the U.S. military began its invasion of Iraq in 2003, TV newscasters broadcast graphic scenes of the tank and troop movements and aerial bombardment. The power of im-agery was vividly demonstrated when tanks entered Baghdad, and one armored vehicle was seen pulling down a large statue of Saddam Hus-sein as throngs of Iraqis celebrated the fall of the dictatorship.

Although modern communications technology permits the wide and rapid dissemination of information, it does not ensure knowledge of, and concern for, international issues. Acquiring knowledge of global issues is of course difficult—in part because of the overabundance of available in-formation but also because of the uneven reporting about international issues. Typically journalists focus on a select number of issues—those where coverage is easily accessible and in which the general public is likely to have an interest. Thus, issues like global terrorism, Iraq's insur-gency, the ongoing Arab–Israeli conflict, and Iran's and North Korea's quests for nuclear arms generally receive wide coverage in the Western media. But when genocide, mass atrocities, or a bloody civil war erupt in Third World countries, the media provide far less coverage, with the re-sult that people are less informed about such deadly conflicts. For exam-ple, although more than one hundred thousand Algerians died from civil strife between militant Muslims and secularists in Algeria from 1992 to 1998, this conflict received virtually no international coverage. Similarly, when the Rwandan genocide campaign erupted in April 1994, the media was largely unavailable to report the rampant killing, in great part be-cause the entire country was engulfed in chaotic violence. Only after the killing had subsided did it become apparent that the mass atrocities had resulted in the deaths of eight hundred thousand persons and the dis-placement of two million Hutus to the Democratic Republic of Congo (DRC).

Of course, reporting immediate events is one thing; developing knowledge about complex global issues is a far more difficult task—one in which interest groups, academic elites, scientific associations, and similar groups play a decisive role. For example, scientists have con-cluded that the earth is getting warmer and that a major cause of such global warming is human behavior. In particular, scientists claim that human-made gasses (mainly carbon dioxide) trap solar radiation, much like the glass of a greenhouse. Consequently, a large portion of global warming is attributed to greenhouse gas emissions, resulting from the use of coal, petroleum, and other carbon-based energy products. Given the complexity of the nature and sources of global warming, governmental and nongovernmental officials have been addressing this global issue for more than two decades. The work of developing and disseminating knowledge about this concern has not been carried out by the media but by governmental agencies, IGOs, NGOs, environmental groups, and advocacy networks. Although numerous global warming conventions (e.g., the Climate Treaty of 1992, the Kyoto Protocol of 1997) have been signed, a comprehensive strategy for reducing global warming gases stills remains to be worked out.

Modern technology not only permits rapid dissemination of international developments, but it also facilitates international advocacy by groups of concerned citizens. These global advocacy networks are essential in addressing international issues, because they serve as a clearinghouse of information, a source for policy alternatives, and a channel for mobilizing public opinion. The important role of international advocacy networks was illustrated in the public policy campaign to ban antipersonnel landmines. The effort, directed by the International Campaign to Ban Landmines, relied heavily on the Internet to coordinate and mobilize public opinion. The initiative was launched in 1992 by citizens in the United States and Britain and grew rapidly with the aid of quick and efficient global communications. The campaign eventually involved the coordination of more than one thousand different NGOs from more than fifty countries. The campaign culminated in 1997 with more than one hundred countries signing an accord banning antipersonnel landmines. The treaty—formally known as the Convention on the Prohibition of the Use, Stockpiling, Production and Transfer of Anti-Personnel Mines and on Their Destruction—went into effect in 1999.[25]

Conclusion

Despite many changes in the IR game, the Westphalian classical system continues to structure contemporary IR. This game is rooted in the following five principles:

1. P 2.1—Viable States Are Sovereign
2. P 2.2—States Must Respect the Autonomy of Other States
3. P 2.3—The Security and Prosperity of States Depend on Their Own Resources
4. P 2.4—States Are Formally Equal
5. P 2.5—A State's Territory Is Inviolable

But the traditional IR game is under strain, and a number of important modifications in the classical model have begun to emerge—in part because of the end of the Cold War and also because of the rapid expansion of international functional interdependence through globalization. Although the emerging postmodern order is still fundamentally rooted in the architecture of Westphalia, the IR game is becoming more complex as nonstate actors and global governance play a more active role in addressing global issues such as human rights, global warming, gender concerns, environmental protection, and religious freedom. As noted previously, the following four principles play an especially important role in the postmodern game:

1. P 2.6—The Role of Coercive Force in Interstate Relations Is Declining
2. P 2.7—The Role of Nonstate Actors Is Expanding
3. P 2.8—The Influence of Global Governance Is Increasing
4. P 2.9—The Influence of Transnational Issues Is Rising

Whether states will become less important in the future world is unclear. What is clear is that important developments are under way in IR, resulting in significant changes in the global context and the way in which the game is played.

RECOMMENDED READINGS

Barber, Benjamin R. *Jihad vs. McWorld: How Globalism and Tribalism Are Reshaping the World* (New York: Ballantine Books, 1996).

Friedman, Thomas L. *The Lexus and the Olive Tree: Understanding Globalization* (New York: Anchor Books, 2000).

Holsti, K. J. *Taming the Sovereign: Institutional Change in International Politics* (New York: Cambridge University Press, 2004).

Jackson, Robert. *The Global Covenant: Human Conduct in a World of States* (New York: Oxford University Press, 2000).

Krasner, Stephen D. *Sovereignty: Organized Hypocrisy* (Princeton, NJ: Princeton University Press, 1999).

Philpott, Daniel. *Revolutions in Sovereignty: How Ideas Shaped Modern International Relations* (Princeton, NJ: Princeton University Press, 2001).

Slaughter, Anne-Marie. *A New World Order* (Princeton, NJ: Princeton University Press, 2004).

THREE

The Players of the IR Game

ON THE MORNING OF SEPTEMBER 11, 2001, nineteen radical Muslim terrorists took control of four jumbo jets and used three of them to attack the World Trade Center in New York City and the Pentagon in Washington, D.C. Because the jets were full of fuel, they resulted in massive fires that caused the collapse of the World Trade Center's 110-story twin towers, major destruction to the Pentagon, and the deaths of more than three thousand persons. Although the hijackers were not soldiers or agents of a government but trained Muslim terrorists, the impact of the 9/11 attacks led the United States to declare war on global terrorism. The irony of the attack was that a nonstate actor had carried out the deadliest single act of aggression against the United States. In response to the perceived terrorist threat, the U.S. government instituted radical changes in domestic security, especially in airline travel, and embarked on a global mission to destroy terrorist networks—a campaign that resulted in the toppling of the Taliban regime in Afghanistan in late 2001.

Most competitive games involve two players or teams. Bridge, for example, is a card game involving two teams with two players each. Major athletic contests like basketball, cricket, or soccer typically involve two teams with a varied number of players. Some board games, such as Chinese checkers or monopoly, can involve four to six players. The IR game, by contrast, involves a large number of players with widely different capacities and interests. Typically, influential players are likely to focus on the global chessboard itself, whereas small, weak players will tend to focus their international ties on regional or topic issues or with neighboring states.

As noted in the previous chapter, the traditional IR game has been played almost exclusively by states. But as the 9/11 events demonstrate, a nonstate actor can profoundly influence international affairs. This chapter therefore explores the evolving role of state and nonstate actors in the international community. In the first section I examine the nature and role of the nation-state, focusing on two key features of states—their primacy and their functional inequality. I then examine four conditions necessary for statehood: self-determination, success in sustaining sovereignty, communal support, and preservation of existing territorial boundaries. In the third section I describe some of the major differences between strong and weak states and some of the challenges posed by the latter to peaceful and prosperous interstate relations. In the concluding section I briefly discuss the growing influence of nonstate players in the IR game.

The Nature and Role of Nation-States

Ever since state sovereignty became the defining feature of the state in 1648 with the Peace of Westphalia, the nation-state has served as the main player of the IR game. Since then, a nation's government would have ultimate responsibility for resolving disputes, promoting economic prosperity, and ensuring domestic order and international security. Although the number of states was fewer than fifty throughout the eighteenth and nineteenth centuries, following World War II, the number of member states increased rapidly, rising to more than 190 by the end of the superpower Cold War in 1990.

Since modern nation-states comprise one or more nations, it is important to differentiate a state from a nation. A *state* is a legal and political concept referring to a well-defined territory controlled by a government and inhabited by a permanent population. From a rudimentary perspective, a state is a legal entity based on land, people, and government. A *nation,* by contrast, is a social and cultural conglomeration of people—a group of individuals who understand each other and have a shared sense of belonging. Although people have been historically associated with such social conglomerations as civilizations, empires, tribes, clans, and racial groups, the modern form of human association is the nation—a social community that shares a common language, culture, religion, history, values, and patterns of behavior. These common ties, which are the foundation for nationality, give rise to preferences and often a desire for political autonomy.

Whether people pursue political self-determination will depend in great measure on the intensity of their group identity. Because political identity is not a fixed attribute but a social construction, varying in time and place, the quest for political self-rule will depend in great measure on the shared myths, common aspirations, and capacity of leaders to mobilize political action. In Northern Ireland, for example, the language and ethnicity are largely the same, but the political aspirations of Catholics and Protestants are radically different: Catholics want a united Ireland, whereas Protestants want to remain a part of the United Kingdom. In Kosovo, the minority Serbs want the territory to continue to remain part of Serbia, whereas the majority Kosovars (Albanian Muslims) want either political autonomy for Kosovo or to become a part of a greater Albania. And in Rwanda, the majority Hutu and minority Tutsi people share a common language and religion but have historically had different social roles in society. Historically, the two peoples have not been able to establish and sustain a tolerant, power-sharing regime. In sum, nations vary in size, strength, and level of development.

States differ in the number of nations that they include. A few modern nation-states, such as Denmark, Ireland, Japan, Norway, and South Korea, are chiefly composed of only one people. Most states, however, are multinational, involving two or more major peoples. Belgium, for example, comprises two distinct peoples with different languages and religions—the Flemings in the northern half of the country and the Walloons in the southern half. Switzerland comprises three distinct regions—a northern German-speaking people, a western French-speaking people, and a southern Italian-speaking people. Many countries, including Iraq, Nigeria, South Africa, and the United States, have three or more major national groups.

Finally, it is important to stress that a state, like a nation, is a social construction—an idea that is used to classify human association and collective action. The state of Israel exists because people live in a geographical territory known as Israel and believe that they are members of a political community known as Israel. Because the state is an idea, when Israel acts in the world, it does so through the actions of individuals in the name of the Israeli state. A state's behavior in the international community is therefore a metaphorical way of describing how people living in a particular nation-state relate collectively with people of other nation-states.

States vary greatly in their ability and willingness to play the IR game. This is so because the nature and institutional capabilities of states differ considerably. Robert Cooper argues that three types of states exist in the contemporary international system: premodern (i.e., fragile or failed) states that are unable to maintain domestic order and fulfill the international responsibilities of sovereign states; modern states that rely on sovereignty and national initiatives to maintain domestic order and fulfill international responsibilities through their developed legal and political institutions; and postmodern states that rely on international institutions to promote national and global interests.[1] Modern states, which represent the largest number, follow the norms of the classical system based on national autonomy. By contrast, postmodern states are found chiefly in Western Europe and represent those states that give up national autonomy in order to strengthen international institutions, especially regional international organization and international law. Premodern states, which represent the smallest group in the contemporary international system, are those nations that have been unable to develop strong institutions in the aftermath of colonial or autocratic rule.

Despite the varied nature of states, they nevertheless share two important features: First, since the world is essentially a state-centric system, states are the dominant players in global politics; and second, because states are highly unequal in their wealth and power, they vary considerably in the capacity to influence global society.

🕮 P 3.1—States Are the Principal Players in the IR Game

States are the primary players in global politics because they are the ultimate decision-making political communities in the world. States are sovereign because they have the authority and a monopoly of force to make and enforce rules within their own territories. Of course, the freedom and autonomy of states is not absolute but is conditional on their fulfillment of commonly accepted duties and responsibilities. This means that a state must use internal sovereignty for the benefit of its people and external sovereignty to foster international peace and order by upholding binding international responsibilities and fostering peaceful conflict resolution.

As noted in Chapter 2, sovereignty does not mean that states are entitled to do whatever they want. Indeed, a state's freedom of action to play the IR game is limited by three factors: its national power resources, the interests and actions of other states, and the degree to which a state's actions promote the international community's common good. These factors are defined as follows:

- 🕮 National power, which is the capacity to determine outcomes, is based on tangible and intangible resources, such as reputation, level of economic development, and military capabilities. The relative power of a state is significant because it affects the range of choices available to that state. The greater a state's national power, the greater its capacity to pursue its foreign policy interests.
- 🕮 A state's freedom of action is also constrained by the likely or actual response of other states. When a state believes that other major players are likely to oppose a foreign policy action, it might be dissuaded from carrying out that action. It can also be compelled to reverse an action. This was illustrated in 1956 when British and French armed forces briefly took control of the Suez Canal after Egypt had nationalized the Anglo-French company that had been running the canal. British and French forces were forced to halt military operations in response to U.S. opposition, which was backed by the threat of economic sanctions.
- 🕮 Finally, states' behaviors are constrained by the need to cooperate with other states in protecting and promoting common global interests. These shared "collective goods" include interests such as global order, international economic prosperity, environmental protection, and humane governance. If global warming is to be

prevented, industrial states need to limit the use of fossil fuels, which contribute to greenhouse gas emissions. Similarly, a state might want to dispose of toxic waste inexpensively by dumping it into ocean waters, far from its territorial boundaries. Such action, however, would be inconsistent with global environmental standards and would be condemned by other states. Thus, although states are independent and free, they are also constrained by global norms.

It is important to stress that the state-centric system can be maintained only if states are viable actors and fulfill their responsibilities domestically and internationally. One of the major challenges in the post–Cold War era has been the rise of fragile and failed states, which profoundly impair the IR game. Not only are failed states incapable of fulfilling international obligations, but when existing states collapse—as was the case in Bosnia, the Democratic Republic of Congo, Haiti, Rwanda, and Somalia in the 1990s—major humanitarian crises result that affect global society. More significantly, state failure also permits subgroups (e.g., terrorist cells, revolutionary movements, or drug cartels) to threaten other states. For example, despite Israel's withdrawal from Gaza in 2005, Islamic militants in that territory have continued to launch crude missiles into neighboring Israel, leading to frequent retaliatory raids by the Israeli Defense Force.

🏛 P 3.2—States Are Unequal Because Their Capabilities Differ

To paraphrase George Orwell, all states are equal but some are more equal than others.[2] Even though the IR game assumes that states are formally equal, states vary considerably in size, wealth, population, and power. As I will argue in Chapter 5, the world is a highly inegalitarian international society, especially economically, militarily, and politically.

From a geopolitical perspective, the post–Cold War world comprises three parts—a superpower, or hegemon, a small core of rich, powerful states, and the periphery (all the other states). The hegemon (the United States) and the core (Britain, France, Germany, Japan, China, and Russia) govern the world. With the exception of a few emerging powers, the world's remaining 190 states participate in the IR game but have little influence in the making and enforcement of rules. A number of peripheral states are making giant strides in improving their national economic and political life and playing a much more influential role in global society. Countries that fit this transitional category include Brazil, a country that has become a major industrial power and that comprises about half of the land in South America, and India, a democratic nation of nearly one billion persons that has achieved significant economic progress since the end of the Cold War by adopting policies conducive to free enterprise. More significantly, failed states can also affect global affairs by exporting problems to neighboring states. From time to time, states in the periphery violate basic rules of the international community by committing aggressive acts, supporting terrorism, or seeking to acquire nuclear weapons. But such exceptions do not alter the fundamental political reality of global society: The world is governed by a coalition of a few powerful states, with the United States playing the dominant role. International society is not a democratic, participatory political system but an oligarchic community.

Although the United States and other core states dominate contemporary global politics by virtue of their superior military, economic, and political capabilities, power is not the sole determinant of their international influence. Principles and ideas also matter. In fact, the core's influence in the modern world derives as much from resources as from the important role of Western ideas in transforming the domestic and foreign policies of states. According to Michael Mandelbaum, three Western ideas, first developed and popularized by President Woodrow Wilson in the early twentieth century, have "conquered" the modern world. These ideas are: 1) the unacceptability of war as an instrument of international conflict resolution; 2) the importance of limited, representative government in protecting and promoting human rights; and 3) the necessity of free enterprise domestically and free trade internationally to promote economic prosperity.[3]

Membership: Joining the Club of States

What are the preconditions, if any, for becoming a member of the international society of states? Although numerous factors have influenced the creation of new states, several principles have played a decisive role. These include the claim of self-determination, success in making and defending the claim of political autonomy, acceptance by other states, and the use of existing boundaries when creating a new state.

🏛 P 3.3—People Have a Right to Self-Determination

Beginning in the late nineteenth century, peoples began demanding political *self-determination*—that is, claiming that nations had an inherent right to govern themselves. The leader most responsible for propagating this idea was President Woodrow Wilson, who justified the claim of political self-rule by linking it with the development of a more democratic, peaceful world order. Wilson claimed that the problem with the international community as it was structured in the early twentieth century lay in the autocratic and unrepresentative nature of some of the leading states, resulting in lack of political legitimacy and global instability. As a result, rather than serving the needs of their citizens and promoting world order, the world's undemocratic regimes tended to participate in a game of domination that subjugated people's interests. What was needed, Wilson believed, was a transformation of global values—with democracy replacing autocracy and self-rule replacing imperial oppression.

Even before Wilson had called for self-determination as a means to construct a more humane and peaceful world, political groups had begun demanding autonomous rule through participatory politics. In the late eighteenth century, with the rise of democratic politics, people began to demand political self-rule. But not until the second half of the nineteenth century did the nation become the central focus of mass politics. The rise of nationality-based mass movements was soon transformed into an ideology known as *nationalism* (see Box 3.1).

Despite Wilson's popularization of the concept, self-determination did not become a part of the international legal lexicon until it was incorporated in treaties. The first to do so explicitly was the UN Charter, which claimed (Art. 1.2 and 55) that the development of peaceful and friendly relations among nations needed to be based on self-determination. In 1960, this right was affirmed by the United Nations in the context of decolonization when the General Assembly adopted the Declaration on the Granting of Independence of Colonial Countries (Res. 1514). One of the resolution's main provisions (Art. 1) makes the bold claim that "all peoples have a right to self-determination." This principle is repeated again in the 1966 International Covenant on Civil and Political Rights (Art. 1).

For Wilson, self-determination was a corollary of democracy: Just as the people had a right to govern themselves within a nation-state, so the nations of the world had a right to govern themselves in the international system.[4] Thus, the fundamental justification for the claim of self-determination was that legitimate decision making needed to be based on consent. Although it is easy to implement the doctrine of consent in homogenous societies, it is far more difficult to apply this notion to multinational states comprising diverse racial, ethnic, and religious groups.[5] Because one people's right to self-determination can conflict with another people's right to territorial integrity, there is no simple way to resolve such claims. Ultimately the right to self-rule is determined by the relative power of those demanding political autonomy. Those who succeed in their quest do so because the configuration of domestic and international forces is on their side.

Although the notion of self-determination did not immediately affect international affairs, following the end of World War II indigenous peoples began demanding increased political autonomy. The growing interest in national autonomy was given impetus by the UN Charter and the

Box 3.1 Nationalism and IR

Nationalism is the political expression of a deep loyalty to one's nation. The fundamental requirement of nationalism is a subjective, psychological predisposition toward people with whom one shares a sense of belonging.[1] As Hans Kohn has observed, nationalism is a "state of mind, in which the supreme loyalty of the individual is felt to be due the nation-state."[2] Essentially, nationalism is the justification and rationale for the claim of political autonomy. Just as theology explains and justifies religious beliefs, so, too, nationalism provides the rationale for the nation-state.

The claim of self-rule is based on the notion that the world is divided into nations, each of which is based on a shared culture, language, and history and entitled to legal autonomy. Like the claim of self-determination, the idea of nationalism is a mixed blessing in the international community. On the one hand, nationalism encourages unity, belonging, and national identity within specific nation-states. It does so by demanding and sustaining political self-rule among persons sharing a sense of belonging. On the other hand, nationalism encourages pluralism, cultural and ethnic diversity, and heterogeneity. By celebrating differences and boundaries, nationalism encourages division and fragmentation in the world. Moreover, nationalism, by encouraging a politics rooted in national identity, can impede the consolidation of global order and international consensus. Even in states comprising multiple nationalities, like Canada, Nigeria, Russia, and Yugoslavia, the quest for a common identity can present a major challenge.

Notes

1 For a discussion of how belonging and nationalism interact, see Michael Ignatieff, *Blood and Belonging: Journeys into the New Nationalism* (New York: Farrar, Straus and Giroux, 1993).

2 Hans Kohn, *Nationalism: Its Meaning and History,* rev. ed. (New York: Van Nostrand, 1965), 9.

international diffusion of decolonization—the idea that colonial states should give up control over territories that they had dominated politically and exploited economically.

But what does the right of self-determination entail? Do all of the world's nations possess this right? Does this right give national groups the right to secede from existing multinational states? Although the UN Charter (Art. 1.2) calls for the promotion of international peace based on respect for "equal rights and self-determination of peoples," it does not specify who a "people" is and it does not define which groups can claim this right. Since the world has tens of thousands of cultural groups based on a variety of affinities (tribal, ethnic, religious, social, economic, and political), the right to self-rule clearly does not apply to all such groups. Clearly a world of ten thousand states or even one thousand states would present extraordinary challenges to the maintenance of world order and the promotion of international economic cooperation. Certainly the governance of an international system of two hundred states is likely to be more feasible than a world with one thousand states.

⚅ P 3.4—Peoples That Succeed in Establishing a State Can Play the IR Game

Historically, the claim to self-rule has depended largely on two factors— the ability of a people to make and sustain a claim of political autonomy and second, the willingness of other states to support and recognize the claim. If a people has the capability and determination to demand self-rule and its demand is not opposed by the international community, then the polity is likely to become a sovereign state, eligible to join the society of states. John le Carré, the Cold War spy novelist, says that a nation is "a people tough enough to grab the land it wants and hang onto it. Period."[6]

Because most nation-states comprise numerous peoples, should sub-national groups be allowed to break away from existing states? For example, should the Chechens be allowed to secede from Russia, the Kurds from Turkey, and the Navajos from the United States? Moreover, because more than ten thousand nations exist in the world, how are statesmen to decide which subnational groups are entitled to self-rule? Since the UN provides no guidelines for determining state eligibility, and since international law has few principles for deciding when ethnic, religious, cultural, or political groups can resort to war to demand political autonomy, joining the club of member states has generally been decided by a people's willingness, determination, and capability to make and sustain the claim of self-determination. In short, the conventional wisdom is that groups that succeed in their self-determination quest and are accepted by other member states are entitled to play the IR game.

In the 1960s and 1970s, during the era of decolonization, the self-determination norm legitimated and guided the transition of more than seventy former colonies from dependency to independence. This transition was carried out in a largely peaceful way—in great part because colonial powers, after concluding that decolonization was inevitable, facilitated the indigenous quest for political self-rule. By the late 1980s, decolonization had run its course and few dependent territories remained. Although numerous ethnic, cultural, religious, and tribal groups

continued to demand political autonomy, the quest for self-determination was now far more daunting because these groups were part of existing sovereign states. Unlike the process of self-determination of former
colonies, which was facilitated by the support from colonial governments, the contemporary quest for political autonomy has faced two significant obstacles.

The first challenge has been the opposition of a neighboring state.
This was illustrated in 1975 when Spain withdrew from Western Sahara,
an arid territory roughly the size of Colorado with a population of about
two hundred sixty thousand, in part because of increased guerrilla activity by Polisario, the armed front of the Saharawi people, who were demanding political self-determination. But rather than achieving political
autonomy, Morocco took over the top two-thirds of the land and Mauritania the other third. In 1979, Mauritania withdrew its claim to the
southern part of Western Sahara, leaving all of the contested territory
under Morocco's control. When Polisario continued sporadic attacks
against Moroccan forces, the government of Morocco built a 1,600-km
sand wall along the territory's western border, thereby significantly diminishing attacks. In 1991 a UN-monitored cease-fire peace accord was
implemented, but subsequent negotiations between Morocco and the
Polisario Front have failed to resolve the dispute over sovereignty. Formally, Western Sahara remains a non–self-governing territory, techni-
cally eligible for self-determination.

Another source of opposition to self-determination arises when a
subnational group seeks to secede from an existing state. When an ethnic, religious, cultural, or political group begins demanding increased
autonomy or even full political independence from a state, the ruling authorities typically use their authority to prevent such action. Because se-
cession results in the diminution of a state's territory, resources, and
people, governments use their monopoly of power to undermine such
initiatives. Thus, when Chechens demanded autonomy from Russia and
resorted to terrorism to advance their demands, the Russian authorities
responded with brutal force. Similarly, when Kosovars (Albanians from
Kosovo, an autonomous territory within the Serbian state) initiated a
guerrilla campaign in 1998 against the governing authorities in order to
press their political claim of self-determination, the Serbian military responded with military action, forcing tens of thousands of Kosovars to
leave their villages and homes. The conflict was resolved only when
NATO, after two months of heavy bombing, forced Serbia to withdraw
its security forces from Kosovo and to allow a NATO peacekeeping force
within the territory. Since then, the United Nations has sought to resolve
the political status of Kosovo (see Box 3.2).

The difficulty in creating a new state from a subnational group is illustrated by the quest for political independence by the Kurds—an ethnic group living in the contiguous area of northwestern Iran, northern

♘   ♘   ♘

Box 3.2 The Difficult Journey toward Statehood:
The Case of Kosovo

Kosovo, a poor territory the size of greater Los Angeles, is a community of two peoples. Of its two million citizens, the vast majority is Muslim Albanians, known as Kosovars; the dominant minority (about 10 percent) is Orthodox Christian Serbs. After the collapse of the Ottoman Empire early in the twentieth century, Serbs conquered Kosovo and imposed control on the territory.[1] Although Kosovo was given significant self-rule during Cold War years, its autonomy came to an abrupt end in 1988 when the Serb government reimposed direct rule. This shift fueled ethnic animosity and intensified Albanian nationalism.

In the mid-1990s, Kosovar nationalists established the Kosovo Liberation Army (KLA) in order to press the claim of Albanian self-determination. In response to growing Albanian violence, Serbia responded with repression, leading tens of thousands of Kosovars to flee their homes and villages. It is estimated by late 1998 some two hundred fifty thousand ethnic Albanians had been displaced and were living in inhumane conditions. Misha Glenny, one of the most astute observers of Balkan politics, noted that the reimposition of Serb rule "transformed Kosovo into a squalid outpost of putrefying colonialism."[2]

When fighting between the KLA and Serb security forces escalated in early 1999, the major powers with an interest in the Balkans, the so-called Contact Group,[3] sought to impose a peace settlement. The proposed agreement, known as the Rambouillet Accord, aimed to halt the fighting by maintaining Serb sovereignty in Kosovo and restoring Kosovo's semiautonomous status. To ensure compliance with the cease-fire, the KLA had to accept demilitarization, and Serbs had to withdraw their army and reduce their police force and allow NATO soldiers to keep the peace. The accord did not attempt to resolve the fundamental political dispute but simply addressed the growing humanitarian crisis. Since the Rambouillet Accord did not address the final status of Kosovo, Kosovars at first opposed the proposed settlement. They only accepted it reluctantly when they recognized that Western states would not offer protection indefinitely to Muslim Albanians. For their part, Serbs found the accord totally unacceptable because the introduction of foreign troops was inconsistent with the sovereignty norm.

When Serbia refused to accept the Rambouillet Accord, NATO began an intense seventy-eight-day air war to compel Serb compliance. When NATO bombers began attacking Kosovo and Serbia, Serbian military and paramilitary forces in Kosovo embarked on a campaign of ethnic cleansing,

(continues)

BOX 3.2 continued

greatly exacerbating humanitarian conditions for Kosovars. Indeed, within a week the ethnic cleansing campaign had forced more than three hundred thousand Kosovars to flee the country. By the time the eleven-week war had ended, nearly eight hundred fifty thousand Kosovars had fled the country to neighboring Albania, Macedonia, and Montenegro.[4] Thus, instead of relieving human suffering, the immediate effect of the war was to greatly aggravate the humanitarian crisis.

The war came to a halt when Serbian president Slobodan Milošević agreed to withdraw all his military and security forces from Kosovo and permit a large NATO peacekeeping force to maintain public order. Despite the introduction of heavily armed NATO soldiers, restoring peace proved to be a significant challenge, especially in controlling Albanian violence and ethnic cleansing. It has been estimated that Muslim Albanians destroyed some one hundred fifty Orthodox churches and forced more than one hundred fifty thousand Serbs to flee their homes and villages. Perhaps the most daunting challenge facing the UN governing authority was the maintenance of law and order in the face of widespread lawlessness and criminality.

Beginning in 2005, UN Special Envoy Martti Ahtisaari, former president of Finland, began negotiations between Kosovar Albanians and Serbs over the future status of Kosovo. After more than a year of talks, the two parties were unable to reconcile their deep differences. Because Serbs viewed Kosovo as part of their country, they were willing to give Kosovars significant self-rule but not sovereignty. For the Kosovars, nothing short of full political independence would be satisfactory. Because bilateral talks failed, the UN Envoy decided to present his own solution. According to Ahtisaari's plan, Kosovo would become independent, but only after a period of international supervision in which the new state demonstrated that it could protect minority rights and carry out its responsibilities as a member state. Although Britain, France, and the United States supported the plan, Russia and China—two countries that have veto authority in the Security Council—were against imposing a settlement, believing that a negotiated agreement was the only acceptable solution.

This case suggests that creating a new state can be a difficult, complex process. If a people make a claim for political autonomy that is uncontested, as was the case with former colonies, statehood can be achieved quickly and easily. But when governments oppose claims of self-determination of subnational groups, the quest for sovereignty can present daunting challenges, as this case demonstrates. Because Serbs have historically regarded Kosovo as a symbolic center of the Serb nation, they will likely continue to oppose statehood for Kosovo. Kosovo's independence will therefore depend on the support of the major powers and the United Nations.

Notes

1 For a description of the nature and effect of Serb conquest of Kosovo, see Noel Malcolm, *Kosovo: A Short History* (New York: HarperPerennial, 1999), 238–263.

2 Misha Glenny, *The Fall of Yugoslavia: The Third Balkans War,* 3rd rev. ed. (New York: Penguin Books, 1996), 67.

3 The Contact Group consists of Britain, France, Germany, Italy, Russia, and the United States.

4 Tim Judah, *Kosovo: War and Revenge* (New Haven, CT: Yale University Press, 2000), 250.

Iraq, and eastern Turkey. The Kurds have been seeking increased autonomy from each of the countries in which they reside, in the hope that someday an independent Kurdistan might emerge. All three states, however, have adamantly opposed not only ethnic and cultural autonomy but also statehood. As of 2006, Iraqi Kurds had achieved a significant level of autonomy, in great part because of the protection that Allied forces gave to them through the establishment of a northern "no fly zone"—thereby prohibiting Saddam Hussein's air force from attacking Kurds. Since the toppling of the Hussein regime in 2003, the United States has encouraged the development of a multinational state in which the distinctive religious and cultural traits of the Kurds, Sunni, and Shia are respected and protected.

In short, political groups that seek statehood are not necessarily entitled to the prize of statehood. Whether they become states ultimately will be determined not by the inherent right of self-determination but by the ability to make and enforce this claim. Political success is determined by power, not justice. As one IR scholar has noted, "Historically, the prize of independence has gone to those powerful or clever or fortunate or merely numerous enough to achieve it."[7] After a nation has achieved statehood, it has the right to exist.

 P 3.5—States Must Be Recognized by Other States before They Can Play the IR Game

Establishing sovereign control over a territory is a necessary but not sufficient condition for membership in the club of member states. To join the society of states also requires that existing member states recognize the claim of self-determination. When an ethnic or cultural group succeeds in establishing sole, uncontested domestic control within a specified territory, it fulfills the fundamental requirement of statehood—namely, final decision-making authority within a state. The monopoly of force within a territory ensures domestic sovereignty, but it does not automatically translate into full membership in the global society of states. If a polity is to enjoy the rights and responsibilities of membership in the society of states, it needs external approval. The existing members of the club must approve of the addition of the new state. This approval is expressed by the international validation of the sovereignty claim. As K. J. Holsti has noted, it is other states that decide which states will join the existing society of states. "The act of recognizing a state," he writes, "in effect creates its special legal status."[8] Taiwan, for example, while enjoying internal sovereignty, is not regarded as a full member state of the international community because states view Taiwan as part of China.

The importance of international recognition is illuminated in the case of East Timor, a former Portuguese colony of about one million persons. When the East Timorese declared independence in 1975, Indonesia refused to accept the claim of autonomy, believing that the entire island of Timor was a part of its territorial boundaries. As a result, Indonesian military forces occupied East Timor and for the next twenty years carried out a pacification campaign against a reluctant people. The conflict left more than one hundred thousand persons dead. But the international community refused to legitimize the Indonesian claim. In response to growing pressure from the United Nations, Indonesia decided to allow a UN-supervised referendum on the future of East Timor. In 1999, an overwhelming majority of the people voted to create an independent state. In response, anti-independence Timorese militias, supported by the Indonesian military, carried out a campaign of retribution, destroying much of the country's infrastructure and killing more than thirteen hundred persons. The UN Security Council responded by establishing a peacekeeping mission, headed by Australian military forces, that restored order and paved the way for the creation of a new state. In 2002, East Timor became an independent state and a member of the United Nations. Regrettably, the nation of one million inhabitants remains fragile, as was demonstrated by an outbreak of bitter fighting among different political groups in mid-2006.

The international community also plays a key role in establishing the boundaries in which groups may pursue self-determination. When leading players think that the disintegration of an existing state is not in the best interests of global order and their own national security, they can use international influence to try to impede the forces of self-determination. The international concern with the dismemberment of states was evident in the early 1990s when Yugoslavian ethnic territories, such as Croatia, Slovenia, and Bosnia-Herzegovina, began demanding independence from the Serb-controlled central government. When civil war broke out in Bosnia-Herzegovina among its three ethnonationalist groups (Serbs, Croats, and Muslims), the leading powers (United States, Britain, France) sought to keep the Bosnian state together, thereby impeding the efforts of Croatia or Serbia to incorporate part of Bosnia into their own territories.

This similar international concern has been expressed toward Iraq. After the government of Saddam Hussein was toppled in 2003, the international community, led by the United States and Britain, sought to establish a cooperative, power-sharing government among the three major ethnic and religious groups—the Shiites, the Sunnis, and the Kurds. Although the Kurds were eager to establish an autonomous, if not independent, state in Iraq's northern region, the United States, the occupying power, demanded that Iraq remain a single political entity. But getting the three major political groups to work together, especially the Sunni Baathist Muslims who have governed Iraq for nearly four decades, has been especially difficult. Dissatisfied with their loss of influence, they have supported an insurgency that has resulted in thousands of civilian casualties from suicide and roadside bombings. The ongoing insurgency in 2007 suggests that the creation of a coherent, unified state is an especially daunting task when one or more warring groups would prefer the collapse and disintegration of the emerging state.

In sum, peoples that succeed in taking control of territory and establishing effective authority within a territory become eligible to play the IR game. By establishing domestic control within a territory they prove that they are sovereign. But if political sovereignty is to become legal sovereignty, then other member states must acknowledge the new state's status as an independent actor. Thus, if a state is to join the club of states, it needs to gain the approval of other states, which is normally expressed through the formal recognition of a state and the willingness to carry out full diplomatic relations with it.

⚘ P 3.6—Prospective States Must Be Based on Former Territorial Boundaries

Finally, emerging nation-states hoping to be admitted into the international community need to fulfill another requirement. The requirement, known in international law as *uti possidetis*, demands that new states be based on existing territorial boundaries. This norm, which developed during the process of decolonization, emerged when indigenous political leaders realized that maintaining colonial borders was essential if the transition from colonial status to political independence was to occur peacefully. Although the existing territorial boundaries of most colonies were arbitrary and not based on ethnic or tribal cleavages, leaders realized that keeping existing boundaries was necessary if the quest for self-determination was to succeed. In time, this norm was accepted as a binding legal precedent in the creation of new states. Thus, when the Czech Republic and Slovakia decided to separate, they did so following existing boundaries. And when East Timor became a separate nation-state, its boundaries along the western front were those established by Portugal when it ruled the territory as a colonial power.

Although the maintenance of territorial boundaries is frequently problematic, the international community has been unwilling to develop an alternative norm on which to devise state boundaries. Reliance on preexisting boundaries might not always provide a satisfying basis for state borders, but until a more reliable norm is developed, precedent is likely to remain a core principle of the international community. Not only is precedent the basis of new state boundaries, but it also remains the foundation for the partition of the world into some 191 distinct nation-states and numerous other non-self-governing territories. The protection and maintenance of this division of the earth has been synthesized into what is called the territorial covenant. The covenant is a set of principles that establishes a framework for creating, maintaining, and revising territorial boundaries. The covenant's key norms are as follows:

1. only existing territorial boundaries are valid;
2. boundary changes made as a result of force or the threat of force are invalid;
3. territorial changes must be made peacefully;
4. territorial changes must be consistent with the principle of self-determination;
5. territorial changes must be based on the consent of those affected by them;
6. the affected parties include both "peoples" and states;
7. the quest to secede from an existing state will not receive international support unless it is based on consent and has involved negotiations; and
8. the territorial boundaries of the seceding state should approximate former administrative boundaries.[9]

These rules essentially seek to preserve order and peace by maintaining the existing boundaries. Any changes in territorial borders need to be carried out peacefully, with indigenous support and the support of other member states.

Strong and Weak States

IR would be relatively stable and predictable if all states were strong and coherent. Regrettably, not all members of global society are capable of maintaining domestic order, protecting human rights, promoting economic growth, and fulfilling international obligations. Indeed, with the end of the Cold War and the collapse of the Soviet Union, the number of fragile or failed states increased, resulting in numerous humanitarian crises. In the early 1990s, for example, the disintegration of Yugoslavia resulted in bitter fighting within Bosnia-Herzegovina among Croats, Muslims, and Serbs, resulting in more than two hundred thousand deaths, widespread human rights abuses, and the dislocation of more than two million people. More than six hundred thousand refugees fled to Germany. Similarly, the collapse of the government of Somalia in 1992 left tribal warlords competing for political control of the state. The civil war not only intensified a famine that originated from drought but impeded the distribution of humanitarian supplies. Although more than three hundred thousand persons had died from hunger, the total number of deaths from famine and fighting would have been considerably higher had the United States not intervened militarily to ensure the distribution of humanitarian food supplies. A third example of a failed state is Haiti. After its people had elected Jean-Bertrand Aristide president, the country's armed forces toppled the government, precipitating a large number of persons seeking to flee the country, many of them to the United States. As a result, a U.S.-led peacekeeping force was introduced in the country in 1994 to restore Aristide to power and to halt the exodus of refugees. Thus, the unrest and instability of states are not solely a matter of domestic concern. As these cases suggest, the breakdown in civic order can result in humanitarian crises and regional instability that may justify, if not demand, foreign intervention.

Several developments have contributed to the weakening or collapse of some states in modern times. To begin with, when the Cold War ended in 1990, superpower interest in developing nations declined greatly. When the United States and the Soviet Union were competing for influence in the world, each superpower gave priority to the stability and prosperity of Third World countries. They did so to maximize their global influence and to ensure that the opposing superpower would not use a regional crisis as a means of extending their power and influence. Not surprisingly, the Cold War involved no direct war between the superpowers but numerous proxy wars, such as the Vietnam War and the Soviet intervention in Afghanistan. Thus when instability and conflict arose in developing countries—such as the Dominican Republic (1965), Ethiopia (mid-1970s), El Salvador (early 1980s), and Angola (mid-1980s)—the superpowers responded with direct or indirect economic and military assistance. Such assistance helped not only to sustain states but also to prevent crises from spreading instability to other states.

A second reason for the rise in fragile states is ethnic, religious, and political conflicts within developing nations. These conflicts have led to "ethnic cleansing," tribal wars, and famine that have resulted in humanitarian crises affecting not only neighboring states but also the international community itself. When Hutus massacred eight hundred thousand Tutsis in 1994, a Tutsi rebel force succeeded in toppling the existing regime, leading more than two million persons to flee to neighboring Congo. And when Albanians in Kosovo (Kosovars) began demanding increased political autonomy from Serbia in 1998, the Serbian government, led by Slobodan Milošević, responded with increased repression and human rights abuses. Because of the humanitarian crisis in Kosovo, NATO authorities demanded that Serbia withdraw its military and police forces from Kosovo. When it failed to do so, NATO responded with an intensive bombing campaign that led to further Serb atrocities against Kosovars. It is estimated that the seventy-eight-day air war intensified ethnic cleansing, displacing hundreds of thousands of Kosovars from their homes and villages, most of them to Macedonia. The war ended only when Serb authorities decided to comply with NATO demands.

Finally, the export of Western ideas, such as limited government and free enterprise, might also have contributed to the weakening of some states. Although constitutional democracy and effective job creation have been shown to be associated with human rights and economic prosperity, the process of developing a free society often undermines existing institutions, resulting in increasing social dislocation, political instability, and corruption. Francis Fukuyama has observed that in its effort to foster economic development through privatization and other market-based reforms, the West has not only helped to reduce the scope of the state in the Third World but has also helped to decrease its capacity.[10] But the diminution of state power is not conducive to domestic or international order. Indeed, state power is essential to make and enforce rules domestically and to preserve world order among sovereign states.

Why are strong states strong? Although scholars differ on the nature and development of a strong state, there is widespread agreement that the following are important to increasing the capacity of state: a modern society and economy, political stability, an effective legal order, an authoritative and impartial judiciary, effective and efficient governmental institutions to make and enforce laws, and cultural values that encourage honesty, trust, cooperation, compliance with the law, and promise keeping. In effect, strong states are those that have well-developed institutions (with formal and informal rules and organizations) to coordinate and regulate human behavior and a moral-cultural environment that provides the values and trust for effective, dependable cooperative action.

The strength of institutions is significantly affected by two intangible factors—legitimacy and social capital. *Legitimacy* is the extent to which people voluntarily accept and support rules and organizations because they consider them valid and beneficial to a nation's well-being. Countries with high levels of legitimacy, such as Denmark, New Zealand, and Israel, tend to enjoy high levels of political stability and efficient and effective methods of conflict resolution.

A nation's strength depends on two types of legitimacy—horizontal and vertical. *Horizontal legitimacy* refers to the scope of inclusiveness (the "we" in states) and depth of commitment to the nation (the degree of shared loyalty). *Vertical legitimacy,* by contrast, refers to the bond of trust and support between rulers and people. The first type of legitimacy is important because it establishes the nature and inclusiveness of a political community and more specifically the criteria for membership. The second type is significant because it defines the nature and basis of governmental authority.[11] Although both types of legitimacy are often in short supply in weak states, the collapse of states in the post–Cold War era has been frequently precipitated by ethnic, religious, or cultural fragmentation, such as the ongoing ethnic and religious conflict in Sudan, or by competition for political power among political leaders, such as continuing domestic political turmoil in Haiti and Somalia. In some cases, the quest for nation building involves ethnic, religious, and political fragmentation, as illustrated in the U.S.-led efforts to build stable, representative governmental institutions in both Afghanistan and Iraq.

Social capital, which represents the level of trust and cooperation existing within society, is important in state building because it provides the moral values and the cultural habits that make possible collective action. Just as economic capital provides the resources to foster investment and job creation, so, too, social capital establishes the cultural patterns and moral values that enable voluntary cooperation and coordination to occur. Although the authority of government is based partly on social capital, the need for the state's coercive power is inversely related to the level of social capital. Thus, a state with a high level of corruption, a low level of confidence and trust in government, and limited voluntary cooperation will necessarily need a higher degree of coercive power to function. On the other hand, states with a high level of trust, voluntary cooperation, and voluntary compliance can function with a far less coercive government.

Table 3.1 contrasts features of strong and weak states. This comparison does not address the power and influence of states, a topic covered in Chapter 5 on political rules. Here our concern is solely with the institutional capacity of states—the ability of states to regulate domestic affairs and play the IR game successfully. Because only strong states have the unity, political and economic strength, and organizational ability to carry out purposeful foreign policies, they are the primary actors that will determine the course of global political affairs. To be sure, fragile states can also indirectly affect the IR game when the effects of war, instability, poverty, and disease spill over into neighboring states or even more distant countries. For example, when large numbers of refugees began fleeing Haiti in 2004 (in small boats) because of continued repression by military authorities, the United States responded with the threat of military intervention. The crisis subsided only when the deposed president, Jean-Bertrand Aristide, was restored to power and backed by UN peacekeeping forces. Similarly, when large numbers of refugees fled civil

TABLE 3.1 Characteristics of Strong and Weak States

Features	Strong States	Weak States
Vertical Legitimacy	High confidence in government; based on competitive elections, free press, free assembly, open dialogue	Low confidence in government; rulers use coercive power to serve their interests; little tolerance
Horizontal Legitimacy	Inclusive of all groups within society	Some ethnic or religious groups excluded
Political Dynamics	Impersonal, impartial application of rules; efficient bureaucracy	Personalistic; government actions favor individuals and groups associated with political leaders
Government Institutions	Strong; can make and enforce rules; institutions can resolve disputes	Fragile; unable to resolve conflicts authoritatively
The Rule of Law	Laws are applied to all and are enforced impartially	Laws are enforced sporadically; the judiciary serves the interests of rulers
Dominant Political Ideas	Human rights, freedom, power based on consent, limited government	No dominant ideas; those with power are entitled to rule
Social Capital	High level of trust; significant levels of voluntary cooperation	Low level of trust; voluntary cooperation is difficult
Level of Corruption	Low	High

unrest in Bosnia and Kosovo in the 1990s, the international community responded with collective peacekeeping missions. In the case of Bosnia, the United Nations first responded with a peacekeeping mission (known as UNPROFOR, or UN Protection Force), and when that failed to keep domestic order, NATO introduced a more powerful peacemaking force (known as SFOR, or NATO Stabilization Force).

Nonstate Players

⚖ P 3.7—Nonstate Actors Can Also Play the IR Game

Although states are the primary actors in the international community, other actors can also participate in the IR game. The principal nonstate actors include:

⚉ formal intergovernmental organizations (IGOs), such as the United Nations, the European Union (EU), and the World Trade Organization (WTO);

⚉ informal governmental networks, such as Group of 8 (G-8);

⚉ nongovernmental organizations (NGOs), such as Amnesty International, Doctors Without Borders, and the International Committee for the Red Cross;

⚉ private international advocacy networks, such as Transparency International, Commission on Sustainable Developed, and the Organization for Economic Cooperation and Development;

⚉ multinational corporations, such as Chase Manhattan Bank, General Electric, and Toyota; and

⚉ transnational religious organizations, like the Vatican and Protestant missionary organizations, such as the Latin American Mission and Wycliff Bible Translators, and religious movements like Muslim fundamentalists and Pentecostal Christians.

Although all of these nonstate actors influence global society, I focus on the two that currently have the greatest impact on the international community—IGOs and NGOs.

IGOs are formal organizations comprising a group of states to pursue a shared international objective. The major difference between IGOs and NGOs is that in the former, actions are taken collectively by official government representatives, whereas in the latter, members represent shared ideas and interests, not the wishes of governments. IGOs, which numbered about two hundred fifty in 2005, can be differentiated in terms of their purposes and scope of membership. Some of these are general purpose global organizations like the United Nations; others are general purpose regional organizations, like the European Union (EU), the League of Arab States, and Organization of American States (OAS). Most IGOs are quite specialized, focusing on specific issues such as the global environment, economic development, health, human rights, and international security. Examples of specialized global organizations include the International Labor Organization (ILO), the World Bank, and the World Health Organization (WHO); examples of specialized regional organizations include the Asia Pacific Economic Cooperation (APEC), the Central American Common Market (CACM), the North Atlantic Treaty Organization (NATO), and the North American Free Trade Agreement (NAFTA).

NGOs are private groups and associations from different countries that have joined together to pursue a shared goal. Some organizations are established to promote a common cause, such as environmental protection, human rights, or peace. Others are created to provide a particular service, such as job creation, protection of wounded soldiers, and disaster relief. Unlike IGOs, NGOs are not established, maintained, or directed by governments. Rather, they are initiated, funded, and managed by citizen groups. Although most societies have numerous national NGOs that influence domestic affairs, here we are concerned only with international NGOs—those that are transnational in scope. Unlike IGOs, which have increased only modestly in size and influence, transnational NGOs have increased their role in the international community even as their number has greatly expanded, rising from fewer than five hundred at the end of World War II to more than sixty-five hundred in 2005.

Conclusion

States are the major players of the IR Game. Despite significant changes in the international order, especially the growing functional integration of the world resulting from globalization, the international order remains fundamentally state-centric. Nevertheless, other actors—especially IGOs, NGOs, advocacy networks, and other groups—have been playing an increasingly important role. On the constructive side, nonstate actors are playing an important role in the international community in facilitating peace and political accommodation, promoting international trade and social cooperation, and encouraging collective action on humanitarian concerns. At the same time, some nonstate actors are also impeding global order and encouraging international instability and war, as was the case with the action of Al Qaeda terrorists on 9/11. Thus, as the number and type of actors proliferate, global politics is becoming increasingly complex. Although diplomacy remains critical in the emerging IR game, the problems and challenges in the new order will demand higher creativity and more diverse skills than those currently employed in the classical game.

As noted previously, the role of states is defined by a number of core principles. These include:

P 3.1—States Are the Principal Players in the IR Game
P 3.2—States Are Unequal because Their Capabilities Differ
P 3.3—People Have a Right to Self-Determination
P 3.4—Peoples that Succeed in Establishing a State Can Play the
     IR Game
P 3.5—States Must Be Recognized by Other States before They Can
     Play the IR Game
P 3.6—Prospective States Must Be Based on Former Territorial
     Boundaries
P. 3.7—Nonstate Actors Can Also Play the IR Game

RECOMMENDED READINGS

Cooper, Robert. *The Breaking of Nations: Order and Chaos in the Twenty-First Century* (New York: Atlantic Monthly Press, 2003).

Friedman, Lawrence M. *The Horizontal Society* (New Haven, CT: Yale University Press, 1999).

Ignatieff, Michael. *Blood and Belonging: Journeys into the New Nationalism* (New York: Noonday Press, 1993).

Karns, Margaret P., and Karen A. Mingst, *International Organizations: The Politics and Processes of Global Governance* (Boulder, CO: Lynne Rienner, 2004).

Strange, Susan. *The Retreat of the State: The Diffusion of Power in the World Economy* (Cambridge: Cambridge University Press, 1996).

FOUR

Goals and Strategies
for Playing the IR Game

IN THE SEVENTEENTH CENTURY, British poet John Donne famously observed, "No man is an island." Just as individual well-being is achieved within a social context, national development necessarily depends on participation in the global society of states. States can of course limit their degree of engagement with other states, but an isolationist policy that totally limits interstate ties will impede the economic, social, and political welfare of its people. During the Cold War, Albania pursued an autarkic, reclusive strategy that prohibited virtually all contact with foreign citizens. The result was an economically and socially stagnant society along with increased human suffering. In practice, therefore, whether a country is large or small, rich or poor, it has little choice but to play the IR Game. A state will maximize its national goals and interests only by engaging other member states in global society.

International relations can be carried out at three different levels: privately through nongovernmental organizations, publicly through intergovernmental interactions, and mixed public-private international transactions. In the first type of relations, private actors—citizen groups, civic associations, business organizations, professional networks, NGOs, and so on—pursue transnational interactions among people and groups from different countries. Examples of such international relations include business transactions, the collaborative work of scholars, tourism, international advocacy groups, and private global communications.

The second and most important type of international relations is government-to-government ties. Fundamentally, the IR game is concerned solely with these intergovernmental relations. Although the most frequent interactions are those carried out by private actors, the most significant relations are those among states.

The third type of international relations involves interaction between the government of one state and the society of another. Such transactions represent a small portion of all international transactions and can be initiated either by a government—as when a major power seeks to influence the public opinion of a foreign society—or by a private actor—as when an NGO seeks to influence the behavior of a government. This type of international interaction was illustrated in the late 1970s by Greenpeace, a global environmental group, when it sought to halt French nuclear testing in the South Pacific, and by international human rights groups in 1990 when they sought to pressure the government of Great Britain to extradite to Spain former Chilean president Augusto Pinochet to stand trial for human rights abuses against Spanish nationals.

In this chapter I explore how states play the IR game by examining the nature and role of foreign policy. In the first part I describe how states seek to advance national interests and how they attempt to reconcile national claims with the pursuit of the global common good. In the second part I assess the nature and role of power, the chief resource in pursuing foreign policy in global society. In the third section, I sketch four types of policies used to advance foreign policy goals: diplomacy, sanctions, threats, and military force.

How to Win: The Nature and Role of Foreign Policy

Although IR is a competitive game, winning does not necessarily involve a winner and a loser. Scholars distinguish between *zero-sum games,* such as chess or football, where the gain of one player or team comes at the expense of another, and *positive-sum games,* where many players or teams can gain (win) without others necessarily losing. Although some international relations, such as a conflict over territory or a war over foreign aggression, are zero-sum games, the bulk of IR is competitive but not conflictual. Fundamentally, interstate relations are a positive-sum game where states coordinate their actions in order to maintain order and harmony in global society and cooperate in promoting shared interests, such as human rights, global economic prosperity, and other international goods. Although all states no doubt desire a peaceful, stable, and prosperous world, they are even more concerned with their own national security, global political influence, and economic prosperity. Just as individuals focus on their own individual and familial prosperity, states are chiefly concerned with their own citizens' welfare. In the IR game, the quest for national well-being is primary; the pursuit of the world's common good is secondary.

Because the tangible and intangible resources of the world are limited and the interests of states are unlimited, interstate competition and conflict are inevitable. To be sure, states can minimize conflict by developing rules and institutions that facilitate cooperation and coordination. Inevitably, however, states will pursue mutually exclusive goals that lead to conflict. Such conflict is often rooted in disputes over issues such as territorial boundaries, political ideology, national security concerns, natural resources, and the economic policies of other states. The challenge in playing the IR game is to maximize national wants and interests without unnecessarily antagonizing other states. When conflict does arise, the challenge is to resolve incompatible goals in the least-costly and -violent way possible.

Winning in the IR game entails maximizing a state's national economic and political welfare while also ensuring the order of global society. States win when they advance their specific national interests and wants. But because national well-being depends in great part on peace, political order, and effective functioning of the global economy, winning in the IR game also entails a peaceful, stable, and economically prosperous world. The IR game therefore entails the pursuit of both global and national interests. The challenge in playing the IR game is therefore to maximize the particular wants and interests of individual societies while also promoting the global common good. A successful strategy must focus on both the national and international levels.

Foreign Policy

Foreign policy can be defined as the expression of a country's vital interests in terms of the interests of other nations. It is, as one scholar has observed, "the face a nation wears to the world."[1] Fundamentally, foreign policy making involves defining general goals and specifying policy objectives and then devising strategies to pursue established goals and objectives.

Foreign policy making is not unlike playing an athletic or board game. To begin with, both foreign policy making and competitive games involve strategy—that is a game plan. In chess, for example, skilled players must combine offensive and defensive tactics in order to prevail against an opponent, and statesmen must rely on a variety of policy instruments in order to maximize the pursuit of national objectives. Additionally, both athletic contests and the IR game involve interactive strategies that are based on an estimate of opponents' capabilities or in response to opponents' actions. For example, in playing football a team will pursue victory by attempting to exploit an opponent's defensive weaknesses or its offensive limitations. And in the IR game, a state will seek to advance its foreign policy goals by using policy instruments and tactics that help it prevail. As in competitive games, statesmen devise strategies not simply based on their own capabilities but also on an assessment of an opponent's resources and political resolve.

The IR game also differs from athletic contests in a significant way. Whereas the logic of winning in athletic or board games is relatively simple, victory in IR is often difficult to define and even elusive. In athletic games, for example, victory is achieved by gaining more points than an opponent or by covering a defined distance in less time than other competitors. But in the IR game winning has no clear definition, because foreign policy entails the pursuit of multiple and ever-changing goals. To be sure, because there is no global authority in the international community, security remains a fundamental goal of states. But states are concerned with other goals as well, and because these are not necessarily complementary, governments must prioritize their wants, and where necessary, reconcile competing and conflicting interests.

Foreign policy is relatively easy among friends who share similar values and goals and respect each others' priorities. When states' ideals, strategies, and resources are radically different, however, foreign policy is likely to be far more challenging. Indeed, Robert Cooper has observed that foreign policy would be easy if it did not involve foreigners.[2] Moreover, when a state seeks to alter the behavior of another, such a foreign policy will require great knowledge, skill, and above all, patience. And because persuading others to change their mind is difficult, often the best strategy is to wait. One diplomat describes this policy—the "diplomacy of patience"—as follows: "The function of diplomacy is often to find a formula—frequently an ambiguous form of words—on which everyone can pretend to agree while they wait for something to change. . . . When it proves impossible to find such a formula, often the best that can be done is to keep talking so that the existence of a 'process' gives everyone an excuse to wait and hope, rather than make things worse by taking action."[3]

🚨 P 4.1—Foreign Policy Is the Means by Which States Pursue Interests in Global Society

A state's foreign policy is represented by the explicit and implicit actions that governments undertake to advance the collective wants and interests of their citizens within the global society. During the Cold War, a major foreign policy goal of the United States was to contain the expansion of Communism by the Soviet Union. To advance this goal, the United States developed numerous political, economic, and military policies and programs. For example, the Marshall Plan was instituted in 1947 to help rebuild the economies of Western Europe that had been destroyed in World War II. To help sustain emerging democratic regimes and to undermine Communist initiatives in foreign countries, especially in Central and Western Europe, the United States established the Central Intelligence Agency (CIA)—an organization tasked to gather foreign intelligence and carry out covert operations. In 1961, President John F. Kennedy established the Alliance for Progress, an initiative to foster economic growth and social reform in Latin America in order to contain the spread of Marxist social revolution. Militarily, the United States initiated the establishment of the North Atlantic Treaty Organization (NATO) in order to deter Soviet aggression against Western Europe.

Although foreign policy making can be conceived as a rational process where decision makers identify and prioritize goals and devise alternative strategies to pursue them in the most efficient and effective manner, in practice, the process of making and implementing foreign policy is not carried out solely through rational calculation by unitary, cohesive states. This is so for a number of reasons. First, although governments of sovereign states have ultimate decision-making responsibility, states are not unitary, coherent actors. Typically, decision making involves numerous governmental agencies, different bureaucratic interests and perspectives, and a pluralistic, divided public opinion that is expressed to and through multiple governmental and nongovernmental organizations. As a result, foreign policy making is a complex, conflictual process. Although the Department of State is the organization responsible for the development and implementation of U.S. foreign policy, it is not the only agency participating in international decisions. Indeed, in most democratic regimes, foreign policy making involves many actors, including citizens, nongovernmental organizations, political leaders, government bureaucrats, and diplomats.

In a seminal study on the Cuban Missile Crisis, Graham Allison argued that the conventional perspective on foreign policy, which he termed the *rational-actor model*, did not fully explain the foreign policy process. Instead, he argued that this rational model needed to be supplemented by two different perspectives—the organizational process model and the bureaucratic politics model.[4] Whereas the rational actor model viewed governmental decision making as a rational process by a unitary state, the other two models emphasized the lack of unity and coherence in the decision-making process. In particular, the *organizational process model* emphasized decision making as the result of outcomes from diverse government agencies, each with their own interests and standard operating procedures (SOPs). Whereas the rational actor perspective views decision making as the result of dispassionate assessment of goals and strategies, the organizational perspective stresses policy making as the by-product of preestablished routines among relevant quasi-independent governmental organizations. Finally, the *bureaucratic politics model* depicts decision making as the result of competition and bargaining among different relevant governmental organizations. Because each participating agency tends to advance its own interests and perspectives, policy making must be seen as the result of bargaining and negotiation among relevant governmental organizations. In effect, the bureaucratic model views decision making as the result of interagency power politics.

A second explanation as to why the foreign policy-making process is not always guided by facts and reason is that government officials might be unwilling or unable to define appropriate goals and to establish appropriate strategies for pursuing such goals. Although decision making can be impaired by ignorance and lack of strategic intelligence (knowledge about an adversary), a far more common reason for failure is overconfidence in achieving desired outcomes. This shortcoming was evident in the U.S. government's decision to topple the Iraqi government of Saddam Hussein in 2003. Although there was little doubt that U.S. armed forces would prevail, decision makers were unduly optimistic about rebuilding an alternative, more humane regime once the Iraqi armed forces had been defeated. But after toppling the Baathist regime, U.S. forces found that nation building was a much more intractable task than the original invasion had been. Indeed, three years after defeating the Hussein government, British and U.S. forces were still battling an ongoing insurgency, seeking to maintain order among warring Sunni and Shia militia.

A more important factor is misperception of international issues and problems, caused frequently by excessive ideological biases or overconfidence in the capacity to effect change. Examples of common misperceptions in international affairs include: underestimating enemy capabilities, oversimplifying issues and problems, misperceiving the intentions of foreign governments, and overestimating the moral purity of one's own actions. The role of misperception in contributing to flawed foreign policies is illustrated in U.S. foreign policy toward Vietnam in the 1960s. Although there were legitimate interests involved in the U.S. commitment to assist the people of South Vietnam in building and sustaining a humane, democratic regime, the excessive ideological commitment to combat Communism led U.S. political leaders to misperceive the nature of the political conflict in Vietnam and to underestimate the military capabilities and strategic tenacity of the revolutionary guerrillas.

Interests: National and Global

When states pursue a foreign policy, they are guided by perceptions of national interests as well as by perceptions of international society's shared interests. National interests are those vital wants of each member state. Global interests, by contrast, are the general interests of the international community itself. Although the two types of interests are related, a sound foreign policy must advance the national interest while also promoting the shared interests of global society. If states pursue only their narrowly defined national interests, the political and moral basis of the international community will suffer. Because the political and economic well-being of states can only be fully realized within a stable and humane international political system, sustaining and promoting the society of states is an important task.

⚄ P 4.2—The National Interest Represents the Fundamental Wants of a Nation

Scholars and public officials refer to the long-term, fundamental wants of states as *national interest*. Because of the stable, persistent nature of states' goals, this concept provides a useful tool for identifying the chief end of foreign policy making—which is to advance the vital interests of states within the international community. Some scholars criticize the idea of national interest because it does not have a fixed operational meaning. But the concept is useful, not because it illuminates specific foreign policy objectives, but because it helps to focus on the permanent, core interests of states and to distinguish them from variable, nonvital concerns. Just as profit making is the major aim of business enterprise, so, too, is the pursuit of national interest the basic foreign policy aim of states.

In a penetrating essay, the noted historian Arthur Schlesinger Jr. argued that foreign policy should be grounded in the national interest, not on morality, ideology, parochial interests, or ephemeral concerns. He claimed that foreign policy is unsustainable when national interest is not its "mainspring." "Without the magnetic compass of national interest," Schlesinger wrote, "there would be no regularity and predictability in international affairs."[5] The noted diplomat George F. Kennan similarly claimed that the aim of foreign policy was to advance the tangible interests of states, not the moral values or sensibilities of their people.[6]

Some critics have argued that the idea of national interest is unnecessarily elastic, obfuscating rather than clarifying the goals of foreign policy. Others have suggested that the notion of national interest is inadequate because it disregards concerns for the global common good. Still others claim that the national interest is simply a tool used to advance greedy, selfish policies. Although the national interest can be misused for short-term, parochial gains, the concept is useful in clarifying the objective of foreign policy, which is to advance the true, long-term interests of states. According to Alexander George and Robert Keohane, national interest can contribute to better foreign policy decision making by helping to "improve judgments regarding the proper ends and goals of foreign policy."[7]

What are the fundamental interests of states? Despite the varied expressions of foreign policy goals by citizens, advocacy groups, and political officials, the basic interests of states have remained largely constant in the modern international system. These interests are security, prosperity, and ideals—with the first being the most foundational.

Survival is the most important state goal, because in the anarchic global society no central authority exists to ensure protection from foreign aggression. One scholar has argued that self-preservation is the most important tangible interest because the fulfillment of other interests depends on survival—that is, on the territorial integrity and political independence of the states.[8] National security is so fundamental that, as Sir Winston Churchill once observed, it needs no political mandate.

Economic well-being, the second vital interest, is important because without economic growth, improving living standards is impossible. Because people, whether in rich or poor lands, desire continued improvements in the physical quality of life, governments are expected to foster economic growth and devise foreign economic policies that are conducive to economic expansion. A growing economy is also important to governments, because national power is dependent on a nation's wealth. Historically, the international influence of a state has depended partly on a country's level of economic development. In his study of wealth and power, historian Paul Kennedy found that the two attributes have been closely linked throughout the centuries. Indeed, he argues that when states devote a disproportionate amount of resources to military security, the result is economic decline.[9]

A third vital interest is the promotion and institutionalization of *ideals*. Such ideals range from ideological and religious beliefs to pragmatic political ideas. The growth of Muslim fundamentalism in the Middle East and Africa, which has resulted in a resurgence of domestic and international politics inspired by Islamic values, illustrates the role of religious values in structuring foreign policy objectives. Ethnic identity can also be an important source of foreign policy ideals. Ethnicity has been an especially strong force in the post–Cold War era among subnational groups demanding political self-determination, such as the Kurds in Iraq (and Iran and Turkey), the Chechens in Russia, and the Montenegrins and Kosovars in the former Yugoslavia. Finally, universal political ideals also serve as a foundational guide in foreign policy. Moral ideals have played a key role in the foreign policy of President George W. Bush, who has made the promotion of human rights and democracy the centerpiece of his national security strategy.

To be sure, the notion of national interest can be misused to defend unlimited national selfishness. However, it must be noted that although an egoistic, imperialistic policy might advance short-term state interests, it is unlikely to promote a nation's political and economic interests in the long run. Thus, if national interest is to serve as a guide, it needs to be enlightened and circumscribed by consideration for the legitimate interests of other states. In calling for a foreign policy rooted in a humane conception of national interest, Theodore Roosevelt observed: "It is neither wise nor right for a nation to disregard its own needs, and it is foolish—and may even be wicked—to think that other nations will disregard theirs. But it is wicked for a nation only to regard its own interest, and foolish to believe that such is the sole motive that actuates any other nation."[10] Roosevelt then went on to argue that the U.S. government should seek to raise the ethical standard of its foreign policy behavior. In sum, *national interest,* when properly conceived, is a useful concept that helps to delineate the fundamental, legitimate goals of states.

☙ P 4.3—The Global Interest Represents the Common Concerns of the International Community

The *global interest* is the common good of the international community. The common good of international society, which is expressed in numerous bilateral and multilateral treaties, conventions, and agreements, focuses on such issues as sustainable economic development, environmental protection, promotion of human dignity, and most importantly, peace. International peace is the foundational global interest because without it a humane, productive world is impossible. In domestic societies, government's most basic task is to use its coercive authority to ensure a humane political order based on the rule of law. But in the international community no global authority exists to resolve interstate disputes and deter war. Thus, if peace and concord are to prevail in global society, states themselves must create the institutions and policies that are conducive to global order.

The pursuit of other common concerns, such as environmental protection, economic prosperity, and human rights, presents a similarly daunting challenge. Because there is no central governing authority to define goals and make and enforce policies, the pursuit of global interests is dependent largely on the voluntary cooperative actions of states. To be sure, cooperative action is encouraged and facilitated by perceived national interests, international legal accords, and global governance structures (e.g., intergovernmental organizations, transnational advocacy networks). But the quest for the global common good—whether it involves the preservation of fish stocks, the maintenance of a clean atmosphere, or the disposal of harmful waste products—is more precarious in international society because no authority exists to allocate behavioral responsibilities to each member state.

The quest to reduce reliance on the use of carbon-based products illustrates the difficulty. Because modernization requires increased energy, and because most energy is generated from fossil fuels, a major challenge in modernization is to reduce reliance on petroleum and to develop alternative sources of energy. In an effort to promote clean air, the world's nations signed a Climate Treaty in 1992 and subsequently agreed to the 1997 Kyoto Protocol, which established pollution-reduction goals. Although there is widespread agreement on the phenomenon of global warming, and although many scientists have concluded that the rise in the earth's temperature is partly a result of carbon gas emissions that capture solar heat (much like a greenhouse), the United States (and several other states) has refused to accept the pollution reductions required by the Kyoto framework. The refusal to accept binding reductions on energy usage is due, among other things, to two factors: the belief that curtailment of carbon-based energy sources would harm the economy and second, the failure to impose reductions on emerging industrial nations. Although it is widely acknowledged that the developed nations are responsible for the largest share of the world's carbon pollution, U.S. officials believe that any international effort to curb carbon emissions must, at a minimum, include India and China, the world's two most populous states and whose industrial development in recent years has led to the highest increases in the rate of carbon consumption.

The challenge in balancing national and global interests is illustrated in the *tragedy of the commons analogy*. The analogy, first articulated in 1833 by economist William Foster Lloyd and popularized in the mid-twentieth century by scientist Garrett Hardin, illustrates the dilemma of reconciling immediate national goals with long-term global interests.[11] According to the analogy, villagers raise livestock on private plots and also on a common pasture. Whereas grazing on private lands is carefully maintained, the communal land deteriorates from its misuse. The problem posed by the commons is: How much grazing should be permitted for each villager, if the goal is to ensure the commons' sustainability? Because the common pasture can only be maintained if limited grazing is allowed, the challenge for the farmers is how to maximize their individual gain without destroying the communal land. If each villager defines his interests in light of the common good, he will place only a limited number of animals in the commons to avoid overgrazing. If villagers, however, pursue their immediate, narrow self-interest, the communal land will be overused, leading to the deterioration of the pasture and the eventual destruction of the commons.

According to Hardin, when property is collectively owned, few incentives exist to promote the long-term common good. For example, when several villagers each add an animal to the common pasture, it leads to their personal gain, even though its long-term cost to the community from the overuse of the commons is distributed to all villagers. Consequently, the incentive to pursue personal gain is stronger and more immediate than the quest for the collective good through self-sacrifice. The tragedy of the commons analogy therefore has important implications for global society, where member states share collective goods like water, air, and marine resources. Because common resources can be overused or misused, states need to ensure that their own actions are not contributing to the deterioration of the commons. The challenge is for states to cooperate in managing and protecting the global environment.

Power: The Essential Resource

⚉ P 4.4—Power Is the Currency Used to Pursue Foreign Policy Goals

Success in the IR game depends largely on states' *power*. Power is important because it is the chief determinant of a state's ability to protect and promote its vital interests in global society. Kenneth Waltz, a leading IR theorist, has observed that power in international relations is significant because it provides states with four important needs: autonomy, freedom of action, a margin of safety, and greater influence in the international community.[12]

Although power is one of the most important elements of international relations, it is also one of the most elusive concepts—in great part because, unlike money in a national economy, it is not a tangible resource that can be easily quantified, but rather a capability. To have power is to be able to determine outcomes, or as one scholar has put it, "to prevail in conflict and to overcome obstacles."[13] But how does one know when they have sufficient power to prevail? Although the behavioral perspective is useful in calling attention to the important purposes and effects of power in IR, viewing power as the ability to get others to do what they would not otherwise do introduces many complexities. In particular, in order to discern the role of power, we need to know 1) what the foreign policy preferences of other states are and 2) which resources—ideas, money, military force—are likely to influence the actions of foreign leaders. But since foreknowledge of others' preferences and perceptions of power is not possible, statesmen are unlikely to assess foreign policy solely from a subjective behavioral perspective. Rather, leaders want a more objective measure of power in order to structure their analyses of relative capabilities and assessment of foreign policy decision making. As a result, leaders tend to think in terms of power as rooted in objective resources, such as territory, population, natural resources, level of economic development, size and quality of the armed force, and intangible resources like national morale, leadership, and quality of government.

Although the role of tangible and intangible resources has varied over time, two resources that continuously play a decisive role in global politics are the size and quality of a state's armed forces and its level of economic development. Military capacity is significant because in the decentralized system of states, military force is the ultimate way of resolving interstate disputes. Although interstate wars have become less frequent in the past century, military power continues to determine the course of interstate politics. The continuing importance of force is illustrated by both its role in major international military conflicts and by the ongoing role of military power in preventing aggression (deterrence) and compelling states to alter their foreign policy behavior (coercive diplomacy). Because all interstate relations are rooted in implicit or explicit threats of force, military capacity is the foundation and indispensable resource of credible foreign policy. To be sure, national interests are normally pursued peacefully through mutual cooperation; but when conflicts arise and disputes cannot be resolved through compromise, a state might resort to coercive diplomacy—threatening the opposing state with military action if it does not comply with the former state's demands.

The second major tangible resource of national power is wealth. A country's productive capacity not only ensures an adequate standard of living for its citizens, but it also provides necessary resources for national security and other state goals. Generally, countries with large national incomes devote more financial resources to the military than states with modest-sized economies. Of course wealth does not ensure a country of significant power. But although wealth might not be a sufficient condition for power, it is clearly a necessary element. Historian Paul Kennedy has shown the close correspondence between wealth and power by arguing that the rise and fall of the great powers has been historically associated with the rise and fall of their economies. Empires, writes Kennedy, are based on wealth, and when a nation's economy declines, it inevitably results in a loss of international influence.[14]

Despite the important role of military and economic resources in determining a state's international influence, resources do not ensure global influence. Because national power is ultimately based on people's subjective assessment of power resources and a government's willingness to use them against other states, power in the final analysis is rooted in perception. And regardless of the validity of such perceptions, it is clear that a state's reputation of power itself contributes to its national power.

Although resources are important in pursuing foreign policy, whether a government can prevail in conflicts will be determined by the ability to use resources in a wise and discriminating manner. Resources are only the investment capital of IR. Whether or not resources are used in a prudent, discriminating fashion to pursue legitimate foreign policy goals will define how effectively a government is pursuing its goals. Therefore, it is important to distinguish between *potential power*—the military and economic resources that can be used to influence and coerce other states— and *actual power*—the effectiveness with which governments use resources to get other states to do what they would not otherwise do. As a result, in the IR game, a state's efficiency in converting resources to actual power is likely to be an important determinant in a government's ability to determine behavioral outcomes of other states. Additionally, it needs to be stressed that although more powerful states are likely to prevail over weaker states, from time to time, states with fewer resources prevail over stronger states. In the two hundred wars since 1800 between strong and weak states (asymmetric conflicts), powerful states have won most of the time. What is surprising is that weak states have prevailed in 30 percent of the cases, with weaker states winning a majority of the wars during the second half of the twentieth century.[15]

Of course, the capacity to influence behavior need not be carried out solely by the use of coercive threats ("sticks") or the promise of benefits ("carrots") from individual states. Another way to influence the actions of other states is to institutionalize power by establishing rules, regimes, and organizations that structure the decision-making choices of others. Although institutions can be the creation of powerful states, such norms and rules will be regarded as more acceptable and less coercive because of their multilateral character.[16] The importance of institutionalizing power is illustrated by postwar U.S. foreign policy, when it sought to promote a stable, humane, and prosperous international system rooted in democratic values and a free international economic order.[17] Although the United States could have promoted these goals alone, it used its considerable power to create institutions that advanced these goals. For example, to promote a free, democratic world, the United States led the way in creating political organizations, like the United Nations and the Organization of American States, and defensive alliance systems, like the Inter-American Treaty of Reciprocal Assistance (the so-called Rio Pact) and the North Atlantic Treaty Organization (NATO). And to advance a liberal international economic order, it played the leading role in establishing organizations like the World Bank and the International Monetary Fund and a multilateral trading arrangement known as the General Agreement on Tariffs and Trade (GATT). These organizations and the values they embody have helped promote international peace and democratic governance and foster global international financial and commercial policies that are conducive to increased economic output.

Finally, it is important to distinguish between two different ways of exerting control on others. Fundamentally, two different strategies are available: a direct strategy called command or *hard power* and an indirect strategy called co-optive or *soft power*.[18] The first seeks to influence the behavior of others through coercive threats or positive inducements. Diplomatic threats, military actions, and economic sanctions are examples of hard power. Soft power, by contrast, seeks to achieve behavioral outcomes by getting others to pursue the goals and behaviors of the home state—to get others to want what you have and want. Examples of soft power include political ideas, economic practices, and cultural values. The victory of free enterprise over state socialism illustrates the important role of ideas in global politics.

Because power is the currency of global politics, a major challenge in playing the IR game is to determine how best to use power to advance the foreign policy interests of states. In the next section, I examine some of the major strategies for pursuing national interests.

Statecraft: The Tools to Maximize Interests

Statecraft is generally defined as the art of conducting the affairs of state—that is, establishing goals and setting strategies for promoting national interests. In global affairs, the major responsibility of statecraft is to prioritize interests in order to distinguish vital from nonvital concerns. A secondary task is to define how those interests should be pursued in global society, ensuring that sufficient resources are available to execute policies successfully. Generally, government officials establish goals and strategies, and trained diplomatic personnel implement a government's foreign policy goals.

In pursuing foreign policy objectives, states have many resources and strategies at their disposal. Three common ways that states have pursued foreign policy objectives are: *negotiation* (reconciling competing and conflicting interests through compromise), *threats* (preventing other actors from carrying out unacceptable behaviors), and *force* (compelling enemies to halt undesirable or harmful actions). During the Cuban missile crisis of 1962, when the Soviet Union installed intermediate ballistic nuclear missiles on the island, President John F. Kennedy was presented with three similar options: persuasion, invasion, and coercion—which one senior U.S. military officer described as "talk 'em out, shoot 'em out, and squeeze 'em out."[19]

States use a variety of approaches to pursue their foreign policy goals. These include:

- Rational persuasion—using logic and data to convince other players;
- Manipulative persuasion—using deception to convince other players;
- Propaganda—disseminating information to the general public in order to alter their perceptions and ideas;
- Sanctions—providing positive (carrots) and negative (sticks) incentives to convince other players to change their behaviors or policies;
- Deterrence—preventing unwanted action through the promise of unacceptable punishment;
- Coercive diplomacy—using military threats to persuade players to change their behavior; and
- Military force—using coercive power to compel a player to change its behavior.

In what follows, I explore the nature and role of four principal foreign policy instruments—diplomacy, economic sanctions, coercive threats, and force.

📖 P 4.5—Diplomacy Can Facilitate the Peaceful Resolution of International Disputes

Diplomacy—the resolution of conflicts through negotiation—is the most fundamental instrument of foreign policy. It is the basic tool of statecraft, because it is the means for developing and promoting common interests and the principal method for peaceful reconciliation of competing and conflicting goals. Typically, such reconciliation is achieved through *compromise*—that is, through the mutual acceptance of a less-than-ideal settlement. In effect, the contesting parties must be willing to accept partial satisfaction, as opposed to the full realization of their goals. Dr. Henry Kissinger, the former U.S. secretary of state, has observed that a negotiated settlement will always appear somewhat unjust and provide only partial satisfaction. "The generality of this dissatisfaction," writes Kissinger, "is a condition of stability because were any one power totally satisfied, all others would be totally dissatisfied."[20]

Historically, the task of representing state interests was undertaken by a cadre of professionals, who carried out their responsibilities with significant authority, flexibility, and secrecy. But as modern science and technology have transformed the world with the resulting instantaneous communication and rapid transportation, foreign policy decision making has become more centralized, leading to a diminution in the role of trained diplomats. In the contemporary world, diplomats continue to play a major role in representing state interests in foreign countries, but the responsibility for major bilateral and multilateral negotiations has shifted to the top political leadership of states. Additionally, diplomacy has become more multilateral as the number of regional and specialized global conferences (summits) has increased to address common economic, environmental, or political concerns (see Box 4.1). For example, the leaders of the industrialized nations—the so-called Group of 8, or G-8—meet annually during the summer months for a two-day economic summit.

From a moral perspective, negotiation is desirable not only because it prevents more costly and violent alternatives but also because it is more likely to result in a lasting peace. When actors fail to resolve a dispute through compromise, they might continue to harbor resentment and seek to achieve a new, more favorable settlement. The rise of Germany in the 1930s and the outbreak of World War II are often attributed to the unduly punitive measures imposed on it by the Treaty of Versailles at the end of World War I. More importantly, however, negotiation provides the most effective way of creating an acceptable, and therefore stable, global order. In a world of sovereign states, the maintenance of global order is most likely to emerge from international cooperation.

🕮 P 4.6—States Can Influence Other States through Economic Sanctions

A second way by which states can persuade other states is by granting economic benefits ("carrots") or imposing economic penalties ("sticks"). Examples of positive sanctions include foreign aid, preferential trade agreements, and increased multilateral loans; negative sanctions include acts such as freezing of foreign assets, suspension of foreign aid, tariff increases, and trade embargo. Although economic sanctions can involve either incentives or penalties, in popular usage they refer primarily to the imposition of economic hardship.

Economic sanctions are a popular foreign policy tool, especially in the United States. One reason for their popularity is that they are viewed as an effective way of sending a message—not only to the recalcitrant state but also to the world community itself. From a public diplomacy

♞   ♞   ♞

Box 4.1 Norms of Diplomacy

When playing the IR game, the following maxims have facilitated effective diplomacy:

1. *Differentiate between vital and nonvital interests* and be prepared to *compromise on nonessentials.* Defining national interests clearly and realistically is a precondition for an effective diplomacy.
2. *Don't be a crusader or moralist.* Moral values should guide and inform the definition of national interest, but should not be the primary guide in foreign policy. Foreign policies guided by morality are likely to impair negotiation and breed international resentment.
3. *Develop knowledge of foreigners.* Because sound diplomacy demands that the messages sent to the receiving state be clearly understood, knowledge of foreign societies—especially their language, history, and culture—is indispensable. This is especially the case when the receiving society is radically different from the nation sending messages. Thus, if diplomatic communication is to be effective across cultures, government officials must possess deep knowledge of foreign values, habits, and traditions, as well as styles of communication.
4. *Practice empathy.* Because foreign policy goals should be pursued in light of the perspectives of other states, sound diplomacy requires knowledge of other states' wants and ideals. Frequently there is more concern with pronouncements and declarations than with ensuring behavioral reform by a foreign state. It is important to place ourselves in other people's shoes, not simply because such a tactic is likely to achieve better outcomes and facilitate bargaining and conflict resolution, but also because empathy is a way to give respect to foreigners.

perspective, sanctions provide an easy way to condemn aggression and oppose injustice. Economic sanctions are also popular because they are viewed as an easy way to punish a state for unacceptable behavior. When a state is involved in aggression, major human rights abuses, or terrorism, other states might respond with individual or collective sanctions in the hope that the target state will desist in its unacceptable behavior. Finally, sanctions are popular because they are perceived as preferable to armed force. Because war is the most costly and destructive tool, the popularity of sanctions derives in great part from the belief that sanctions are a morally preferable alternative to violence. When U.S. senators were debating whether or not to go to war against Iraq in 2003, a

5. *Be patient.* Because people typically resist change, influencing the behavior and ideas of others is difficult. This is especially the case for foreigners, because they are likely to think and act differently from nationals. Consequently, the quest to influence the foreign policy behavior of other states will require serious and prolonged engagement. One diplomat has written that "lasting results need lasting commitment."[1]

6. *Focus on outcomes, not values or positions.* A common error in foreign affairs is to focus on the errors, mistakes, or unacceptable beliefs of other states rather than on the desired behavioral outcomes. Roger Fisher, a conflict resolution specialist, has written, "the formulation and reformulation of the decision we seek is . . . the single most important element in the successful conduct of foreign affairs."[2]

7. When direct negotiations are unproductive, *get the help of outsiders.* Intermediaries can assist conflict resolution by diffusing passions, gathering relevant information, generating alternative solutions, and facilitating communication. Major powers can facilitate third-party negotiations by facilitating communication and encouraging antagonists. President Jimmy Carter illustrated the important role of outside pressure during the 1978 Camp David negotiations, which resulted in a peace accord between President Anwar Sadat of Egypt and Prime Minister Menachem Begin of Israel.

Notes

1 Robert Cooper, *The Breaking of Nations: Order and Chaos in the Twenty-First Century* (New York: Atlantic Monthly Press, 2003), 126.

2 Roger Fisher, *International Conflict for Beginners* (New York: Harper & Row, 1969), 75.

common refrain among opponents of war was to let "sanctions do their work," in the belief that the economic hardship would in time encourage the Iraqi regime to alter its policies.

Economic sanctions are imposed for a variety of reasons. One goal is to punish a state for committing illegal, unjust behavior. When Libya was implicated in the downing of PamAm Flight 103 in 1988, which led to the deaths of more than 250 persons, the U.S. government responded by imposing stiff economic sanctions. These measures remained in effect for nearly fifteen years and were lifted only after the Libyan government of Mu'ammar Gadhafi admitted guilt and provided compensation to victims. A second reason for imposing sanctions is to communicate individual or collective disapproval of behavior. When South Africa persisted in maintaining racial segregation (apartheid), Western states imposed a variety of trade and financial restrictions that greatly curtailed its economic growth. Third, sanctions are imposed in order to foster policy change in a target state. The core assumption of sanctions is that increased economic adversity will lead to behavioral change—that punishment and isolation will encourage reform.[21]

Do sanctions work? Whether or not economic sanctions are an effective foreign policy tool will depend on what goals are sought. If the aim is to punish a state for its aggression or human rights abuses or to send a message about a regime's injustice, then sanctions are likely to work, because effectiveness will be determined solely by the extent of economic coercion.[22] If the goal is behavioral change, however, then success is likely to be far more elusive. Indeed, Charles Kindleberger asserts, "most sanctions are not effective,"[23] and Margaret Doxey concludes her study of sanctions by noting that "in none of the cases analyzed . . . have economic sanctions succeeded in producing the desired result."[24] In a statistical study of sanctions from 1946 to 1989, sanctions achieved behavioral change in only 34 percent of the cases. Moreover, the study found that during the first half of the Cold War era, sanctions were much more effective than in the second half.[25]

What explains sanctions' ineffectiveness? One possible reason is that punishment and hardship do not necessarily encourage political change. Indeed, sanctions can contribute to greater political resolve, as demonstrated by the Cuban government's response to the long-term economic sanctions imposed by the United States on the island after Fidel Castro instituted Communism domestically and revolutionary politics internationally. A second reason why sanctions are ineffective is that the harm is borne disproportionately by citizens, with government decision makers finding ways of overcoming their losses. Finally, sanctions are suspect because economic hardship cannot be targeted solely on decision makers and military officials. Because moral theory demands that war must discriminate between civilians and leaders, noncombatants and combatants, the inability to target hardship on government officials undermines their perceived moral superiority over war. The significant humanitarian costs of comprehensive economic sanctions were amply evident in Iraq in the mid-1990s, when it was estimated that more than half a million children had died from direct and indirect effects of U.N.-imposed sanctions following the end of the 1991 Gulf War.

🁢 P 4.7—States Can Influence Other States through Military Threats

Threatening military action is a third way that states can try to influence the behavior of foreign states. Fundamentally, threats—which can be

made implicitly or explicitly—are used either to deter or to coerce. The first option, *deterrence,* seeks to prevent an opponent state from carrying out undesirable behaviors by promising unacceptable punishment. Perhaps the significant example of this foreign policy tool was the threat of nuclear retaliation during the Cold War. According to the logic of nuclear deterrence, the United States sought to deter Soviet aggression by promising unacceptable retaliation. To ensure that this retaliatory threat was credible, the United States developed three major ways of delivering nuclear bombs (land-based long-range missiles, sea-based missiles, and bombers). According to deterrence theory, the preservation of peace rested not on the prevention of a nuclear attack but on the certainty of unacceptable retaliation (second strike) after being attacked (first strike).

The second option, *coercive diplomacy,* seeks to compel a state to do something or to stop doing something through the promise of compelling force. This foreign policy tool was dramatically illustrated in the Persian Gulf in 1991. After Iraqi armed forces invaded Kuwait in August 1990, the United States, with the support of numerous other states, condemned Iraq's aggression and called for the immediate termination of its occupation. After nearly six months of preparing a large multinational force, the United States—with the support of numerous Security Council resolutions—demanded that Saddam Hussein withdraw his forces from Kuwait or face forceful expulsion. When he refused to comply with the coercive diplomatic demands, the U.S.-led forces carried out a month of aerial bombardment followed by a brief four-day ground assault that resulted in the defeat of Iraqi forces and the restoration of Kuwaiti sovereignty.

It is important to stress that both deterrence and coercive diplomacy seek to achieve political objectives peacefully. Unlike war, deterrent or coercive threats involve only the possible use of force. Whether or not the threatening state resorts to military action is determined by the response of the opponent: If a state disregards the threat, it will either be punished (because of the failure of deterrence) or compelled (because of the failure of coercive threats). Although several factors are likely to affect the credibility of threats, two factors are of special significance: first, the size, quality, and preparedness of armed forces and second, the willingness to use force in deterring and compelling enemy states. The credibility of deterrence and coercive diplomacy rests in large measure on relative military capabilities and the perceived will to use those capabilities in achieving foreign policy goals. Thus, military theorists assume that the greater the relative military resources and perceived certainty of action, the more effective deterrence and coercive diplomacy are likely to be.

Because both deterrence and coercive diplomacy seek to realize foreign policy objectives with threats rather than applied coercion, they are more economical and efficient uses of military power than war. Not surprisingly, both passive threats (deterrence) and active threats (coercive diplomacy) are the most common use of military power in the IR game. But these tools are likely to remain effective only so long as they are credible. If threats are made without adequate resources or will, bluff is likely to be called, compromising a state's foreign policy and damaging its international reputation.

⌂ P 4.8—States Can Compel Other States with Force

The fourth major instrument of foreign policy is coercive power, or force. When states are unable to promote or defend their vital interests through diplomacy, sanctions, or threats, they might resort to armed force—the most extreme foreign policy tool. Armed force is the ultimate instrument in the international community, because no global institution exists with the authority to ensure order, protect rights of member states, or resolve interstate conflicts impartially and decisively.

Although most international relations are carried out peacefully, inevitably states pursue opposing goals that lead to major conflicts. When states are unable to peacefully resolve disputes involving vital interests, they might decide to use coercive force after exhausting all other alternatives, including sanctions and coercive diplomacy. Historically, the most prevalent type of armed conflict was international war. But in modern times, as the lethality of armed violence has increased, domestic or internal war has become the most frequent type of armed conflict. Such wars are fueled by political groups seeking to gain control of government, by a disgruntled ethnic group demanding political self-determination, or by a political group seeking to transform the nature of the state. Military historian John Keegan has written that contemporary wars are not only a means to resolve international conflicts but also a "vehicle with which the embittered, the dispossessed, the naked of the earth, the hungry masses yearning to breathe free, express their anger, jealousies and pent-up urge to violence."[26]

When disputes involve vital interests, such as national honor or territorial security, resolving conflicts through diplomatic negotiation can prove difficult, if not impossible. Generally the most intractable international disputes involve the creation of new states, national security concerns, and territorial claims. The issue of political sovereignty is especially difficult because sovereignty cannot be compromised: Territory either belongs to one group or to another, not to both. Therefore it is not surprising that territorial conflicts like the Northern Ireland dispute between Catholic Nationalists and Protestant Unionists, the Bosnian war between Croats, Serbs, and Muslims over the nature and boundaries of a Bosnian state, the ongoing Arab–Israeli dispute over a Palestinian state, and the quest for Kosovo's political autonomy from Serbia have involved significant violence.

Although war was viewed among European leaders as an acceptable way to carry out foreign policy up until the early twentieth century, war became less legitimate as its lethality increased. Not surprisingly, as war became more destructive, it also became less frequent and was increasingly regarded as an illegitimate policy instrument. In the nineteenth century, the Prussian strategist Carl von Clausewitz could argue in his classic study *On War* that war was a purposeful political action designed to achieve a state's vital interests. In his view, war—which he regarded as a "political instrument, a continuation of political activity by other means"[27]—was like a wrestling match in which each player used physical force to try to compel the opponent. However, following the highly destructive World War I, which resulted in more than twenty million civilian and military casualties, political leaders began to question the legitimacy of force as a policy instrument. Indeed, the establishment of a collective security system under the League of Nations, the newly created global governance system, coupled with efforts to outlaw war and strengthen international law, was a direct by-product of the growing disillusionment with a global order that settled disputes ultimately through war. As I note in Chapter 7, the United Nations system is based on the assumption that force is only legitimate under two conditions—in response to aggression (Art. 51) and when sanctioned by the Security Council in the service of global peace.

Conclusion

In playing the IR game, states pursue their national interests through foreign policy. Because maximizing national interests can only be achieved within a stable, prosperous international order, states also are concerned with the global interest—that is, with promoting international peace, humane democratic states, and a growing, prosperous global economy. Because no global government exists in international society, the pursuit of national or global interests is carried out by each state using power, the currency of the IR game. Whether power is used directly or indirectly, positively or negatively, it is always an underlying element in interstate relations. Even when officials are using peaceful diplomacy to pursue shared goals and to resolve disputes, power remains an ever-present reality. The challenge in the IR game is to maximize the pursuit of national and global interests in the most peaceful, effective, and efficient way. How states balance their national interests with the claims of global society remains one of the major political and moral challenges of global politics.

In playing the IR game, states should keep in mind the following principles discussed in this chapter:

P 4.1—Foreign Policy Is the Means by Which States Pursue Interests in Global Society

P 4.2—The National Interest Represents the Fundamental Wants of a Nation

P 4.3—The Global Interest Represents the Common Concerns of the International Community

P 4.4—Power Is the Currency Used to Pursue Foreign Policy Goals

P 4.5—Diplomacy Can Facilitate the Peaceful Resolution of International Disputes

P 4.6—States Can Influence Other States through Economic Sanctions

P 4.7—States Can Influence Other States through Military Threats

P 4.8—States Can Compel Other States with Force

RECOMMENDED READINGS

Baldwin, David A. *Economic Statecraft* (Princeton, NJ: Princeton University Press, 1985).

Finnemore, Martha. *National Interests in International Society* (Ithaca, NY: Cornell University Press, 1996).

Kagan, Donald. *On the Origins of War and the Preservation of Peace* (New York: Doubleday, 1995).

Keohane, Robert O., and Joseph S. Nye. *Power and Interdependence,* 3d ed. (New York: Longman, 2001).

Kissinger, Henry. *Diplomacy* (New York: Simon and Schuster, 1994).

Nicolson, Harold. *Diplomacy,* 3d ed. (New York: Oxford University Press, 1973).

Ross, Dennis. *Statecraft (and How to Resore America's Standing in the World)* (New York: Farrar, Straus, and Giroux, 2007).

PART TWO

Principles and Rules of the IR Game

FIVE

Political Rules of the IR Game

ON AUGUST 2, 1990, Iraq invaded its tiny neighbor Kuwait. Iraq's military forces smashed Kuwait's small defensive forces and within two days controlled the entire country. Iraq claimed that it had taken this action to reclaim oil resources along its southern border that it believed were being unjustly shared with Kuwait. Additionally, Saddam Hussein, Iraq's dictator, believed that Kuwait was guilty of "financial aggression" because it had been pumping more than its quota assigned by the Organization of Petroleum Exporting Countries (OPEC), leading to a fall in petroleum prices. Although Hussein no doubt assumed that Western nations would condemn Iraq's territorial aggression, he calculated that no state within the region would be able to challenge his invasion. He failed, however, to anticipate the U.S.'s determination to redress this flagrant and illegal intervention. As a result of U.S. initiatives, the United Nations Security Council passed more than a dozen resolutions condemning Iraq and demanding the swift restoration of Kuwait's sovereignty. When Iraq failed to comply with the demand to withdraw its forces, a large multilateral force, spearheaded by the United States, initiated war against Iraq. The war involved more than a month of heavy bombing followed by a ground invasion that resulted in the rapid capitulation of Iraqi ground forces.

This brazen act of aggression is illustrative of the anarchic character of the international community and of the uncertainty of territorial security in such a system. Because honoring state sovereignty is a principal obligation of member states (see Chapter 2), Iraq's invasion was a violation of Kuwait's sovereignty and therefore a criminal act. Iraq's disregard of a basic norm raises a number of important questions: Do political rules exist, or are the alleged "rules" simply suggestions? If political rules govern the international community, what makes them legitimate? Finally, who is responsible for their enforcement?

This chapter examines the nature and role of the political rules of global society. In the first part, I describe different conceptions of global society and how these alternative perspectives affect the playing of the IR game. Although a number of paradigms influence IR, I focus on the two most influential perspectives on the international community—realism and idealism—and then describe how these alternative perspectives are likely to affect strategy. In the second section, I describe basic political rules of the IR game. Even though there is no uniform view of the global political system, there is nonetheless significant consensus about foundational political rules and norms of global society. I sketch the most important of these, distinguishing between primary and secondary rules.

Alternative Conceptions of Global Society

Assumptions and beliefs play an important role in how we conceive of the world. Thus, when scholars theorize about global politics, they do so using *paradigms,* intellectual constructs, that filter perceptions, guide the acquisition of knowledge, and reinforce or undermine beliefs. These cognitive maps or worldviews affect all aspects of human life, including international politics. Thus, when we begin thinking about the world and global politics, we do so with some beliefs, ideas, and concepts already in place. The more one theorizes about a subject, the more developed a worldview is likely to become. The two major paradigms of the IR game are realism and idealism.

Realism

Realism, the oldest and most influential approach to global politics, dates from the origins of political thought in ancient Greek civilization. The historian Thucydides, author of the classic *History of the Peloponnesian War,* is often regarded as the father of realism. Other ancient and modern thinkers who contributed significantly to the development of this tradition include St. Augustine, Niccolò Machiavelli, and Thomas Hobbes. In modern times scholars like Herbert Butterfield, E. H. Carr, George Kennan, and Reinhold Niebuhr contributed significantly to the refinement and application of the realist perspective to international affairs. Hans Morgenthau, author of *Politics among Nations,* the first widely used IR text in the United States, was arguably the most influential American realist of the twentieth century. Realism's dominance in domestic and global politics does not derive from its ancient roots, its wide public appeal, or its adherence by decision makers. Rather, realism holds sway because of its explanatory power, the ability to explain the logic of international political behavior.

Realism is expressed in a variety of perspectives. Some scholars emphasize human nature, others focus on the decentralized structure of global society, and still others emphasize the competitive, offensive nature of political competition among states.[1] Despite the plurality of realist traditions, realism is a coherent paradigm that is characterized by a number of distinctive elements. These include: a pessimistic view of human nature, the prevalence of conflict and competition, a state-centric focus, an anarchic political system, a priority on security, and an emphasis on power. I briefly examine each of these features.

First, realists are pessimistic about the quest for peace, justice, and international cooperation. This pessimism is rooted not in the frailty of reason or the inadequacy of institutions, but in human nature itself. Because individuals and groups give priority to their own interests, often in disregard for or at the expense of the interests of others, the establishment of a peaceful and just community is a difficult, unending task. International order is not an automatic by-product of international affairs. Rather, it must be constructed by fostering compromise among the conflicting, egoistic interests of states and by balancing and counterbalancing the power of states.

A second, related characteristic of realism is the competitive, conflictual nature of interstate relations. Because wants exceed the supply of resources, states continuously compete to maximize their share of available resources. Such competition makes cooperation at times difficult and can result in major conflict. The difficulty in reconciling competing interests is illustrated by the challenge in negotiating arms control agreements, devising international trade agreements, or promoting international initiatives to reduce global pollution. Realists believe cooperation among states is possible but that it will always remain uncertain because of the limited level of trust in global society.[2]

Third, realism assumes that the primary actors in global society are states. Although other actors play the IR game (e.g., international organizations, multinational corporations, NGOs, religious groups, advocacy networks), the primary player is the nation-state. Although institutions can facilitate cooperation and coordination of policies, in the final analysis such cooperation is possible only when states will it.

Fourth, realism assumes that the international community is anarchic—that is, without a central authority to resolve disputes. Essentially, the world is a *self-help system* where security and well-being are ensured by each state's capabilities and resources. One scholar has written that such a system is one "in which those who do not help themselves, or who do so less effectively than others, will fail to prosper, will lay themselves open to dangers, will suffer."[3] Because no common authority exists in the world, the security and prosperity is determined chiefly by each state. And because survival is not assured, the most fundamental interest is survival.

Fifth, realism gives precedence to security over other national interests. The priority of security derives from the fact that the territorial integrity and political independence of a country are basic to all other national concerns. Without survival, the protection of culture and the promotion of economic prosperity are meaningless. Kenneth Waltz argues that survival is the ground of action—not because states always explicitly seek security, but because the anarchic world structure requires that states take care of their own survival.[4] Because the political independence and territorial integrity of states are not assured, each state must provide for its own defense. As Robert Cooper, a British diplomat, has observed, when it comes to national security, "it is largely a world of every country for itself."[5]

Finally, realism emphasizes national power. As mentioned in the previous chapter, power is the fundamental currency of international relations. Because of the inherent conflict among states and the absence of a common power to ensure security, states need to maximize national power. According to some realists, power is so important that it is not only a means, but also an end in itself. For example, Hans Morgenthau, who defined politics as a struggle for power, thought that the prudent statesman was an official who thought and acted in terms of "interest defined as power."[6] If leaders disregarded power, Morgenthau warned, they would become victims of those who had learned to acquire and use it.

Idealism/Institutionalism

Unlike the tradition of realism, which focuses on existing realities, *idealism* emphasizes ideals and hopes for a better, more peaceful world. Idealism is idealistic because it is concerned with bringing about changes that are conducive to a more humane, just global system. The foundation of political idealism is an optimistic view of human relationships and a belief that harmonious, peaceful, and just communal relations can be secured through institutions based on consent and the rule of law. Because of the faith placed on human institutions, the IR tradition of idealism is often referred to as *institutionalism*.

This tradition is grounded in a number of assumptions. First, it holds an optimistic perspective about human nature, social and political life, and interstate relations. Not only are people assumed to be fundamentally good, beneficent, and rational, but their collective actions are similarly assumed to be guided by reason and concern for the common good. When wars arise among states, this suggests that ideological passion and greed have overcome reason. Moreover, the poverty and injustice in the world is not owing to human evil, but rather to flawed social and economic structures that foster injustice. Some idealists have espoused the utopian conviction that the states' fundamental interests are complementary rather than competitive—a notion that historian E. H. Carr defined as the "doctrine of the harmony of interests."[7] This doctrine, popular with many British officials in the nineteenth century, was expressed in the belief that free trade led to international peace.

A second assumption of this tradition is the belief that international institutions can play a significant role in global affairs. Just as human rights are secured in domestic society through constitutional procedures and the rule of law, so, too, can international order and justice be pursued through international institutions—norms, rules, laws, and organizations that structure interstate behavior and help promote international cooperation. Although international law is relatively weak in global society, it nonetheless plays an important role in structuring IR. Similarly, although international organizations have limited independent authority, they nevertheless contribute to maintaining global order and preventing the spread of conflict.

And third, idealism emphasizes the role of moral values in defining foreign policy goals and strategies. Whereas realism's struggle for power leaves little room for moral judgment in international relations, idealism emphasizes moral norms in the development and implementation of foreign policy. Indeed, idealists assume that moral values must play an important role in inspiring political action to affect change and in providing a vision for a more peaceful and humane world.

Although idealism's roots are found in ancient political thought, the application of this tradition to domestic society and the international community developed greatly in modern times, expressing itself in four distinct strands.

The first strand, *political liberalism,* emerged in the seventeenth and eighteenth centuries with the writings of Thomas Hobbes, John Locke, Jean Jacques Rousseau, and other political theorists. According to this perspective, people have basic rights. The central political challenge is how to secure and protect those rights, especially human liberty, in a communal context. Because the major impediment to individual freedom had been tyranny, the protection of individual rights demanded a limited, constitutional government—one based on consent. For liberals, therefore, the major purpose of constitutional government was to secure human rights through constrained political power.

A second major perspective is *internationalism,* an approach that emphasizes the role of domestic structures in determining the nature of global relations. According to Immanuel Kant, a nineteenth-century German philosopher, peace among states is best achieved through an informal federation of republican regimes. Although Kant thought that some centralization of global power was necessary, international institutions alone were insufficient to ensure order. In his view, a humane global order could emerge only if states themselves were based on limited, constitutional authority.[8] In the twentieth and twenty-first centuries, two U.S. presidents, Woodrow Wilson and George W. Bush, strongly emphasized the need for democratic government as a foundation for global order. Whereas Wilson was far more concerned with promoting global order through open, transparent decision making and stronger international law and organizations, Bush placed far more emphasis on the need to help transform autocracies into more democratic governments. According to the so-called Bush doctrine, not only does democracy foster human rights, but such regimes also make international peace more feasible.

The third expression of idealism is *liberal institutionalism*. Although building on the internationalist strand, this contemporary perspective assumes that peace and cooperation are rooted in the work of global institutions, not simply the goodwill of states. Specifically, institutionalism assumes that global cooperation is a direct by-product of the work of international law, international governmental organizations, and informal global regimes that help to promote world order and to foster global prosperity. Institutionalists are confident that the political architecture of multilateral rules, norms, and organizations can structure the behavior of states. Institutions, in other words, are not simply the aggregation of state interests, but are independent actors that can influence the political dynamics of the international community.

The fourth type of idealism, *globalism,* is a direct by-product of liberal institutionalism. According to the globalist perspective, many of the world's major problems—such as crime across borders, transnational terrorist organizations and movements, environmental dangers like global warming, and the transnational spread of infectious diseases like AIDs—are increasingly global and therefore require new institutions to address such challenges. Ironically, globalists do not favor world government. Rather, they assume that the most effective way to address the growing transnational challenges is by establishing new and varied forms of global governance that lead to a more developed "global civil society." Such a society will comprise "networks" of international organizations, national governments, the private sectors, professional associations, labor unions, and nongovernmental organizations. Thus, whereas the institutionalist perspective views the world as a society of states that achieves unity and cooperation through international institutions, the globalist worldview regards the world itself as a global community that is structured around more inclusive forms of global governance.[9]

Alternative Strategies

Because realism and idealism present contrasting visions of the world, how global problems are perceived and addressed will depend partly on the prevailing assumptions and beliefs among decision makers. Because paradigms structure perceptions and guide the foreign policy decision-making process, players' strategies in the IR game will necessarily depend on players' worldviews, as well as their perceptions of other states' worldviews. As a result, in playing the IR game, players will necessarily be influenced by their own paradigms as well as the perceived paradigms of opponent states. In what follows, I sketch some distinctive traits for each alternative strategy.

Because political realism emphasizes the danger and insecurity of global society and the conflictual and competitive nature of international relations, political realism gives precedence to a number of strategic principles. These include the following:

- Maximize national power. Because security is not assured, players can acquire as much power and wealth as possible to ensure that they can overcome any major threat.
- Build alliances. Given the anarchic nature of global society, states must work cooperatively with other like-minded states to maximize their security and promote shared political and economic interests; the development of political and military alliances can contribute to global order by strengthening deterrence.
- Make power a priority. Because military force is the ultimate instrument of power, players must ensure that they have the necessary military resources to effectively deter any potential threat and to use force to compel an enemy when vital interests are at stake.
- Protect state sovereignty. Because states are the primary institutions that ensure domestic order and secure human rights, states need to maintain their freedom of action; although international institutions can help coordinate state actions, shifting governmental responsibilities from states to international organizations is premature and should be opposed.
- Focus on the national interest. A prudent foreign policy must be guided by the national interest; this does not mean that a state disregards the common global good but that national interests are defined in light of the shared interests of other states; when conflict arises between the national interest and the global interest, states should give precedence to the former.
- When pursuing vital interests, do not rely on international institutions. Although global institutions can facilitate cooperation and coordination on secondary issues, they are not reliable in ensuring the security and well-being of member states; additionally, because they have no authority to define problems and ensure compliance, it is unwise to place trust in global institutions; and because all community life depends on trust, states can build trust by cooperating with other member states; but in developing common policies, statesmen must remember to verify compliance, or as former President Ronald Reagan observed frequently, "trust but verify."
- Pursue multilateralism but be prepared to act unilaterally. When feasible, states should pursue their interests cooperatively with other states; but when multilateral institutions are an impediment to vital interests, multilateralism needs to give way to unilateral action; it is important to recall that goals and purposes define coalitions, not the other way around.

In contrast to realism, the institutional tradition emphasizes strategic norms that encourage and rely on greater global governance. Because the world is not, to use Thomas Hobbes's description, "a war of all against all," but rather an imperfect, uncertain society of states, security is not the overriding concern of states. Rather, states pursue a wide variety of political, economic, cultural, social, and environmental interests. Foreign policy is the means to advance these broad interests through individual and collective action. Some important strategic principles of the idealist perspective include the following:

⚉ Institutionalize power. Rather than relying directly on coercive threats, use international norms, regimes, and organizations to influence the behavior of other states; because institutions are multilateral in character, they are regarded as a more acceptable (legitimate) form of power.

⚉ Use soft power rather than hard power. Instead of relying on direct threats or positive rewards to influence behavior, use the indirect strategy of soft power by modeling ideals, values, cultural norms, and economic practices; soft power, like institutional power, is a more acceptable way to influence behavior, because it encourages behavioral change by getting others to want to incorporate your values and behaviors because of their inherent desirability.

⚉ Comply with international law and the decisions of international organizations. By following existing rules and working through international organizations, states can foster global order.

⚉ Strengthen global governance. States can reduce insecurity and promote global cooperation in the anarchic international community by shifting decision-making authority from member states to global institutions.

⚉ Pursue both national and global interests in foreign policy. Because the well-being of nations is partly dependent on the health of global society, states should pursue their long-term interests by balancing narrow self-interests with the general collective interests of global society.

⚉ Multilateral action is generally preferable to unilateral action. To promote international harmony and foster international political consensus, states should pursue their foreign policy interests through multilateral channels where possible; a multilateral approach is likely to result in greater individual and collective gains than one that is solely unilateral.

International cooperation and coordination are likely to be easier among players sharing a similar worldview. This is so because shared values and assumptions are likely to reduce misperception and foster additional shared ideas and values. When players use different paradigms, however, coordinating policies and reconciling conflicting goals are likely to present greater challenges. How should states play the IR game when they rely on different ideological perspectives? The challenge of playing the IR game from two different vantage points is illustrated in the contemporary tensions between the United States and Western Europe. The tensions are not simply over policy issues or over the dominant role of the United States in world politics. Rather, the tensions are rooted in different worldviews—with Europe's perspective giving preference to international institutions and to social and economic issues and the U.S. perspective giving greater emphasis to sovereignty, security, and human rights rooted in a democratic government. Robert Kagan has famously described the two strategies of the United States and Europe as follows: "Americans are from Mars and Europeans are from Venus: They agree on little and understand one another less and less."[10]

Thus, in playing the IR game it is important to distinguish between conflicts that are based on different worldviews and those that are rooted in tangible and intangible interests. To the extent that disputes involve concrete, tangible issues, such conflicts are potentially amenable to peaceful resolution through diplomatic negotiation. But when disputes are rooted in ideology, religion, or opposing paradigms, compromise is unlikely to be sufficient to reconcile the antagonism. Rather, when confronting intractable disputes, knowledge and understanding of an opponent's religious and political worldview will be indispensable. Only then can communication occur to facilitate some partial resolution of the conflict.

Primary Political Rules

Political rules are those regularized, customary practices that states have adopted as members of the society of states. Because no world parliament exists, the rules that states have devised have emerged from their voluntary, autonomous actions. These behaviors have arisen out of a quest for two opposing goals—freedom and membership in global society. On the one hand, sovereign states seek to maximize their national interests and in particular their economic well-being and territorial security, even in disregard for or at the expense of the interests of other states. On the other hand, states voluntarily circumscribe their autonomy in order to be a part of the international community. Membership in the global society is important because states' fundamental goals can be secured only if a stable, humane, and prosperous world is sustained.

The society of states is sustained through political, economic, legal, and moral rules. Here I focus on political rules that have emerged from the voluntary practices of states. I differentiate between two types—

those rules that are foundational to the security and well-being of individual states and those that are conducive to the peace and welfare of the world. The first set of rules, which are based on the sovereignty and power of states, are associated with the traditional global order. The second set of rules is associated with the emerging postmodern system and is less decisive in the contemporary world.

≜ R 5.1—Make the Safety of Your Country a Top Priority

Viable nation-states have a right to exist and to protect themselves from foreign aggression. Just as individuals have a natural right to defend themselves from attack, so, too, states have an inherent right to protect themselves from foreign aggression. The right of self-defense is therefore a basic rule of the IR game—a right explicitly enshrined in the United Nations system. Article 51 of the UN Charter states: "Nothing in the present Charter shall impair the inherent right of individual or collective self-defense if an armed attack occurs against a Member of the United Nations, until the Security Council has taken measures necessary to maintain international peace and security."

Even though the divisions and boundaries of the world might not be founded on justice, the map of the world is regarded sacrosanct. Peaceful international relations are based on the legitimacy of existing cartography. Although the map of the world might not be just, any effort to use force or the threat of force to change the map is prohibited. The IR game thus assumes that the status quo is the foundation for peaceful international relations.

In domestic societies the security of persons is assured by the existence of governmental institutions that ensure compliance with laws and punishment of criminal wrongdoing. But because the international community is a self-help system, where each state is ultimately responsible for its own security, states devote a significant portion of public resources to maintain armed forces, ostensibly to protect their people and territory from potential foreign attacks.[11] In 2004, for example, total world military expenditures were estimated at nearly one trillion dollars ($975 billion), with the United States accounting for nearly half of this amount. Other leading spenders on military forces included the United Kingdom ($47 billion), France ($46 billion), Japan ($42 billion) and China ($35 billion). Countries with high military expenditures as a percentage of their gross domestic product (GDP) included Angola (4.7 percent), Burundi (5.9 percent), Israel (9.1 percent), Jordan (8.9 percent), Kuwait (9.0 percent), Oman (12.2 percent), Singapore (5.9 percent), and Turkey (4.9 percent).[12]

Because of their incredible destructive power, nuclear weapons are the most prized instruments of national security. The nuclear club currently includes the following states: the United States, Russia, Britain, France, China, Israel, India, and Pakistan. North Korea claims to have acquired such weapons, and South Africa declared in the late 1980s that it destroyed the few nuclear devices that it had developed. Other states, including Libya, Iraq, and Iran, have sought to acquire nuclear weapons. The expansion of the nuclear club is contrary to the widely shared norm of nonproliferation—the idea that states that do not have nuclear arms should not seek to acquire them.

R 5.2—Take Care of Your Nation First, Then Worry about Others

This rule, which no doubt appears unduly selfish, even cynical, derives from the anarchic structure of global society. In such a society of independent states, each sovereign community is first and foremost responsible for its own security and welfare. In such a system, the first duty of the state is to protect its citizens and to advance their economic and social well-being through a foreign policy based on national, not global, interests. Indeed, foreign policy is generally defined as the process by which states pursue their national interests in light of the interests of other states.

This does not mean that states should not care for the needs and wants of other peoples. From a moral, even strategic perspective, it might be desirable and at times necessary to assist other nations. Giving financial aid to poor countries, promoting environmental protection abroad, and protecting human rights in war-ravaged states are considered desirable, not essential, policies in the Westphalian system. During the Cold War, for example, the United States gave significant financial assistance to developing nations. And although humanitarian impulses were no doubt a motive in seeking to improve the quality of life in poor lands, the fundamental justification for most foreign aid was based on its perceived national interest: The promotion of Third World prosperity would inhibit the spread of Communist regimes and, secondarily, provide a market for U.S. exports.

R 5.3—Resolve Disputes Peacefully

One of the most fundamental regulative rules of IR is that states must resolve conflicts in a peaceful manner. International peace would be relatively easy to maintain if every state were fully satisfied and did not seek to expand its territory, resources, and relative share of power and wealth. Because demand for resources exceeds their supply, states compete over the distribution of scarce resources, inevitably leading to conflict. If disputes involve vital interests, states might threaten coercive action or even resort to force. When states make explicit threats or commit aggression, victim states can respond in one of four ways: 1) they can acquiesce and do nothing, 2) they can use diplomacy and seek to resolve disputes through negotiations, 3) they can threaten punishment, and 4) they can retaliate with force. Of these options, only the first two are consistent with the responsibility to maintain a peaceful and stable international order. But maintaining peace at all costs will inevitably reinforce injustice and create the basis for future conflict. The danger of appeasement—making peace the only value—was dramatically illustrated in 1938, when then British Prime Minister Neville Chamberlain accepted Germany's annexation of the Sudetenland (the western Czech territory bordering Germany) in return for Hitler's promise not to acquire further European lands. Chamberlain returned to London announcing that "peace is at hand," only to discover that World War II would break out soon thereafter. Thus, the quest for long-term international order can only be fulfilled when justice is reconciled with peace.

Because the international society of states is anarchic, there is no central authority to resolve conflicts. And because conflict resolution is carried out by states themselves, countries must pursue their foreign policy interests in a peaceful, nonthreatening manner if world order is to be maintained. A stable, peaceful international community is possible only when states pursue foreign policy goals peacefully—a rule that is enshrined in numerous important multilateral treaties as well as the charters of major international organizations. For example, Articles 2.3 and 2.4 of the United Nations Charter state, respectively: "All members shall settle their international disputes by peaceful means in such a manner that international peace and security, and justice, are not endangered," and "All Members shall refrain in their international relations from the threat or use of force." Despite the widespread acknowledgment of the duty to refrain from using force, violence has nevertheless remained a common occurrence in world politics. Indeed, as the late French scholar Raymond Aron observed, war is the preeminent symbol of IR because it represents the final way of settling interstate conflicts.[13]

In domestic society peace and justice are maintained through the rule of law. Thus, when a crime is committed, the offender is held to account so that future crime is deterred and the fundamental moral order of society is sustained. In international society there is no sovereign entity that can hold criminal states to account. If justice is to be maintained, member states themselves have to respond to unjust, illegal actions by using threats or even coercive force. The legitimacy of force is clearly illustrated in Britain's response to Argentina's aggression in the Falkland Islands (Islas Malvinas) in April 1982. Although sovereignty of the islands has been contested for more than a century, the sudden resort to force by Argentina was clearly a violation of the duty to resolve disputes peacefully. Thus, when Argentina committed aggression against

a small group of islands in the southern Atlantic Ocean, the only re-
course for Britain was to acquiesce or to expel Argentine military forces.
Britain chose the latter course of action. As diplomat Robert Cooper has
observed, "when Argentina chose to operate according to the rules of
Clausewitz rather than those of Kant, Britain had to respond on the
same level."[14]

States have developed a variety of tools and approaches to foster international peace and inhibit war. Some of these instruments of conflict
resolution rely indirectly on the application of international law (arbitration), and others involve the direct role of neutral intermediaries. Third
parties can help clarify sources of the conflict and help illuminate relevant facts (conciliation) or identify common ground between the antagonists and develop alternatives for resolving the dispute (mediation).
Intermediaries can even be entrusted with the responsibility of issuing a
binding judgment (arbitration).

The most significant war prevention approaches are not legal or political but structural. These efforts seek to prevent war by managing
power to inhibit the use of force. One way of managing power is through
an informal, flexible system of *balance of power*—an approach used by
the major powers of Europe in the early part of the nineteenth century.
At the Congress of Vienna (1815), Austria-Hungary, England, France,
Prussia, and Russia established a system known as the Concert of Europe that sought to maintain a balance of power and inhibit the centralization of power in the hands of any one state. When this system failed
to prevent World War I, the leading states decided that a different way of
managing global power was needed.

The system that they created and institutionalized in the League of
Nations (1919–1945), the world's first major formal international peacekeeping organization, was *collective security*. This approach sought to inhibit war by promising that an aggressor state would be punished with
the combined power of all other member states. The basic idea of collective security is captured in the claim that "an attack on one is an attack
on all." The theory assumes that states will not commit aggression if they
know that their act would be repulsed by the combined power of all
other community members. But as with the European balance of power
system, the League of Nations was unable to prevent war. Consequently,
after the Allied powers (Britain, Russia, and the United States) had defeated the Axis powers (Germany, Italy, and Japan) in World War II, the
victorious states created a new international organization, the United
Nations, to prevent war. Unlike the League of Nations, however, the
United Nations did not allow each member state to decide individually
whether or not they would respond to aggression and threats to international peace. Instead, the UN entrusted the responsibility of peacekeeping and peacemaking to a fifteen-member committee (the Security
Council) in which the major powers (Britain, China, France, Russia, and
the United States) play a decisive role.

🖹 R 5.4—Do What Is Necessary to Protect Vital Interests

Because states compete for scarce resources (power, honor, territory, money) in global society, conflict is inevitable. States pursue a wide variety of interests in the international community, most of them specific and nonvital. When conflicts arise over nonvital issues or concerns that are amenable to compromise, then peaceful negotiation is likely to result in reconciliation. But when issues involve vital interests like honor, security, and territory, conflict resolution is likely to be far more elusive. According to this rule, when a conflict involves a vital interest, a state must do whatever is necessary to protect its interests. It must seek to win—and do so at the lowest cost and with the least violence.

In addressing major conflicts, statesmen have three different strategies that they can pursue: diplomacy, sanctions, and military coercion—words, money, and force. The first alternative relies on reason, bargaining, and a willingness by the parties to accept a less than ideal settlement. Negotiation succeeds when both parties remain only partially satisfied with the agreement but fully satisfied that the dispute has been resolved. The second alternative involves use of positive inducements and negative threats to achieve a resolution. Fundamentally, a state uses carrots and sticks to try to influence an opponent. The goal is to get an enemy to alter its actions through the promise of conditional benefits and penalties. As I write, the United States and the European Union are seeking to dissuade Iran from pursuing a uranium enrichment program, because they fear that Iran is seeking to build nuclear weapons. Iran, a major oil exporter, claims that its uranium program is solely for the peaceful purpose of nuclear energy production. To date, Iran has resisted all positive inducements, claiming that as a sovereign power it has the right to pursue nuclear energy. The third alternative is force—the option sketched at the outset of the chapter when a U.S.-led coalition ended Iraq's occupation of Kuwait in 1991. According to the Westphalian system, military force is a legitimate way to defend vital interests after all other alternatives have been exhausted.

Given the destructiveness of war, states have developed numerous legal conventions to limit violence in war, and moral and religious theorists have developed the just war tradition (see Box 8.1) for structuring moral reasoning about war. Although I examine some of these legal and moral guidelines in Chapters 7 and 8, Box 5.1 presents some widely used IR principles for judging the use of force.

🖹 R 5.5—Keep Your Powder Dry

This rule suggests that states should maintain a high state of military preparedness to cope with potential harm. Because the intentions of

♟   ♟   ♟

Box 5.1 Principles for Using Force

Scholars and decision makers have found the following principles helpful in determining when and how armed force should be used to advance foreign policy goals:

1. *Exhaust All Other Alternatives before Resorting to Force:* This is an important principle not only because political morality and the international legal order demand it, but also because the effectiveness of force is inversely related to its use. Overreliance on force is likely to be counterproductive, providing decreasing deterrent and compellent power with increasing dependence on force.

2. *Do Not Overestimate Your Capabilities:* One of the most difficult challenges for the statesman is to develop an accurate assessment of a state's relative power. Indeed, John Stoessinger argues that the misperception of relative power is one of the major causes of war.[1] Estimating relative power is difficult for several reasons: first, because power is not measured simply by the quality and quantity of armaments; second, because an enemy's resolve is difficult to estimate; and third, because power is determined partly by strategy— that is, how force is used. In predicting the outcomes of military conflicts, the balance of interests and resolve are more significant than the balance of power.

3. *Rely on Deterrence and Coercive Diplomacy, Not Force:* Threats are not only more economical than force, but they also are frequently successful in achieving foreign policy goals, provided the promise of military action is credible and appropriate. The two major ways that states threaten others is through deterrence and coercive diplomacy. Deterrence, it will be recalled, seeks to prevent unwanted action by the threat of unacceptable punishment. Coercive diplomacy, by contrast, seeks behavioral compliance through the explicit or implicit promise of military action. Military threat, the most common way that military power is used, is the foundation of defense policy. If deterrence and coercive diplomacy are to be credible, they must fulfill two conditions: First, a state must possess the resources to inflict disproportionate harm and second, the threat must be backed by will—by the belief that the promised military action will be carried out.

4. *Do Not Bluff:* Bluff occurs when a state makes a threat that it is incapable or unwilling to fulfill. Bluffing is harmful because it undermines deterrence and coercive diplomacy. It might be possible to bluff

(continues)

BOX 5.1 continued

once, but after an enemy state concludes that threats are not credible, the efficacy of a threat will vanish.

5. *Resort to Force Only if You Can Win:* Carl von Clausewitz, the famous nineteenth-century Prussian officer and military strategist, once observed that war was simply politics by force—or, as he put it, "a continuation of political activity by other means."[2] The resort to force is undertaken in the belief that desired political objectives can be achieved through force. But to prevail politically, the enemy must be defeated. Given the destructive nature of war, the resort to force should be undertaken only if one is likely to prevail militarily. This is why the just war theory demands that before resorting to war, the use of armed action must have a high probability of success.

6. *Maximize the Legitimacy of Force:* Because legitimacy (i.e., acceptability because an act is perceived as inherently correct) tends to be inversely related to unilateralism, the use of force is likely to be perceived as acceptable and morally valid when other countries, especially major powers, give explicit or tacit support to the coercive action. To be sure, when aggression occurs or vital interests are threatened, states have the right of self-defense—a right codified in international law and enshrined in the UN Charter. In such conflicts, where legitimacy is inherent, multilateral support for the victim can help defeat the aggressor but is not legally or morally necessary. For example, after Argentina invaded the Falkland Islands in April 1982, the United Kingdom responded by sending a large naval force that defeated the occupying forces. Although the British action was unilateral, it was regarded as a legitimate response to Argentina's blatant aggression.[3]

7. *Although Force Can Impose Order, Only Legitimacy Ensures a Stable Peace:* The advantage of achieving a political settlement through negotiation is that an agreement involves voluntary acceptance of the terms of the accord. When a settlement is achieved through coercion, the defeated party will continue to desire more favorable terms. Imposition, in other words, does not resolve the desires of a subjugated people—but simply postpones the day of reckoning.[4]

Notes

1 John G. Stoessinger, *Why Nations Go to War* (New York: St. Martin's Press, 1974), 227.

2 Carl von Clausewitz, *On War*, trans. Michael Howard and Peter Paret (Princeton, NJ: Princeton University Press, 1976), 87.

3 Sometimes the quest for legitimacy is far more difficult, as was the case with NATO's 1999 war with Yugoslavia. In response to Serbian "ethnic cleansing" of Al-

banians in Kosovo, a small territory governed by Yugoslavia (Serbia), Western powers demanded that Yugoslavia withdraw its military forces from the small territory. When Slobodan Milošević, the country's president, refused, NATO carried out an intensive bombing campaign that forced Yugoslavia's capitulation. Although the defense of human rights in Kosovo was considered morally valid by most observers, the failure of Western powers to gain Security Council approval led a number of analysts to question the legitimacy of this war.

4 After defeating the Axis powers in World War I, the Allies imposed a harsh settlement on Germany in the Treaty of Versailles. The postwar peace, however, was short-lived. Indeed, because of its lost prestige and power, Germany pursued nationalistic policies in the 1930s that led to the outbreak of World War II. Thus, although force can create order in the short run, a long-term peace can be achieved only when the major powers view international boundaries and political and economic conditions as legitimate.

states are unknown, foreign policy, like the weather, is unpredictable. Therefore a prudent foreign policy must prepare for a variety of contingencies. This truth was captured by President George W. Bush, who stated, in response to North Korea's testing of ballistic missiles on July 4, 2006, that "we must plan for the worst and hope for the best."

Preparing for harmful developments does not mean that states have evil intentions, or that trust and cooperation are impossible. Rather, it implies that states must take into account the possibility that some states might become dissatisfied with the status quo and seek to change existing conditions through force. Moreover, conditions and relationships can change with little warning. As John Mearsheimer has observed, "intentions can change quickly, so a state's intentions can be benign one day and malign the next."[15] A prudent foreign policy must therefore include a wide array of options, ranging from positive, harmonious strategies to coercive actions designed to defend and compel through force.

♟ R 5.6—Mind Your Own Business

According to this rule, because states are responsible for their own affairs, they should respect the territorial sovereignty and political independence of other states. Deliberate interference in the internal affairs of other states is prohibited. As I noted in Chapter 2 (P 2.2), one of the most basic responsibilities of member states is to respect others' sovereignty by not seeking to undermine the authority and decisions of foreign governments. In effect, sovereignty and nonintervention are two sides of the same coin. This does not mean that a state is prohibited from influencing public opinion through legitimate instruments of democratic participation. Nor does it mean that foreign associations and NGOs must refrain from seeking to alter the foreign policy decisions of other states. Rather, nonintervention means that states should not usurp the decision-making authority of other states, whether by covert operations or overt military intervention.

This rule has come under great pressure in the post–Cold War era, with a rise in gross human rights abuses, especially so-called ethnic cleansing and genocide. Although some of these abuses derive from the unjust policies of dictators, the most serious violations are a result of civil wars over the control of the state. How should the leading powers have responded to the Bosnian civil war that resulted in two hundred thousand deaths and two million refugees and displaced persons? When Hutu extremists embarked on an extermination campaign against the minority Tutsi in 1994, were the major powers duty-bound to honor Rwanda's sovereignty? Partly because of the rise in weak and failed states, the international community is slowly coming to realize that the hollowed norm of state sovereignty might have to give way to foreign intervention when states are unable to fulfill their basic responsibility to protect human rights. Thus, under the emerging postmodern order the nonintervention rule is giving way to a new rule—the need to protect human rights.

⁂ R 5.7—Build Coalitions and Alliances to Advance Foreign Policy Interests Multilaterally

A major power might have the luxury of pursuing foreign policy objectives unilaterally. Most states, however, collaborate with others in advancing their interests. They do so formally through global, regional, and specialized organizations and other multilateral institutions and informally through coalitions, alliances, and specialized networks. International organizations have the advantage of providing increased security through the centralization of power as well as distributing the responsibility and burdens when addressing major international problems. Most importantly, institutionalizing international cooperation helps build stable relationships among member states and contributes to global order. An illustration of the important role of coalitions is the Non-Aligned Movement (NAM), which was established in the 1950s to advance the political and economic interests of poor countries by remaining apart from the ideological conflict of the two superpowers—the Soviet Union and the United States. Another example of the important role of multilateral cooperation is the United Nations Conference on Trade and Development (UNCTAD), established in 1964. The aim of UNCTAD, which met quadrennially, was to help foster an international economic order that was conducive to the development of poor nations.

Even dominant powers find it useful to pursue foreign policy interests through coalitions and alliances. Early in the Cold War, the United States decided to use its considerable power to advance security, democracy, and economic prosperity by creating institutions like NATO and the World Bank. The institutionalization of its influence made U.S. power more legitimate and therefore more acceptable. When the United States demanded that Iraq withdraw from Kuwait, it relied on Security Council resolutions and a multinational coalition of military forces. The importance of multilateral cooperation is also illustrated in the Group of Eight (G-8)—the heads of state of the leading industrial states and Russia that meet annually to discuss shared economic and political concerns. Although the G-8 rarely takes decisive actions, the forum provides an excellent opportunity for the world's political leaders to identify key global issues and to develop common strategies.

Secondary Political Rules

As I noted in Chapter 2, important changes are under way in the international system. I noted that the emerging postmodern order was characterized by a declining role of coercive power in interstate relations, a growing influence of nonstate actors, an increasing role of global governance, and a growing importance of transnational concerns. In view of the shift toward a postmodern order, a number of new rules are being developed and institutionalized. Unlike primary political rules, which continue to regulate most IR behavior, the rules of the emerging postmodern order vary widely in interpretation and application. Moreover, because the idealist tradition emphasizes voluntary cooperation and the growing role of law and institutions, idealists are likely to emphasize compliance with these rules. For their part, realists are likely to play the IR game using only primary rules.

⚜ R 5.8—Support International Institutions, but Do Not Rely on Them for Your Nation's Prosperity or Security

This rule emphasizes the need to support global institutions, especially international law (IL) and intergovernmental organizations (IGOs). States reinforce international legal order by complying with its precepts and strengthen global organizations by encouraging and facilitating collective action. Although IL and IGOs can help maintain international order and promote global cooperation, a nation's security and welfare are ultimately dependent on its own power and resources. In short, international institutions contribute significantly to world order but are unable to care for the welfare of each member state.

As I make plain in Chapter 7, although international law contributes significantly to global order by structuring the international behavior of states, it nevertheless is weak, especially when confronting aggression and other types of major international crimes. Still, international law provides important rules to regulate behavior in areas of shared concern. For example, the law of the sea helps to regulate international-maritime activity by establishing important rules in areas such as territorial waters, jurisdiction in the high seas, environmental protection, and conservation of marine life. Similarly, the laws of war potentially limit human suffering by, among other things, seeking to protect civilians and to provide humane treatment for prisoners. Because no sovereign authority exists to apply and enforce international legal obligations, however, compliance with international law is uncertain, even in the most favorable circumstances. This is especially the case when important issues are at stake. Thus, when Nicaragua sued the United States in the International Court of Justice, the world's "supreme court," because of alleged violation of its sovereignty, the United States responded by contesting the court's jurisdiction, and when that failed, disregarding the court's proceedings and final judgment.

The most significant IGOs are those that seek to promote international order on a global basis (the United Nations) or within specific geographical regions (like the African Union and the Organization of American States). Most IGOs, however, are limited in their ability to regulate the behavior of states or to channel collective action. This is because most IGOs are not authoritative institutions capable of actions that are independent of the joint preferences of their member states. Arguably, the most developed IGO is the European Union (EU), an organization of twenty-seven European states that has sought to build regional political unity through the processes of social and economic integration. The high level of EU institutional development is evident by its supranational authority—that is, the ability of the organization's decision-making structures to make decisions and establish policies without the explicit consent of its member states.

No other IGO has realized the level of institutional development of the EU. Most IGOs function as consensus-based institutions where action is possible only when substantial agreement can be realized. To the extent that the United Nations promotes global order, for example, it does so through consensus involving, at a minimum, the leading powers, especially the five permanent members of the Security Council (Britain, China, France, Russia, and the United States). When consensus is achieved, as was the case in the 1991 Gulf War, then UN-based action is possible. But when the major powers are undecided, as in the 1994 genocide in Rwanda and the 2005–2006 humanitarian crisis in Darfur,

Sudan, then the United Nations will discuss, evaluate, declare, and condemn but take no action. The demand for consensus also impairs decision making at the regional level. When NATO began an air war against Yugoslavia in 1999, for example, member states needed to agree on the strategy and tactics—a requirement that greatly increased the complexity of military strategy.

Ironically, the most influential intergovernmental organizations are specialized agencies like the International Monetary Fund (IMF), the World Trade Organization (WTO), and the World Health Organization (WHO). The success of such organizations is owing to the fact that they pursue limited objectives in narrowly defined areas of common concern. The WHO has been exceptionally effective in virtually eliminating some diseases, and the WTO, along with its predecessor organization, the General Agreement on Tariffs and Trade (GATT), has been able to foster international trade by reducing trade barriers and by helping to resolve commercial disputes.

Finally, it is important to stress that idealists and realists will apply this rule differently. Because realists emphasize the anarchic architecture of the international community, they will emphasize national autonomy and doubt the efficacy of voluntary cooperative action, especially in maintaining international institutions. As a result, they are likely to give precedence to their own resources over those of international organizations. By contrast, idealists will give priority to global institutions and therefore emphasize the first part of the rule—namely, the obligation of supporting international institutions.

🏛 R 5.9—Protect Human Rights in Other Nations When Feasible

As noted earlier, a basic rule of the classical game is the duty to honor the sovereignty of other states. Although nonintervention is an important principle, it is not absolute, because the norm presupposes states that are capable and willing to fulfill international obligations. Sovereignty protects the autonomy of states, but only if states fulfill their obligations—that is, to not threaten other states and to protect the human rights of their people. The right of political independence, in other words, is conditional on the peaceful and benign intentions of regimes toward other countries and toward their own people. Thus, when states fail to live up to their responsibilities they lose their legitimacy, making room for other states to intervene in their internal affairs.

Rule 5.9 demands that human rights take precedence over sovereignty. When civil wars threaten widespread human suffering or a regime perpetuates genocide, the international community has a responsibility to intervene to protect innocent civilians. The problem with placing responsibility on the international community is that the community remains weak, unable to take decisive action. Global society is not yet ready to take on the responsibilities of sending force into harm's way to protect innocent civilians. The United Nations periodically creates peacekeeping forces to keep warring parties apart. But these multinational police forces are introduced not to make peace or to protect civilians; rather, their only task is to maintain a negotiated peace settlement. If military action is needed to protect human rights, then the UN Security Council must authorize peace enforcement action in terms of Chapter VII of the UN Charter. The problem with this option is that the permanent members of the Security Council rarely concur on peace enforcement missions. The UN did authorize collective action to end Iraq's occupation of Kuwait in 1991, but this action was unusual in the annals of UN history.

If human rights are sacrosanct and the major powers are politically unable to take collective action to protect people from atrocities, then perhaps individual states or a group of like-minded states need to assume the responsibility to protect human rights through military action. If this step is taken, however, it is important that all peaceful alternatives have been exhausted before embarking on a military intervention. This is, of course, what happened in the spring of 1999 when NATO initiated a humanitarian war against Yugoslavia without UN authorization. NATO took the unilateral action, because Russia and China, both permanent members of the Security Council, opposed military action against Yugoslavia. Western powers, by contrast, believed that Serb ethnic cleansing and human rights abuses against Kosovars constituted a grave threat to regional peace and to the moral foundation of global society. As a result, NATO demanded that Serb security forces leave Kosovo or face war. When President Milošević refused to comply with NATO's demands, it initiated a seventy-eight-day bombing campaign that eventually forced Yugoslavia's compliance.

The appropriateness of foreign intervention was illustrated in 2001, when U.S. military forces intervened in Somalia. At the time, hundreds of thousands of people were dying from starvation, and because the government had ceased to function, no central authority existed to ensure that food aid reached starving people. Instead, warlords used international aid to advance their own political power, preventing humanitarian aid from reaching people in distress. In 1994, an even more destructive humanitarian crisis unfolded in the small African country of Rwanda. In the early 1990s, the United Nations brokered a peace accord that called for power sharing between the country's two ethnic groups—the majority Hutus and the minority Tutsis. In April 1994, the ruling Hutus embarked on an extermination campaign to eliminate all Tutsis in order to prevent a power-sharing government from being established. Because the UN Security Council failed to authorize an adequate military force to halt the killing, the three-month genocide left more than eight hundred thousand persons dead. A third humanitarian crisis emerged in

Bosnia-Herzegovina in 1992, when its three ethnic groups began fighting over the territorial division of this multiethnic state. The war persisted until 1995, when the parties accepted a peace accord backed by NATO military forces. But during the three years of ethnic fighting more than two hundred thousand persons died, and more than two million were displaced from their villages.

In view of the unprecedented human rights abuses resulting from failed states, UN Secretary-General Kofi Annan called on the international community, in 1999 and again in 2000, to develop consensus on when and how foreign intervention for human rights purposes is permissible. In response to this call, the Canadian government established an international commission of distinguished political leaders and scholars to investigate this topic. In 2001, the commission issued its report, which is one of the most careful analyses of the challenge of reconciling human rights with sovereignty. In its report, titled "The Responsibility to Protect," the commission argued that because sovereignty involved a duty to care for people, when states were unwilling or incapable of caring for human rights, the international community should assume this responsibility. The commission did not call for foreign intervention. Rather, it claimed that when a regime was unable or unwilling to protect human rights, "the principle of nonintervention yields to the international responsibility to protect."[16] In effect, the commission wanted the Security Council to determine when and how UN-sanctioned armed forces could be used to protect people.

⚑ R 5.10—Promote and Protect Global Public Goods

In Chapter 3, I defined the global interest as the common good of the international community. A key element of this global interest is the promotion and protection of *global public goods*. Collective or public goods are ideas, values, practices, resources, and conditions that benefit everyone in a society or community. Global public goods are those collective goods that extend across borders, generations, and national or ethnic divisions. Examples of such goods include peace, financial stability, poverty reduction, clean air, environmental protection, and conservation of the species; examples of collective "bads"—harmful and detrimental conditions and practices in the international community—include war, international financial instability, air pollution, global warming, and deforestation.

Public goods have two characteristics: First, their enjoyment is not diluted or compromised as the good's usage is extended to others. This means that goods like clean air, knowledge, or highways can be enjoyed by all persons in society without adverse consequences to the good itself. Second, no person can be excluded from enjoying a public good. If global warming is halted through dramatic reductions in carbon emissions, for example, every country benefits, regardless of whether it contributed to the reduction of global warming gasses. Just as domestic communities are sustained through the provision of public goods for all of its members, so the international community similarly depends on the availability of global public goods to help sustain order, peace, and economic prosperity among states. Without collective goods, global welfare would decline with the rise of public "bads"—war and instability, increased terrorism from weak states, more ocean pollution, environmental degradation, and a rise in infectious diseases.

Who provides for public goods? Although some collective goods arise spontaneously within domestic society through the self-interested behaviors of individuals,[17] the government plays an important function in directly providing some public goods (e.g., national security, airline safety) and by indirectly fostering public goods by regulating human behavior to minimize harm (from automobile accidents, from corruption in corporations, e.g., by promoting automobile safety and protecting consumers from harmful substances). The role of government in providing institutional "safety nets" is important because of the so-called *free-rider problem*. The problem arises from the temptation to use freely available public goods without paying for them, or even helping to maintain them. Thus, the development and maintenance of collective goods is generally easier in smaller, close-knit communities where strong group loyalty exists among members. As the size of community increases, it becomes easier for individuals and groups to rely on others for the provision of collective goods.

Given the temptation to "free ride" in global society, securing dependable behavioral commitments to the development of global public goods is important. One way of achieving compliance is through treaties and conventions—as was demonstrated by the banning of ozone-depleting gasses with the signing of the Montreal Protocol in 1987. After scientists had conclusively demonstrated that chlorofluorocarbons (CFCs) were reducing the earth's atmospheric ozone (a type of oxygen that helps to protect the earth from the sun's harmful ultraviolet rays), the developed industrial states agreed to eliminate the use of CFCs. One of the reasons for the success in the elimination of CFCs, which were used in aerosol sprays and refrigeration, was that the industries were able to develop safe alternative products. This has not been the case with fossil fuels, which are the source for most world energy, but which also are chiefly responsible for global warming gasses. Thus, although states desire to reduce the atmospheric effects of carbon emissions, they are even more concerned with short-term economic growth, which can only be sustained with increasing availability of energy. In short, although global collective goods are important to the international community, the provision of such goods will continue to present major challenges.

Conclusion

Because peoples' perspectives and values affect their perceptions of the international system and of individual states, worldviews or paradigms have a profound impact on how foreign policy is carried out. As a result, when playing the IR game, it is important to be aware of one's own ideals and perspectives as well as those of other states. Additionally, because the international system is shifting from a modern to a postmodern structure, players need to be aware that the traditional rules of the classical game are being supplemented with a number of emerging rules. In this time of transition, players would be well advised to continue to abide by the primary or fundamental political rules of the IR game. These rules, to repeat, include the following:

R 5.1—Make the Safety of Your Country a Top Priority
R 5.2—Take Care of Your Nation First, Then Worry about Others
R 5.3—Resolve Disputes Peacefully
R 5.4—Do What Is Necessary to Protect Vital Interests
R 5.5—Keep Your Powder Dry
R 5.6—Mind Your Own Business
R 5.7—Build Coalitions and Alliances to Advance Foreign Policy
        Interests Multilaterally

In view of the increasing integration of the modern world, states should also seek to observe the three rules of the emerging postmodern world:

R 5.8—Support International Institutions, but Do Not Rely on Them
        for Your Nation's Prosperity or Security
R 5.9—Protect Human Rights in Other Nations When Feasible
R 5.10—Promote and Protect Global Public Goods

RECOMMENDED READINGS

Doyle, Michael W. *Ways of War and Peace: Realism, Liberalism, and Socialism* (New York: Norton, 1997).

Keohane, Robert O. *Power and Governance in a Partially Globalized World* (London: Routledge, 2002).

Mandelbaum, Michael. *The Case for Goliath: How America Acts as the World's Government in the Twenty-first Century* (New York: Public Affairs, 2005).

Mearsheimer, John J. *The Tragedy of Great Power Politics* (New York: W. W. Norton, 2001).

Morgenthau, Hans J. *Politics among Nations: The Struggle for Power and Peace,* 5th ed. (New York: Random House, 1978).

Singer, Max, and Aaron Wildavsky, *The Real World Order: Zones of Peace/Zones of Turmoil* (Chatham, NJ: Chatham House Publishers, 1993).

Waltz, Kenneth. *Theory of International Politics* (Reading, PA: Addison-Wesley, 1979).

SIX

Economic Rules of the IR Game

STATE POWER DEPENDS ON national wealth, and national wealth depends largely on a country's economic output. Consequently, the level and growth rate of a country's economy greatly influences a state's capacity to play the IR game. When a nation's economy is growing, tax revenues are likely to increase, thereby providing additional resources for national security, foreign aid, global goods, and other related public concerns. At the same time, economic development is important in providing employment and investment opportunities that can help meet human needs and provide opportunities for productive work. If a country is poor and unable to meet fundamental human needs, it is unlikely to be a strong state. Economic growth is therefore important not only in building a coherent and vigorous state but also in generating power resources that allow it to help structure global politics.

The growth and development of countries' economies is a multifaceted process involving environmental, geographical, cultural, social, political, financial, and technological elements. Although foreign elements—including foreign capital, international trade, and foreign investment—can contribute to a country's economic growth and development, wealth creation is fundamentally a domestic process achieved when the necessary preconditions are in place and the political, social, and economic environment is conducive to business enterprise. Some of these preconditions include political order, an impartial and effective enforcement of law, protection of property rights, cultural values that are conducive to efficient production, high quality of infrastructure, a highly educated workforce, and limited governmental interference in business enterprise.

Although economic success depends primarily on domestic conditions, the promotion of economic growth and development is not determined solely by the economic dynamics within countries. Rather, participation in the global economy through international trade, foreign direct investment, the internationalization of production, and transnational movement of technology and capital can enhance economic growth. It does so by attracting investment capital and by increasing the size of markets, which in turn facilitate economic specialization and make possible more efficient production through economies of scale (lowering unit costs by increasing the scale of production). Thus, countries with relatively low wages can produce and export labor-intensive goods more efficiently than industrial states, while knowledge-based economies can produce and export technology-intensive goods to less-modern countries.

This chapter analyzes the nature of international economic relations in the context of global politics. IR scholars call this area of analysis *international political economy*, or IPE. Whereas economics is concerned primarily with the efficient production and distribution of goods and services and political science is chiefly concerned with governance, IPE focuses on the interaction of markets and states in the international community. From the perspective of IPE, the functioning of the global economy is determined by the interplay of markets and governments. Economic and technological forces shape the interests and policies of states as well as the international political relations of states. At the same time, states establish the domestic and international rules of the economic game of production and distribution of goods and services. As I noted in Chapters 4 and 5, states seek to maximize national interests, cooperating with other states when goals are shared, confronting other states when goals are in conflict, and always competing with other states to increase their relative share of scarce resources. Moreover, the order of global society arises not from a central authority but rather from the ongoing political interaction of states, especially the major powers of the world. This fundamental anarchic framework of political relations establishes the context in which national economic forces operate in the international community.

In this chapter I examine key ideas, principles, institutions, and rules of the contemporary international economic order. The chapter has four parts. In the first section, I describe the process of modern wealth creation that has led to extraordinary improvements in living conditions for many of the world's people and to increasing economic inequalities among states. Secondly, I present distinctive features of a market economy and contrast it with two alternative approaches—mercantilism and state socialism. Because capitalism has become the dominant approach to wealth creation, I explore the nature of markets and why a decentralized economic order is conducive to efficient production and distribution of goods and services. Then I illuminate the nature of market economics by describing key principles of a capitalist approach. In the third and fourth parts, I describe the principal international economic institutions and the dominant rules structuring modern international economic relations.

World Economic Development

One of the major achievements of modern times has been the extraordinary rise in the standard of living of a large portion of the world's population. Perhaps the best indicator of the improvement in the human condition has been the dramatic increase in life expectancy. At the beginning of the twentieth century, for example, longevity for men and women in the United States was less than fifty years, but because of improvements in health care and general living conditions, life expectancy had risen to nearly seventy-seven years at the beginning of the twenty-first century. Although the quality of life varies greatly among countries, it is significant that most nations have experienced major improvements in living conditions and longevity, in life expectancy in particular.[1] For many developing nations, however, the rapid expansion of population—resulting from the rapid decline in infant mortality because of improved medical care—has inhibited a rise in per capita income. Poor countries with a population growth of 3 percent or more, such as Bangladesh, Haiti, and Pakistan, must grow economically at a minimum rate of 3 percent per year simply to maintain existing levels of average personal income.[2] Moreover, the benefits of economic expansion are often distributed unequally, even in countries that achieve moderate economic growth.

Despite rapid population growth, unequal distribution of income within and among countries, and human suffering caused by civil war, ethnic strife, and revolutionary instability, many developing nations in Asia, Africa, and Latin America nevertheless have experienced significant improvements in the quality of life from economic modernization, especially in the last three decades of the twentieth century. These improvements are evident in the rise in average living conditions, as measured by the human development index (HDI), an indicator devised by the United Nations to measure the physical quality of life.[3] In virtually every country for which data are available, the HDI increased during the 1980s and 1990s. Although some countries suffered temporary declines in their HDI coefficients because of civil war, maladministration, and disease,[4] in nearly every country the average quality of life increased during the latter part of the twentieth century.

What explains the significant improvements in living conditions in countries like Brazil, Chile, China, Ghana, Indonesia, the Republic of Korea, Singapore, and Thailand? Although numerous factors have contributed to the rise in living conditions in low- and middle-income countries, economic growth has played the decisive role. Such growth has been possible because societies have accepted a worldview that emphasizes economic progress through persistent and deliberate human initiatives. This modern perspective—differing dramatically from the static worldview of traditional societies, in which people's fate is determined at birth—assumes that savings and investment along with modern science and technology can foster increased economic output. This dynamic view, sometimes called the *modernization thesis,* declares wealth to be a human creation rather than the discovery or acquisition of resources. Some of the major tenets of this modernization perspective include the following:

1. *Modern wealth is a human creation:* Whereas wealth in traditional societies was gained by acquiring land and resources, modern wealth is based primarily on producing goods and services. Businesses that produce goods and services most efficiently will tend to prosper the most. Economic growth occurs through improvements in economic efficiency. Such improvements necessitate replacing old ways of producing goods and services with new, more efficient processes. The creation of modern wealth is therefore carried out through a process of "creative destruction."

2. *Wealth creation is based chiefly on human attributes, not tangible resources:* Although labor, land, capital, and technology contribute to growth, the emphasis on tangible resources is misplaced because development has little to do with the possession of resources.[5] Rather, economic growth is based principally on ideas, techniques, information, and other intangibles that foster higher productivity through better motivation, superior organization, and more efficient use of resources. According to economist P. T. Bauer, human capabilities and attitudes combined with a society's social and political climate are principal determinants of development. He argues that differences in these factors "largely explain differences in levels of economic achievement and rates of material progress."[6]

3. *Wealth creation is a dynamic process that can lead to ever-increasing output:* In a traditional society, where wealth is based on resources and is largely fixed, the increase in wealth for one group will necessarily lead to a decline in resources for other groups. In modern economics, by contrast, wealth creation is a dynamic process where wealth can be increased continually and where all producers and consumers can benefit from a rise in total economic output. Modern wealth creation is therefore a positive-sum process, where all can potentially benefit. Of course, economic gains are not ensured but will depend on the level and efficiency of economic output. Factors that contribute to economic output involve environmental conditions like a strong, beneficent state, stable political and economic institutions, and a modern infrastructure and more specific economic elements like the quality of labor skills, the level of capital investment, and the degree of technological innovation.

4. *The level of economic prosperity depends on a country's productive capacity:* Because modern wealth is a human creation, national prosperity is not fixed but varies in accordance with the country's economic capabilities. As a result, nations can develop or decay, rise or decline. At the beginning of the twentieth century Argentina was ranked among the top ten economies in the world. Some thinkers believed that Argentina had greater prospects for

economic growth and development than the United States. A century later, the United States was the leading economy in the world, with a per capita income of more than $40,000, whereas Argentina's per capita income was less than $5,000, or one-eighth of the U.S. income. In the 1960s, Ghana and South Korea had roughly the same standard of living, yet by the 1990s per capita income of South Korea was nearly ten times that of Ghana. In the 1960s, China was considered one of the poorest countries in the world, but after instituting a wide variety of economic reforms in the 1970s and 1980s, the economy began to grow at an average annual rate of 8 to 10 percent. If China can maintain its current economic growth rate, some economists estimate that China could overtake the United States as the leading world economy by 2040.[7] India, the second most populous country in the world, has also undertaken major economic reforms, resulting in significant increases in national economic output. Throughout the Cold War era, India followed statist policies that impeded job creation, but beginning in the early 1990s, India adopted market-based policies that led to significant domestic and foreign investment and a dramatic rise in economic growth.

Modern wealth creation has resulted in unprecedented international inequalities. In 1820, for example, the richest country in the world had a real per capita income about four and a half times as high as the poorest. By 1913, the ratio was fifteen to one, and by 1950 it had increased to forty-two to one. In 2000, the ratio was seventy-one to one.[8] The rising international economic inequalities are not a result of the increasing poverty of the world's population. Rather, they are a consequence of an increasing rise in the standard of living for those citizens dwelling in modern, economically prosperous societies.

In light of the modern economic history of countries, modern economic growth supports the following propositions:

- 🕮 Wealth is chiefly a human creation. It is based primarily on the production of goods and services that are desired by people rather than on extracting resources from the earth. Modern wealth is made, not found.
- 🕮 Economic growth is important, because it is necessary in order to improve a society's standard of living. Without growth there can be no increase in economic output, and without increased productivity there can be no improvement in the physical quality of life.
- 🕮 Increased economic output has historically resulted from greater production inputs (like labor and minerals) and from more efficient use of given inputs. For example, whereas one farmer could feed, on average, three to five people a hundred years ago, now

one farmer can produce sufficient food for more than one hundred persons.

ᾊ Increased economic efficiency is an important source of economic expansion in the modern world. Factors that contribute to increased productive efficiency include the quality of labor skills, capital investment, technological innovation, and a hospitable business environment—that is, one that provides essential public goods, such as political order, the rule of law, and the protection of property rights.

ᾊ Domestic conditions that facilitate economic growth include: order, the rule of law, stable monetary system, protection of property rights, high level of trust (social capital), little corruption, high level of honesty and frugality, and a priority on material improvement.

ᾊ The economic success of countries depends on the quality of the state. Well-governed countries have more successful economies that poorly governed states.

ᾊ Because national wealth is determined by a country's level of economic output, countries will rise (and fall) economically based on their level of economic output.

ᾊ The most effective way to reduce poverty is to expand national wealth through increased productivity.

The Market Economy and Its Alternatives

Historically, countries have pursued economic development through a variety of strategies. Since the emergence of the Westphalian order, the three principal economic strategies that have been used are mercantilism, state socialism, and capitalism. In the twenty-first century, capitalism has become not only the dominant strategy for most nations but the prevailing theory of wealth creation. Twenty or thirty years ago, however, the dominance of the market economy could not have been predicted. In fact, during much of the twentieth century, especially the Cold War years, theorists and leaders carried out a vigorous debate over the relative merits of a decentralized, private enterprise system versus a centralized, command economy. This debate came to an end only when the communist theory of political economy was jettisoned by the Soviet Union in 1990, leading other countries to do so as well. Robert Heilbroner describes the decisive ascendance of capitalism and the precipitous collapse of state socialism as follows:

> Less than seventy-five years after it officially began, the contest between capitalism and socialism is over: capitalism has won. The Soviet

Union, China, and Eastern Europe have given us the clearest possible proof that capitalism organizes the material affairs of humankind more satisfactorily than socialism: that however inequitably or irresponsibly the marketplace may distribute goods, it does so better than the queues of planned economy; however mindless the culture of commercialism, it is more attractive than state moralism; and however deceptive the ideology of a business civilization, it is more believable than a socialist one.[9]

In what follows I examine key principles of a market economy. Before doing so, however, I briefly describe the nature of mercantilism and state socialism—the principal alternative economic strategies that have been used by states since the Westphalian order came into being.

Alternative Systems

During the sixteenth and seventeenth centuries, some imperial states— notably Spain and Portugal—sought to maximize national wealth by acquiring precious metals and regulating commerce. This strategy of economic nationalism—known as *mercantilism*—assumed that national economic policy could be manipulated to national advantage. According to mercantilist doctrine, states could maximize national wealth by taxing trade, especially with colonies, and by achieving a positive balance of trade—that is, where the value of exports exceeded the value of imports. Because a state could achieve a trade surplus only when another state ran a trade deficit, it was impossible for all nations to gain from trade. Thus, mercantilist doctrine regarded commerce (like power) as a zero-sum process, where the gain of one nation must come at the expense of another. This strategy proved wanting not only because of its static view of wealth creation but also because it focused on the creation of national public savings rather than on the improvement of the consumers' economic welfare.

Although mercantilism is no longer practiced as it once was in the seventeenth century, the impulse to influence production and commerce in order to maximize national wealth continues to be expressed in a variety of ways. The newer efforts to gain national economic advantage are often called *neomercantilism* and involve a variety of initiatives of state-directed free enterprise. The aim of these efforts—sometimes referred to as industrial policy and strategic trade policy—is to maximize national income through government regulations and incentives.[10] Unlike crude protectionist initiatives that seek to curtail imports through quotas and tariffs, strategic trade is far more subtle in the manner in which is seeks to influence commerce. But like traditional mercantilism, its goal of directing production and managing trade is to maximize national income in the anarchic, decentralized international society of states.

The second approach, *state socialism*, was based on Marxist economic analysis. According to Karl Marx, a German social and economic theorist (1818–1883), capitalism was unsustainable because the demand for profits by capitalist investors' would result in the increasing exploitation of workers and the eventual suffocation of the capitalist economic system itself. Marx therefore predicted that capitalism would eventually collapse and be replaced by a classless economic order. Marxism's economic predictions, however, have not been fulfilled. The failure of Marx's economic analysis is owing to a variety of factors, including his failure to anticipate the collective power of labor unions, to appreciate the important role of technology and management in the production of goods and services, and most importantly to foresee the inherent human longing for freedom—to be able to produce and consume goods and services freely.

In the twentieth century, state socialism was expressed in two distinct forms—a radical form known as *communism* and a moderate version known as *democratic socialism.* The radical form, which was first developed in Russia and then practiced in countries like China, Cuba, and North Korea, was based on an ideology rooted in the political economy of Marxism and the theory of political organization of Vladimir Lenin, the leader who first institutionalized communism in Russia. According to communist ideology, since markets were assumed to be ineffective in meeting the fundamental needs of society, state socialism was necessary to ensure effective production and distribution of goods and services. This meant that a primary task of government was to directly manage all major aspects of national economic life through central planning. But communism would not have become a major global ideology had it been chiefly concerned with economics. Rather, the global expansion of communism was owing to the ideology's Leninist theory of political action and organization—a theory that directed a group of leaders (the vanguard) to direct workers (the proletariat) in revolutionary action. The Cold War, a forty-five-year conflict between totalitarian Communist Soviet Union and democratic capitalist United States, was of course similar to other great-power disputes in other historical eras. But the intensity and intractability of the conflict was a result of the competing worldviews that helped to sustain it with ideological zeal.

The moderate version, which was practiced by many Western European nations following World War II, left investment and production decisions largely in private hands but used high taxation to provide for a broad range of public goods, including health, education, and social and economic welfare. Although democratic socialism remains popular in some European states, state socialism is virtually extinct. The death of state socialism occurred when China and Russia, the two major experiments in command economics, gave up central economic planning in favor of market economics.

The Market Economy

As noted previously, the dominant theory of wealth creation in the modern world is the market economy, or capitalism. Unlike a *command economy*, where the state regulates and directs the major economic decisions of society, a *market economy* is one where individual consumers and producers are the chief decision makers. In his landmark book *The Wealth of Nations*, published in 1776, Adam Smith argued that the most effective way to foster national economic prosperity and promote individual welfare was through the market—a system in which people freely buy and sell goods and services to satisfy human needs and wants. According to Smith, the market coordinates economic activity through the voluntary actions of producers and consumers. The "magic" of the market is that it creates and distributes goods and services without anybody being in charge. These voluntary actions do not lead to chaotic, unpredictable human behaviors, however, but rather to relatively stable institutions. The stability of markets is rooted in the so-called law of demand, which holds that people will buy more of a good as its relative price falls and less as it rises, and that individuals will buy more goods and services as their relative income increases and less as it falls.

According to market economics, the pursuit of economic self-interest fosters productive efficiency, stimulates job creation, and promotes market stability. As Martin Wolf has observed, "self-interest, coordinated through the market, motivates people to invent, produce and sell a vast array of goods, services and assets."[11] Most surprisingly, Smith argued that when individuals pursue their own self-interest, their actions will not only maximize their individual welfare but will also foster society's general welfare. Smith referred to this miracle of maximizing collective well-being through the self-interested actions of individuals as the "invisible hand."

Sir Winston Churchill, the famous World War II British prime minister, once noted that democracy was a bad form of government, except that it was better than its alternatives. Similarly, capitalism is not a perfect economic system, but it is better at generating wealth than any other system devised and practiced by humans. To begin with, capitalism is not a cure-all for society's social and economic problems. It does not ensure the eradication of poverty, nor does it guarantee full employment. Moreover, capitalism does not eliminate economic instability. Still, a free-market approach dominates modern economic life because, as Robert Gilpin has noted, it is "the most successful wealth-creating economic system that the world has ever known."[12]

The market economy is based on several key principles. I next describe some of the most important of these.

≜ P 6.1—Markets Are Economically Desirable

As noted previously, the magic of markets is that, by facilitating voluntary exchange between producers and consumers, they maximize economic output. Because nobody is in charge of making goods and services, production is determined by consumer demand. And because consumers are guided by their own self-interest, they will buy desired goods at the lowest cost. Because producers are also guided by self-interest, they seek to maximize profits by selling the most goods possible. Producers will therefore risk capital in order to satisfy consumers' material wants by offering the best products at the lowest cost. Because technological innovation perpetually makes available new and better products, capitalism is fundamentally a process of creative destruction. Economic efficiency is continuously leading to new and better ways to make new and better products. Moreover, as consumer demand shifts, producers respond by halting production for unwanted goods and investing in new initiatives.

≜ P 6.2—Governments Can Help Markets Work

A market economy involves specific "rules of the economic game," such as legal protection of property rights, the sanctity of contracts, access to reliable economic information, and competition among firms. Because these rules are not self-enforcing, public authority must ensure that the essential procedures and practices of a free economy are maintained and periodically amended in response to changing circumstances and community needs. Besides making rules, government must serve as a referee, ensuring that markets remain competitive and that producers play by the rules of the game. In short, the role of government is not to produce goods and services but to ensure a stable and supportive context for private economic transactions. As economist Milton Friedman observed in his classic *Capitalism and Freedom,* government must maintain law and order to prevent coercion of one individual by another, enforce private contracts, define property rights, interpret and enforce such rights, and provide a monetary framework.[13]

The state can perform the tasks of rule maker and umpire only if government is itself limited, open, accountable, and transparent. Because government holds a monopoly of power within the state, rulers are often tempted to use their political power to secure economic gains through corruption and by establishing policies that benefit the ruling class

Economic Rules of the IR Game 🏛 131

rather than society as a whole. Thus, if a market economy is to succeed, it needs a good, beneficent state where property is protected, contracts enforced, and corruption punished.

One of the disquieting facts about the world is the significant and rising economic inequalities among countries. To a significant extent, the major cause of contemporary international income gaps is the difference in the quality of the state. Because a major determinant of economic growth is the quality of government, states that are weak, corrupt, and malgoverned are likely to be poor, with little prospect for improving average per capita income. By contrast, countries with limited, accountable, and constitutional governments are likely to be far more prosperous. The quality of government matters because a society characterized by crime, mistrust, and corruption is unlikely to encourage business investment. By contrast, constitutional regimes are likely to be far more effective in encouraging business enterprise and fostering job creation. In sum, because economic success depends on the quality of the state, Martin Wolf argues that the inequality in the quality of states guarantees continued inequality among individuals.[14]

🏛 P 6.3—Markets Work Best When Governmental Interference Is Limited

Because markets are based on voluntary exchange between producers and consumers, they are most efficient when transaction costs are kept to a minimum. Because most voluntary economic exchange is carried out through intermediaries, transactions are never wholly free. Rather, they typically involve some costs for information and the purchase or sale of commodities themselves. Historically, government has raised revenue by taxing commercial activity and by imposing income taxes on individuals and corporations. Although governments need income to carry out their regulatory work, taxes are an impediment to economic efficiency. Consequently, the market economy works best when the role of government is limited.

As noted previously, governments play a crucial role in protecting property rights, enforcing contracts, and maintaining a stable currency. But beyond these basic tasks, government intervention might be necessary to overcome unexpected "market failures" and to provide public goods, such as education, highways, airline safety, financial stability, public health, and product safety, that are conducive to economic growth. In the United States, for example, public safety is provided by numerous agencies at the national level (e.g., Department of Homeland Security, the Federal Bureau of Investigation, and the Department of Defense) as well as at the state and local levels (the state and local police). Additionally, the Food and Drug Administration (FDA) is responsible for protecting public health by regulating food and pharmaceutical products, and the Federal Aviation Administration (FAA) ensures the safety of civil aviation by regulating domestic air traffic and establishing aircraft safety standards.

◱ P 6.4—Capital Investment Is Necessary to Increase Economic Output

Historically, economic growth has resulted from increased availability of production inputs, such as labor and minerals, and from a rise in economic output from given inputs. Because increased productive efficiency is the most important source of economic growth, investment in capital is crucial to developing new and better products at lower costs. Such capital is important because it makes possible improvements in labor skills, technological innovation, and management and marketing. In a market economy, the interests of business leaders and consumers are coordinated through self-interest. Business leaders will risk capital in order to maximize a return on investment. But investment will result in profit only if a firm provides goods and services demanded by consumers. In turn, consumers' self-interest is ensured when they are able to purchase the commodities that they want for the lowest cost.

◱ P 6.5—International Trade Can Facilitate Economic Growth

International commerce can encourage economic expansion for two principal reasons. First, global trade increases the size of markets, thereby facilitating specialization and economies of scale. As a result, companies can design and produce goods and services not only for their domestic market, but for consumers throughout the world. For example, Nokia, a Finnish telecommunications company, is a leading producer of mobile telephones. Because Finland has a population of only five million people, most of its products are made and sold in foreign countries. Indeed, although the design and development of new cell phone technology is carried out at its headquarters in Helsinki, Nokia has ten manufacturing and assembly plants in Europe, the Americas, and Asia that produce nine hundred thousand units per day using 275 million parts.

A second reason why trade fosters growth is its emphasis on the production of goods and services in which countries have a relative economic advantage. The idea that countries have different productive capacities gave rise to the *theory of comparative advantage,* the cornerstone of the liberal theory of international trade. This theory holds that national economic welfare is maximized when countries produce goods and services in which they are comparatively efficient. British economist

David Ricardo demonstrated in the early nineteenth century that because countries have different productive endowments (i.e., different levels of natural resources, labor skills, technology, etc.), they have different relative production capabilities. As a result, countries should produce goods and services in which they have a comparative economic advantage. Unlike Smith, who argued that countries should trade when they had an absolute advantage, Ricardo argued that countries should trade even if they could produce all goods more efficiently. In short, national economic welfare is maximized when countries produce goods in which they have a relative economic advantage and import goods and services that can be produced more efficiently in other countries.

The doctrine of comparative advantage has been more recently supplemented with the idea of *competitive advantage*. Whereas the original formulation of the doctrine was based on different factor endowments, Michael Porter has argued that countries can develop new technologies and products that give firms and nations competitive advantages over other firms and nations.[15] For example, in the late 1990s Apple Computer developed a digital music player called the IPod. Because of its simplicity of design, small size, and ease in the downloading of songs, this product has been an overwhelming economic success, leading to the development of smaller and more powerful IPods. Because of Apple's commanding lead in digital music players, it maintains a global competitive advantage in 2007. Competitive advantage is even more important in the development of complex products like passenger aircraft, electric-powered cars, or large television monitors, which involve significant time and investment in research and development. Not surprisingly, two large corporations—a U.S. company (Boeing) and a European conglomerate (Airbus)—dominate the global market of jumbo jets.

Despite the extraordinary economic growth of China, India, and other developing nations using market economics, numerous scholars, public officials, and social and political groups continue to oppose global capitalism. They view this process as detrimental to the social traditions of traditional societies, inimical to the well-being of people, and incapable of lifting the masses out of poverty. For some critics, the global capitalist system is a way of making developed countries more economically prosperous at the expense of the low-income countries. In Box 6.1, I explore some of the major criticisms of the pervasive practices and institutions of global capitalism.

Institutions of the Global Economy

In the aftermath of World War II, Western leaders decided that the most effective way to promote a peaceful and prosperous world was to encourage the development of democratic regimes and to foster economic

♙   ♙   ♙

Box 6.1 Global Economic Backlash

The international influence of global capitalism became so pervasive following the collapse of the Soviet Union that economist John Gray termed the system "imperial laissez-faire,"[1] and political scientists Edward Luttwak and Peter Evans called it "turbo-capitalism"[2] and "hegemonic globalization,"[3] respectively. Although these and other critics acknowledged that the rapid expansion of modern market economics had resulted in beneficial developments, they also claimed that the rapid extension of market systems had resulted in many harmful outcomes. Because of the disruption to traditional social norms and economic dislocation wrought by globalization, numerous groups began to oppose the further deregulation of the global economy. These opposition groups—sometimes collectively called the global justice movement—involve labor organizations, environmental movements, social groups, and advocacy networks. Some of the major criticisms of global capitalism include the following:

1. *It accentuates inequalities within and among states.* James Mittelman, an IR professor, observes that the problem with the expansion of market economies is that the benefits go to those who are ready to compete in the global economy. Moreover, because states vary in their level of development as well as their level of participation in the global economy, the results from globalization are highly uneven. Countries that are prepared to compete in the global economy are likely to benefit from foreign trade, whereas those that are not well prepared are likely to derive fewer gains. Consequently, economic globalization will result in asymmetrical outcomes. As Harvard political economist Dani Rodrik has noted, economic globalization exposes a "deep fault line" between workers who have the skills and mobility to flourish in a market economy and those who either do not have these advantages or who perceive the expansion of unregulated markets as contrary to their nation's social norms and communal order.[4]

2. *It undermines traditional cultures and threatens social institutions.* Because economic modernization is achieved by increasing productive efficiency, modern industries place great emphasis on a skilled and well-managed labor force that uses modern science and technology. Because economic efficiency requires workers with a "modern mind-set," the spread of global capitalism leads inexorably to modifications in cultural traditions and behavioral patterns. Thus, when Western apparel industries establish plants in developing countries like Cambodia and Vietnam, they introduce work standards and routines that often challenge existing cultural and social norms. More-

over, when McDonalds fast-food restaurants have been introduced in some European centers, some people (most notably some French groups) have objected strenuously to this development for cultural, political, and social reasons.

3. *It exacerbates tensions between social classes and nations.* John Gray writes that although the expansion of global capitalism has made the world smaller and more integrated, it has not made the world more peaceful or more liberal. Indeed, he argues that the expansion of the international market has increased tensions among social groups and intensified nationalism.[5] Because economic globalization increases labor and capital mobility, modern firms continuously strive to maximize profits by developing new and better goods and services and reducing production costs. This process of "creative destruction" can have an especially damaging role on communities when factories are closed or transferred to foreign countries. Additionally, capitalism can play an inflammatory role between ethnic minorities and citizens, especially when foreign minorities control a large portion of a nation's commerce, as is the case in many developing countries. Amy Chua, a law professor who has investigated the economic impact of ethnic minorities in poor countries, writes that the spread of "free market democracy" in such countries is "a principal, aggravating cause of group hatred and ethnic violence throughout the non-Western world."[6] Finally, international financial mobility can inflame nativist sentiments when global capitalism is perceived as a cause of job loss and de-industrialization. Pat Buchanan, a former senior presidential advisor and Republican presidential candidate, writes that because U.S. influence is based on national wealth, the United States should pursue a policy of economic nationalism. "Free trade is not free," he writes. He therefore suggests that the United States should disengage partially from the global economy.[7]

Notes

1 John Gray, *False Dawn: The Delusions of Global Capitalism* (London: Granta Books, 1998).

2 Edward Luttwak, *Turbo-Capitalism* (New York: HarperCollins, 1999).

3 Peter Evans, "Counterhegemonic Globalization: Transnational Social Movements in the Contemporary Global Political Economy (2005)," in *The Globalization and Development Reader: Perspectives on Development and Global Change,* ed. J. Timmons Roberts and Amy Bellone Hite (Oxford: Blackwell Publishing, 2007), 420–442.

4 Dani Rodrik, "Has Globalization Gone Too Far?" in *The Globalization and Development Reader: Perspectives on Development and Global Change,* ed. J. Timmons Roberts and Amy Bellone Hite (Oxford: Blackwell Publishing, 2007), 313.

(continues)

BOX 6.1 continued

5 John Gray, "The World Is Round," *The New York Review of Books* (August 11, 2005), 14.
6 Amy Chua, *World on Fire: How Exporting Free Market Democracy Breeds Ethnic Hatred and Global Instability* (New York: Doubleday, 2003), 9.
7 Patrick J. Buchanan, "Free Trade Is Not Free," in *Global Backlash: Citizen Initiatives for a Just World Economy,* ed. Robin Broad (Boulder, CO: Rowman & Littlefield, 2002), 34–37.

development through a stable and relatively free international economic order. In effect Western leaders decided that after the war had ended a liberal international political and economic order should be established—one based on democratic governance and relatively free trade. Fundamentally, the liberal approach to global economics involves the extension of market economics from the state to the world. Just as workers should produce goods and services in which they have expertise and buy desired goods and services in which they do not have expertise, so, too, should countries specialize, exporting products they can produce more efficiently and importing those goods and services produced more efficiently by other nations. According to liberal trade theory, global welfare is increased through international economic efficiency.

The core ideas for this global market economy were first developed by British and U.S. leaders at Bretton Woods, Vermont, in 1944, where they decided that in order to promote global economic prosperity, nations would need to collaborate in creating institutions and policies conducive to global trade. In particular, leaders decided that if global economic prosperity was to be facilitated, three goals would need to be pursued: 1) a reduction of trade barriers, 2) establishment of a stable and efficient international monetary system, and 3) creation of a source of low-interest loans to facilitate economic reconstruction and economic growth in impoverished nations. After the war, three institutions were established to advance these goals—the General Agreement on Tariffs and Trade (GATT), the International Monetary Fund (IMF), and the International Bank for Reconstruction and Development (IBRD), or World Bank.

GATT, a Geneva-based multilateral institution, was established in 1947 to facilitate the reduction of tariff and nontariff barriers. GATT was based on two premises: 1) that trade should be governed by multilateral rules rather than unilateral actions or bilateral agreements and 2) that trade should be nondiscriminatory—that is, that trade preferences granted to one member state must be granted to all member states. Throughout the Cold War years GATT carried out a series of multilateral trade negotiations, or "rounds," that resulted in major tariff reductions. The two most successful were the Kennedy Round (1964–1967) and the Uruguay Round (1986–1993), each of which resulted in tariff reductions of 35 to 40 percent. As a result of trade liberalization, international commerce increased dramatically, rising from $94 billion in total world exports in 1955 to more than $4 trillion in 1994 and more than $10 trillion in 2005. Equally important, the share of world economic output (gross domestic product) more than doubled from 1965 (7.6 percent) to 2005 (14.7 percent).

In 1995, GATT was superseded by the more powerful World Trade Organization (WTO). In contrast to GATT, the WTO has more extensive and more binding rules governing international commerce and has greater authority to resolve trade disputes. In 2005, the WTO had 149 member states, accounting for nearly 97 percent of world trade. Interestingly, although Cuba and China are members of WTO, countries like Iran, Iraq, Russia, and Vietnam are not. In 2001, the WTO initiated a major round of trade negotiations focusing on agriculture, services, and intellectual property. The talks—known as the Doha (Qatar) Round— were supposed to conclude in 2005, but Europe, the United States, and leading emerging states were unable to reach agreement on agricultural subsidies and intellectual property rights (IPR).

The second institution, the IMF, was established to facilitate international economic transactions. Because each country has its own currency, international commerce can occur only if an efficient international monetary system exists that facilitates transnational payments. Such a system must, at a minimum, provide relatively stable exchange rates, so that financial and commercial transactions are predictable, and provide a source of international financial reserves to cope with balance of payments disequilibria. If a country is to effectively meet its foreign financial obligations, it will have to acquire foreign exchange—that is, foreign currencies with which to pay for imports. The principal means by which states generate foreign exchange is by accumulating financial reserves through trade or loans. These surplus funds can then be exchanged for foreign currencies to buy imports. Thus, one of the goals of an effective international monetary system is to facilitate efficient and predictable currency convertibility.

Because the IMF failed to establish an international reserve currency, the U.S. dollar became the de facto basis of international exchange. Because the United States guaranteed a fixed value to the dollar ($35 could be converted into one ounce of gold), the dollar provided a stable foundation for international commerce. Because the United States was unwilling to serve as the world's central banker, it terminated gold convertibility in 1972, thereby ushering in a system of flexible exchange rates.[16] Under this new decentralized system, currently in effect, the value of a currency is determined by a currency's supply and demand. In light of growing international trade, the volume of foreign exchange trading—that is, the buying and selling of national currencies—has increased dramatically, rising from about $200 billion per day in 1986 to more about $1.5 trillion in the late 1990s.[17]

The second major purpose of the IMF is to serve as a lender of last resort to countries experiencing monetary instability. When countries suffer from major financial disequilibria because of a rise in the cost of petroleum, high inflation, or a persistent balance of payments deficit, investors and currency traders might lose confidence in a country's economy, leading to a decline in its currency valuation. Because a stable international financial order is crucial to a prosperous international economic order, the IMF has a pool of funds from which short-term financial transfers are made available to countries in need. Typically, the IMF conditions financial aid on domestic economic reforms.

The third major international economic organization, the World Bank, was established to provide states with low-interest loans for major economic development projects. Originally, the bank focused on the reconstruction of war-torn Europe, but in the 1950s it shifted its focus to the economic development of Third World nations. At the beginning of the twenty-first century, the World Bank had a portfolio of more than $22 billion, allowing the bank to disburse more than $2.5 billion annually. Although this amount is not insignificant, it is relatively small when compared with all the bilateral loans and grants from developed countries to poor and emerging markets and is dwarfed by the much larger private financial transfers through foreign direct and foreign portfolio investment. As a result, the role of the World Bank has diminished relative to other sources of capital.

International Economic Rules

How should a country play the international economic game? Should it focus on stimulating economic growth, or should it concentrate on meeting the basic needs of its people? Should poor countries pursue strategies different from those of advanced economies? Moreover, should a government seek to focus on export-led growth, or should it simply concentrate on creating policies and institutions that are conducive to productive efficiency? Finally, should the state pursue strategic trade policies that encourage development in high-tech industries, like commercial aircraft or computers? Given the dominance of liberal political economy in the contemporary world, I describe five widely accepted rules based on this economic perspective.

⚉ R 6.1—Make Economic Growth a Priority

The most basic governmental economic task is to create an environment that encourages job creation. This means that the government must maintain sound fiscal and monetary policies, establish rules that foster sustainable development, inhibit inflationary policies, and restrict the scope of government in economic life. Historically, rulers have used political power to satisfy their own wants and to cultivate populist support by establishing public policies that are beneficial to particular groups of people. For example, in the late 1940s, the Argentine dictator Juan Domingo Perón expanded public works and established government programs and policies that favored the labor class. Although his initiatives won him strong backing from workers, the immediate and long-term legacy of his policies greatly harmed the economy of Argentina. Other countries—most notably former communist regimes like China and the Soviet Union and current regimes like Cuba and North Korea—have pursued central planning. Under this model, the task of job creation was in the hands of the government, which not only directed investment but regulated production and distribution of goods and services. Although statist policies have been effective in providing basic educational and health services and in achieving some economic success in sectors targeted by the state, central planning has not been effective in meeting consumer wants or in fostering society's overall economic expansion.

A second impediment to job creation has been the temptation to focus on domestic and international redistribution of income. To be sure, the state has an important role in helping to provide essential services, such as basic education, national security, and health, and to ensure that fiscal policies contribute to an economic order that is perceived as fair and legitimate. But when governments focus on redistribution of income, the initiatives are often detrimental to economic growth, because public officials become concerned with transfers rather than the creation of new employment. Some countries—notably Denmark, the Netherlands, and Sweden—have been able to combine successfully job creation with expansive social welfare services supported by high consumption and income taxes. But most countries that have sought to redistribute income domestically or internationally have failed to maintain an environment conducive to job creation. Thus, if a choice must be made between fostering growth or redistribution, the former is generally preferable.

Table 6.1 contrasts two different approaches to meeting the needs of the poor. In country A, which emphasizes economic growth, the nation's wealth doubles in time, and the conditions of the poor improve absolutely (from 1 unit to 1.5 units), although their share of total income declines (from 10 percent to 7.5 percent). In country B, which emphasizes redistribution, the nation's income declines slightly, but although

TABLE 6.1 Comparison of Growth and Redistribution Models

Country A (growth)	Country B (redistribution)
Year 1 100 units; poor get 10 per capita income for the poor: 1	Year 1 100 units; poor get 10 per capita income for the poor: 1
Year 10 200 units; poor get 15 per capita income for the poor: 1.5	Year 10 90 units; poor get 11 per capita income for the poor: 1.1

the poor's relative share increases from 10 percent to 12, the per capita income for the poor increases marginally—from 1 unit to 1.1 units. This comparison suggests that a focus on growth is more likely to uplift the conditions of the poor than is a redistributive program.

The advantages of a growth model have been amply demonstrated in recent decades and confirmed by empirical research, which has demonstrated that economic growth benefits poor nations and poor people.[18] The post–Cold War experience of Vietnam illustrates this. After the Soviet Union collapsed, Vietnamese political leaders began pursuing market-based economic policies and increased integration in the global economy. These reforms led to dramatic increases in economic growth that greatly benefited the poor. Whereas 51 percent of the Vietnamese were living in abject poverty (earning less than one dollar per day) in 1990, by 2006 the percentage of extremely poor people had been reduced to 8 percent.[19]

🏛 R 6.2—Nurture Economic Growth through a Market Economy

Because a country's level of economic development is a major determinant of its capacity to play the IR game, wealth creation is the most fundamental economic requirement of the state. And because markets are the most efficient institutions to facilitate job creation, states should establish policies and institutions that nurture a market economy. As noted previously, government has an important role to play in fostering economic growth, but its task is not to produce goods and services but rather to establish and enforce rules that ensure a stable, competitive market. The beneficial effects of market policies are illustrated by the dramatic improvements in Ireland's economy following the implementation of market-friendly reforms that were instituted in the late 1980s and early 1990s. These reforms included lowering corporate taxes, abolishing government agencies, reducing governmental regulations, increasing incentives for foreign direct investment, easing controls over foreign port-

TABLE 6.2 Trade and Economic Growth of Selected Countries, 1990 to 2003

Country	Exports as a Percentage of GDP 1990–2003	1990–2003	Average Annual Economic Growth Rate
Argentina	10	25	2.3
Belgium	71	82	2.1
Brazil	8	17	2.6
Chile	35	36	5.6
China	18	34	9.6
Haiti	18	13	−0.8
Hungary	31	65	2.4
India	7	14	5.9
Ireland	57	94	7.7
Netherlands	54	65	2.7
Sierra Leone	22	22	−3.2
Sweden	30	44	2.3
Tanzania	13	18	3.7
Vietnam	36	60	7.5

SOURCE: Data from World Bank, *World Development Indicators, 2005* (Washington, DC: World Bank, 2005), 198–200, 230–232.

folio investment, maintaining low inflation, and ensuring a stable fiscal environment. As a result, Ireland's economic growth rate increased dramatically, rising from an average annual rate of 3.2 percent during the 1980s to 7.7 percent during the 1990s. To illustrate the dramatic turnabout, in 1987 the Irish Republic's per capita income hovered at 63 percent of the United Kingdom's, but by 2003 its per capita income of $25,500 was $3,200 higher than the UK's. Because of Ireland's chronic unemployment and low growth rate, one of its major exports has been people. But since its economic boom, Ireland's historic migration patterns have shifted: For the first time in modern history Ireland is experiencing net immigration, as Irish people return to their homeland.

🍁 R 6.3—Participate in the Global Economy

Because economic growth can be encouraged through international trade and global financial transfers, countries should participate in the global economy as much as possible. As Table 6.2 suggests, countries vary greatly in the extent to which they engage in the global economy, and not surprisingly, countries that are actively engaged in international trade tend to have higher levels of economic growth than countries that are less engaged. Countries might, for political or other reasons, constrain the inflow of goods, services, and investment capital from foreign countries, but such protectionism comes at a significant economic cost to the home country. On the other hand, countries can deliberately pursue economic growth by instituting domestic policies conducive to exports. This strategy of export-led growth has been followed by a number of emerging economies, including China, India, Ireland, Malaysia, Singapore, and South Korea. As the data in Table 6.2 suggest, countries that foster trade (as evidenced by the rise in exports as a percentage of the gross domestic product) tend to also have fast growing economies. Indeed, countries with high growth rates in exports (Argentina, Brazil, Hungary, India, Ireland, Korea, Malaysia, and Vietnam) had higher average rates of economic growth than those with low or stable rates in exports.

R 6.4—Pursue Free Trade

Free trade is advantageous because it allows consumers to purchase the greatest number of goods and services at the lowest cost. According to most economists, the gains from free trade are so obvious that even if other countries maintain trade restrictions, open trade is still the best overall policy for a society. This is so because a country with an open economy is likely to gain more from cheaper imports than it is likely to lose from unfair practices that reduce exports. But as Robert Gilpin has noted, one of the major paradoxes of international trade is that, even though it greatly benefits the welfare of its citizens, trade liberalization is constantly being threatened by protectionism.[20]

The temptation to regulate trade arises from a number of sources. First, governments might seek to limit imports in order to protect domestic economic interests from foreign competition. But protectionism is at best a short-term solution, even when it is given to protect new (referred to as "infant") industries. When governments give temporary protection to industries, they protect them from international competition and thereby prevent the process of "creative destruction" to occur. Thus, when protection is offered, as was the case for many years to Argentina's industries, it prevents consumers from acquiring better, less-expensive products, and it thereby distorts domestic production. Rather than concentrating on production in which Argentina had a comparative or competitive advantage, it protected domestic industries for social or political reasons. Once Argentina adopted a more open economy, economic production began to increase rapidly.

A second reason why governments try to regulate commerce is the belief that a nation's economic prosperity is achieved through a positive trade balance where exports exceed imports. The widespread assumption is that a trade deficit is bad and a surplus is good. This view is typically based on the belief that a country's balance of payments is like a checking account, where income and expenditures must be equal to avoid an overdraft. Because in personal banking the goal is always to maintain a surplus for unexpected contingencies, some observers assume that a country should also accumulate reserves through persistent trade surpluses. If the aim of economic activity is to establish a large national savings account, as was the case under mercantilism, then perhaps continued surpluses could be viewed as sound policy. But if the aim of economic production is to satisfy consumer wants, then a trade surplus is no guarantee of economic success.

Indeed, a trade deficit might be owing to the relative strength of an economy rather than to its weakness. If a country's economy is strong and growing relative to others, the demand for imports will be high, whereas the slow growth in foreign countries limits demand for a nation's exports. This imbalance in growth rates can therefore contribute to a trade deficit. In addition, a strong economy is likely to attract foreign investment and further appreciate the value of a country's currency. Such currency appreciation will result in more expensive exports and less expensive imports, thereby exacerbating a trade imbalance. Thus, the belief that a positive balance of trade is necessarily economically preferable to a negative balance of trade is unsustainable.

Another way to understand the interrelationship between trade and capital is to recognize that credits and debits in a country's balance of payments must always balance according to international accounting rules. Because the current account in goods and services and the capital account are integrated in the balance of payments, a trade deficit is covered with foreign financial agreements—that is, IOUs or other promises of debt repayment. For example, when the United States ran a trade deficit of about $200 billion in 2005, the U.S. government met this "imbalance" by selling U.S. Treasury Bonds and other debt instruments to countries with which the United States had a trade deficit. The deficit was thus covered by the purchase of U.S. financial assets, which increased the U.S. debt with foreign countries.

To some degree, the pursuit of free trade is being increasingly bypassed by the phenomenon of globalization. As the world has become more integrated, production of goods and services is increasingly a multinational process, where the manufacture of products like cars and computers is dependent on components from many different countries. And with the growing importance of transnational knowledge pools and low-cost international communication, economic innovation and services are occurring without human migration. In *The World Is Flat*, Thomas Friedman argues convincingly that, because of modern information technology, territorial boundaries no longer ensure the maintenance of a hierarchical world where the rich, developed nations dominate the peripheral poor nations.[21] Indeed, because a well-educated worker in India, Romania, or Uruguay can have access to nearly the same information, software, and tools as that of a British or U.S. worker, corporations in developed countries are "outsourcing" some of their work. But unlike traditional importation of labor, modern outsourcing occurs by transferring production and services to workers in other countries.

R 6.5—Support a Stable and Efficient International Economic Order

Just as international peace is a collective good created by states, so, too, the maintenance of a stable and prosperous international economic order demands support from states. As noted previously, the extraordinary expansion of wealth creation has been made possible by the dissemination and institutionalization of ideas, practices, and policies that have stimulated business enterprise within and across national boundaries. However, the policies and institutions of the global economy are not self-sustaining. Indeed, the liberal order can only be sustained if states, especially the major powers, support the rules and institutions of the international economy. Thus, the liberal international economic order will be effective only if it rests on a strong political foundation.[22]

Such a foundation demands that states support the major trade and financial organizations, including the WTO and IMF, and seek to strengthen international trade and monetary policies by working multilaterally to ensure stability, efficiency, and financial liquidity of the global economy. Because states compete for scarce economic resources, they must resist the temptation of focusing solely on short-term national economic interests and because states benefit from the international flows of goods, services, and investment capital, protecting the international economic order is also an important state interest, albeit one that is more distant and less immediate. When commercial or financial conflicts arise, states must seek to resolve disputes without threatening the system itself. Because trade and investment presuppose a high level of transnational trust (sometimes called social capital), confidence in the international economy is essential to global economic prosperity.

Finally, states contribute most directly to the stability and prosperity of the global economy by maintaining sound domestic fiscal and monetary policies. When countries pursue inflationary policies, maintain persistent balance of payments deficits, or peg their currency at an artificially high level, foreign investors and foreign exchange traders might lose confidence in the long-term viability of the economy. And when they do, they will withdraw investment capital, sell securities, and trade off the national currency. This is what happened in the Asian financial crisis of 1997–1998, when Indonesia, Malaysia, the Philippines, South Korea, and Thailand all suffered a reduction in national income of about 15 percent.[23]

Conclusion

Although the world has witnessed a dramatic rise in living conditions, a large number of people still remain in abject poverty. The key to reducing poverty is to facilitate economic growth. Although countries can institute domestic reforms that foster economic expansion, states must also participate in the global economy. Because economic growth is positively correlated with the level of economic openness, government should resist the temptation of seeking to manipulate domestic and international economic affairs. Rather, states should establish the fundamental rules of the economic game and allow markets to determine the most efficient way of producing and distributing goods and services. Only in limited cases should states bypass the market to provide collective goods for a society's people.

In playing the IR game, states would be well advised to abide by the following principles discussed in this chapter:

P 6.1—Markets Are Economically Desirable
P 6.2—Governments Can Help Markets Work
P 6.3—Markets Work Best When Governmental Interference Is
    Limited
P 6.4—Capital Investment Is Necessary to Increase Economic
    Output
P 6.5—International Trade Can Facilitate Economic Growth

Additionally, in pursuing economic development and seeking to increase national income, governments should develop public policies based on the following five rules:

R 6.1—Make Economic Growth a Priority
R 6.2—Nurture Growth through a Market Economy
R 6.3—Participate in the Global Economy
R 6.4—Pursue Free Trade
R 6.5—Support a Stable and Efficient International Economic
    Order

RECOMMENDED READINGS

Easterly, William. *The White Man's Burden: Why the West's Efforts to Aid the Rest Have Done So Much Ill and So Little Good* (New York: Penguin Press, 2006).
Friedman, Thomas L. *The World Is Flat: A Brief History of the Twenty-First Century* (New York: Farrar, Straus, and Giroux, 2005).
Gilpin, Robert. *Global Political Economy: Understanding the International Economic Order* (Princeton, NJ: Princeton University Press, 2001).

Landes, David S. *The Wealth and Poverty of Nations: Why Some Are So Rich and Some So Poor* (New York: W. W. Norton, 1999).

Sachs, Jeffrey D. *The End of Poverty: Economic Possibilities for Our Time* (New York: Penguin Press, 2005).

Stiglitz, Joseph E. *Globalization and Its Discontents* (New York: W. W. Norton, 2002).

Wolf, Martin. *Why Globalization Works* (New Haven, CT: Yale University Press, 2004).

SEVEN

Legal Rules of the IR Game

ON NOVEMBER 4, 1979, Iranian revolutionaries stormed the U.S. Embassy in Tehran, taking fifty-three diplomats hostage. After failing to gain their release, the United States asked the International Court of Justice (ICJ)—commonly known as the World Court—to intervene in the dispute. Specifically, the U.S. government requested that the court declare Iran's actions a violation of international law and order the immediate release of all hostages. Soon thereafter, the ICJ gave a preliminary judgment. After declaring that the inviolability of diplomatic envoys and embassies was a foundational rule for peaceful interstate relations, it declared that Iran was obligated to immediately return the embassy to the U.S. government and release the hostages.

In its final judgment in May 1980, the court decided that 1) Iran had violated and was still violating international law, 2) the Iranian government must restore the embassy premises to the U.S. government, and 3) reparations must be made to the U.S. government. Iran did not recognize the World Court's jurisdiction and allowed the student militants to continue to hold the hostages. They were not released until January 1981, when Ronald Reagan became president.

The ICJ is not always so unsuccessful, however. About four years later, the court settled a territorial dispute between the United States and Canada involving some thirty thousand nautical square miles of sea off the northeastern coast of North America. Although claims to the territory had long been contested, the conflict became significant in the 1970s with the rising acceptance of exclusive economic zones (EEZ), which allowed states to claim territorial waters up to two hundred nautical miles off their coastline for exclusive economic use. In view of the economic potential for fishing and offshore oil drilling in the contested waters, both Canada and the United States began to press their respective interests more vigorously. And after failing to resolve the dispute through negotiations, the parties asked the ICJ to arbitrate the conflict. Specifically, Canada and the United States requested that the court appoint a panel of five Western ICJ judges (one each from United States, Canada, Italy, France, and West Germany) and issue a binding settlement. In October 1984, the court issued its decision, granting two-thirds of the contested waters to the United Sates and one-third to Canada.

As suggested in the two previous chapters, political and economic rules play a decisive role in the IR game. This is not the case with international law, the topic that we address here, or international political morality, the subject covered in the next chapter. The major challenge posed by skeptics concerns the legal status of international law and its effectiveness as a regulator of states' behavior. Echoing the skeptical perspective, former U.S. judge and Supreme Court nominee Robert Bork has noted that a major difficulty with international law is that "it converts what are essentially problems of international morality, as defined by a particular political community, into arguments about law that are largely drained of morality."[1] Others have questioned the validity of international law because of the absence of a central global authority to ensure compliance. Abba Eban, an Israeli statesman and diplomat, once quipped, "international law is the law which the wicked do not obey and which the righteous do not enforce."[2]

These two cases illustrate some of the possibilities and limits of international law in resolving interstate disputes. U.S. Senator Daniel Moynihan has written: "International law exists. It is not an option. It is a fact."[3] This is especially true of the principle of inviolability of diplomatic premises and personnel, perhaps the most basic and widely accepted norm of international law. Still, after violating this basic principle, Iran refused to accept the World Court's jurisdiction and to follow its subsequent verdict. The case with the United States and Canada, by contrast, shows a willingness to accept the court's judgment, owing in part to the two countries' shared political and legal perspectives as well as to a common conception of the nature of the territorial dispute.

This chapter examines the role of international law in global society. I begin by describing distinctive features of international law, including how such law is made and how it is enforced. In the second section I describe macro international law, focusing on the foundational principles of the legal order established with the creation of the United Nations system. In the third section I describe micro international law, focusing on legal rules in several areas of concern.

The Nature and Role of International Law

The Nature of International Law

International law is commonly defined as a body of rules that states and other players accept as binding obligations in their mutual interactions. This definition calls attention to three features of international law. First, international law is a body of rules comprising an integrated and logically related set of imperative norms. These norms cluster around

Table 7.1 Selected Rules in Four Types of International Law

Jurisdiction
 1. States have exclusive jurisdiction over people and property within national boundaries.
 2. Diplomats and diplomatic premises are exempt from host state jurisdiction.
 3. States may prosecute their nationals for crimes committed abroad.
 4. States may prosecute aliens for crimes committed in their territory according to their own legal procedures and standards, not those of the alien's state.
 5. States may expropriate foreign property provided it is done for public purpose and compensation is adequate and prompt.

Law of the Sea
 6. States have exclusive jurisdiction over territorial waters (twelve nautical miles).
 7. States may claim an exclusive economic zone (two hundred nautical miles).
 8. States can enforce their laws against foreign merchant ships in their internal waters.
 9. Ships have a right of "innocent passage" through international straits.
 10. States have the right to use the high seas.
 11. Every ship in international waters must be under the jurisdiction of the flag state.

Airspace/Outer Space
 12. States have exclusive jurisdiction over their airspace.
 13. Airplanes do not possess the right of innocent passage. Use of airspace requires consent.
 14. In international airspace, aircraft must be under the jurisdiction of the flag state.

War
 15. The intentional killing of unarmed civilians is not permitted.
 16. Soldiers may not kill or wound military personnel who have surrendered.
 17. Hospitals may not be seized or attacked in wartime.
 18. Prisoners of war are entitled to humane treatment; torture is prohibited.
 19. Taking or killing hostages is prohibited.

key topics of international concern, such as the rights and duties of states, jurisdiction over nationals and aliens, the law of the sea, and the law of international organizations. Table 7.1, which lists some key norms of international law, illustrates some of those topics.

Second, international law applies chiefly to states. Historically, the major aim of international law has been to provide rules for guiding and judging the behavior of states. Because states have been the primary subjects of international law, corporations, transnational associations, and individuals have been viewed as secondary subjects that could receive legal protection only through their respective states. In the latter part of the twentieth century, however, individuals and other nonstate actors have increasingly been recognized as subjects of international law themselves. The Nuremburg and Tokyo Military Tribunals, for example, brought legal charges against Nazi and Imperial Japanese military officers for violating fundamental norms of international law. Specifically, the Axis leaders were charged with committing three types of crimes—war crimes, crimes against humanity, and crimes against peace.

Third, international law depends on a higher degree of voluntary compliance than does domestic law. Because there is no central political authority in the international community to make, interpret, and enforce international law, compliance with international law is dependent ultimately on the willingness of states to abide by the widely accepted principles and rules of international law. Gerhard von Glahn titled his introductory international law text "law among nations" because he believed that the principles and rules of international law represent "not law above nations or supranational law but law among nations, *jus inter gentes*."[4] The status of international law is therefore ambiguous: States are subject to its norms but, as sovereign political communities, are not fully bound by them. For example, when Iran refused to participate in the U.S. versus Iran case, there was no international organization that could compel Iran to participate in the ICJ proceedings and no global authority that could enforce the court's judgment.

Making International Law

Because no international institutions exist in global society with the authority to make international legal rules, how is international law made? Whereas governments make and change law in domestic society, the making and development of law in the international community is carried out through the individual and collective actions of states. More specifically, it is developed through formal treaties and conventions and informal processes, such as conferences, declarations, and multilateral agreements, as well as the imposition of rules by the great powers. According to Article 38 of the Statute of the International Court of Justice (ICJ), the principal sources of international law are international treaties and agreements, custom, general principles of law, and the judicial decisions and teachings of influential writers on international law. In what follows, I explain how treaties, custom, and principles contribute to the development of international law. I also suggest that universal moral norms can be viewed as a potential source of international law.

International treaties are the most important source of international law. A treaty (or convention) is a formal written agreement between states, creating binding legal obligations for the signatories. Treaties are important because they create explicit agreement, codify common goals and expectations, and create, on the basis of voluntary consent, binding obligations. Treaties include specific agreements between two or more states as well as general conventions and charters for universal, regional, and specialized organizations. Because treaties are based on consent, legal scholars tend to regard them as the source of international law's legitimacy and the basis of the international legal order. According to Michael Akehurst, "treaties are the maids of all work in international law."[5]

The extent to which law is created through treaties depends of course on the nature of the treaty and the level of compliance with its provisions. Some treaties simply codify existing customs. This was the case of the Vienna Convention on Diplomatic Relations of 1961, which codified numerous customs on the rights and responsibilities of diplomatic agents. Other treaties establish new rules through deliberate joint action of government leaders. Examples of such accords include: the Nuclear Nonproliferation Treaty of 1968, which established new standards for regulating the use and transfer of nuclear technology and fissionable materials; the Landmines Treaty of 1999, which banned the production, transfer, and use of antipersonnel landmines; and the 1987 Montreal Protocol, an agreement that prohibited the production and use of ozone depleting chlorofluorocarbons (CFCs).

The second most important source of international law is custom—that body of widely shared practices and behaviors of states. For custom to be considered a source of law, two conditions must exist: The custom must be widespread among nations, and the practice must be regarded as an expression or manifestation of law. Custom does not include just any regular pattern of state behavior but only those widely accepted practices that are recognized as binding on states. What makes customary rules a source of international law is their universality and repeated usage. For example, in the seventeenth century, states began claiming exclusive jurisdiction over three nautical miles of adjacent sea, based on the fact that a cannon's range was roughly that distance. As states increasingly acknowledged this custom-based jurisdictional limit, it became part of the customary law of the sea. Similarly in the 1950s, Ecuador and Peru began claiming exclusive fishing rights over territorial waters extending two hundred nautical miles from their coastlines. The United States and other major powers resisted this claim. In time, however, a growing number of states began claiming an exclusive economic zone (EEZ) of two hundred nautical miles, and by the early 1980s, this claim was regarded as customary law.[6]

The *Paquette Havana* case, heard by the U.S. Supreme Court in 1900, illustrates the important role of customary norms in international relations. The case involved two Spanish fishing vessels that U.S. naval forces had captured off the coast of Florida at the start of the Spanish-American War. The owners of the Spanish vessels sued the U.S. government to recover the loss of the ships and cargo. The Supreme Court ruled in favor of the Spanish claimant, because the U.S. naval vessels had violated the customary legal norm of exempting unarmed coastal fishing vessels from capture in wartime when they are solely engaged in peaceful commercial activities.

The third source of international law is general principles. Although scholars differ on the source and proper scope of such principles, there is nevertheless widespread agreement that foundational principles undergird international law. Some jurists claim that principles must be derived from domestic law, and others regard them as rooted in the international system itself. Those who take the narrow path argue that general principles include only those ideas and principles from well-developed domestic legal systems. Two examples of such principles include equal treatment before the law and "good faith" in negotiation. Other scholars argue that the international legal order itself gives rise to principles that achieve authoritative status as they contribute to conflict resolution and advance human rights and international justice. Two important examples of such principles are *pacta sunt servanda* (treaties must be observed) and *rebus sic stantibus* (treaties must change when circumstances change). The first principle, rooted in the need to keep promises if community is to be sustained, is generally regarded as the bedrock of international law. The second principle suggests that when a treaty's original conditions change significantly, its legitimacy is lost.

Finally, international law is rooted in moral values. Morality—sometimes denoted as natural law or simply higher law—can also serve as a basis for international law. Although this source is not mentioned in Article 38 of the ICJ Statute, it is clear that many jurists believe that moral norms provide an important basis for determining acceptable international behavior. Such moral norms establish a foundation for affirming human rights, promoting peacekeeping, caring for prisoners in wartime, and protecting civilians in war. According to the normative perspective, some principles and values are so fundamental to human life that no state may ever willfully disregard them. Indeed, neither the policies of government nor the consent of citizens can legitimize an unjust action that is contrary to the higher law. The fact that statutory (positive) law cannot override natural law is a basic principle of moral law. This principle, which was the basis for the Nuremberg Trials at the end of World War II, led Allied prosecutors to try Nazi leaders for their war crimes and "crimes against humanity," even though they justified their actions as having been authorized by sovereign German authority. The normative perspective thus claims that when moral law and state action conflict, the former takes precedence.

More recently, international lawyers have developed the idea of *jus cogens* ("compelling law") to identify conditions or actions that are never morally permissible. According to this new principle, some international norms are peremptory (or absolute) and must never be violated. Accordingly, treaties that violate a peremptory norm (Vienna Convention on the Law of Treaties, Art. 53) are considered null and void. Although there is no consensus as to which practices are prohibited by the *jus cogens*, jurists generally acknowledge that piracy, genocide, slavery, torture, and crimes against humanity are peremptory norms.

Changing International Law

One of the key issues of international law is the problem of how to change law peacefully. Fundamentally, there are two ways of altering laws in domestic society—through peaceful means, using the institutional machinery of government, and through violence. When the institutional structures of society fail to bring about needed reforms through peaceful means, political groups might resort to violence to bring them about or, in the extreme, topple a regime. Because violence is an "illegal" form of political change, it is normally used only as a last resort. The responsibility of government, of course, is to maintain law and order by thwarting and punishing "illegal" behavior.

Violence is relatively infrequent in domestic political societies that enjoy democratic governance, in contrast with the more conflictual relations between sovereign states. The reason for higher levels of naked power and violence in the world community lies in the absence of developed institutional mechanisms to make and enforce rules. The interest groups, political parties, and legislatures that facilitate peaceful change in domestic society do not exist in international society, contributing to weak procedures to bring about global reforms. These institutions are weak or absent and do not have the legitimacy of their domestic counterparts. As a result, the procedures and institutions available for carrying out global legal reforms are comparatively underdeveloped.

An important vehicle for making and changing international law is the periodic specialized conference. Examples of such law-creating conferences include the Hague Conferences of 1899 and 1907, which codified, among other things, rules of war and procedures for international arbitration and conflict resolution, and the Third UN Conference on the Law of the Sea (UNCLOS III), which resulted in the 1982 UN Convention on the Law of the Sea. The UNCLOS III convention codified existing international maritime customs and established new norms in a number of major areas, including territorial waters, the high seas, and economic zones. Although international conferences can contribute to the making of conventions and treaties, they are not equivalent to domestic legislatures. States are not bound by the proposed international norms until they ratify the conventions or treaties.

Another vehicle for bringing about international legal change is an *international regime*.[7] Regimes are widely accepted rules, norms, and behavior patterns within a particular issue area of the international community. As countries establish closer cooperation in specialized areas of shared concern (e.g., foreign investment, refugees, deep-sea fishing, environmental protection, and waste disposal), they develop informal principles and procedures codifying the shared, voluntary patterns of behavior. Regimes are important because they encourage the development of procedures and norms that facilitate coordination and cooperation among states. Although such rules and procedures are not themselves international law, they provide the shared practices through which international law can be developed. In effect, regimes serve as a "halfway house" between an anarchic system and a law-abiding community, contributing quasi-legal norms that can subsequently be transformed into law as the procedures and rules gain acceptance.

A third approach to changing international law is through informal and incremental actions of individual states. When a large number of states begin to challenge existing norms, their "illegal" behaviors can precipitate a change in the law. In the early 1950s, when customary international law allowed states a maximum of twelve nautical miles of exclusive control over adjacent waters, Chile, Ecuador, and Peru began claiming a two-hundred-nautical-mile exclusive fishing zone. Because the United States considered such action illegal, it refused to recognize the extended fishing claims. Thus, when U.S. vessels were captured and confiscated for violating Ecuador's claim, the U.S. government decided to provide financial aid to fishing vessels to cover fines for "illegal" fishing and the release of the captured ship. By the late 1970s, however, a growing number of states, including the United States, began accepting the larger zone, which precipitated a change in international law that was codified in the 1983 Law of the Sea Convention. In altering international law through incremental adjustments, it is important that the proposed norms be widely accepted. If the new norm is effectively challenged by other states, especially more powerful states, it is unlikely that it will become part of the body of international law. Thus, when Mu'ammar Gadhafi began claiming in 1981 that the Gulf of Sidra, located off the coast of Libya and historically regarded as international waters, was part of Libya's territorial waters, the United States decided to challenge a claim it regarded as arbitrary. To affirm the Western claim that the Gulf of Sidra was a part of international waters, President Reagan ordered a naval task force into those waters in August 1981. When Libya sought to challenge the action by sending up fighters, U.S. F-14 jets protecting the task force shot down the two incoming Libyan planes. In short, modifying or extending existing norms can only be realized if there is broad support for such changes.

One of the continuing debates in international relations is whether international law is law or simply a moral aspiration or a shared expectation. Whether international law is regarded as law or morality will depend of course on how the law itself is defined. In Box 7.1, I briefly explore part of this debate by focusing on some major misconceptions about international law.

♘ ♘ ♘

Box 7.1 Is International Law Really Law?

Fundamentally, there are two major approaches to law—the realist and the behaviorist. The realist school, based on the command theory of law, holds that only law upheld by force is law. This is the view of the famous seventeenth-century British political theorist Thomas Hobbes, who wrote in *Leviathan*, his masterpiece, that "covenants without swords are but words" and that "where there is no common power, there is no law." The chief requirement for an effective legal system, according to this conception, is the ability of government to ensure compliance through the threat or use of the state's monopoly of force. During the nineteenth century, the English writer John Austin provided the most celebrated articulation of this legal perspective when he defined law as "the command of the sovereign."[1] Because law required not only clear rules but also an institution to enforce them, international law was not "law" but rather "positive international morality." The columnist George Will reflected this perspective when he observed that the notion of international law is problematic because of the lack of international consensus about norms. "Besides," asked Will, "can there be law among sovereign nations—law where there is no sovereign to adjudicate and enforce judgments?"[2]

In contrast to the realist approach, behaviorists emphasize the *habits of compliance*. For them law embodies the rules and norms that community participants are in the habit of fulfilling and find it in their interest to do so. The key to an effective legal system is *legitimacy*—understood as the voluntary acceptance of rules and the governmental institutions that make them. International legal order will be regarded as legitimate if the institutions for making, interpreting, and enforcing rules are viewed as acceptable and if the rules themselves have widespread support. In effect, a credible legal system needs to be based on implicit or explicit consent.

Those who suggest that international law is largely a myth rather than a reality do so because they assume that force is essential for compliance. But as Roger Fisher, a scholar of international law and negotiation, notes, the idea that law requires force is based on several misconceptions.[3] First, law does not work only because it is a command backed by force. There are times, he argues, when governments obey the decisions of courts, even though they possess superior force to disregard such legal action. For example, when steel workers went on strike in 1950 and forced the steel mills to close, President Truman used executive power to open the mills and keep them running. The Supreme Court, however, ruled that Truman's action was illegal and ordered him to cease running the companies. He complied with the action, even though he could have used the military

(continues)

BOX 7.1 continued

forces at his disposal to defy the court. Similarly, when the Supreme Court declared in 1972 that President Richard Nixon had to turn over secret tapes, the president complied with the court verdict because of the widely accepted binding authority of the court.

A second misconception regarding international law is that the only way to influence foreign governments is through force. According to this myth, international legal norms are incapable of influencing the actions of states, because only individual or collective military power can effectively bring about behavioral change in another state. But as noted earlier, military power is only one instrument of statecraft. Other significant elements of power that do not involve military force include widely shared norms and procedures, international public opinion, rational argumentation and negotiation, and moral suasion. Although force might serve as the ultimate arbiter of international decision making, it is not the only means to influence another state.

A third misconception is that law only restrains. According to Fisher, law is not only a set of rules prohibiting action but also a set of guidelines and principles affecting the choices and interests of individuals and political communities. Law, in other words, is both a positive force in guiding the aims and goals of states and a restraining force in restricting selfish behavior. The emphasis on the absence of international governmental machinery and the weakness of negative sanctions tends to focus attention on the failure and weakness of international law and to obscure the extent to which it is obeyed. Louis Henkin, a leading scholar of international law, writes: "What matters is not whether the international system has legislative, judicial, or executive branches, corresponding to those we have become accustomed to seek in a domestic society; what matters is whether international law is reflected in the policies of nations and in relations between nations . . . whether law is observed, whether it governs or influences behavior."[4]

Hedley Bull has noted that compliance with international law is generally higher than is commonly supposed. He writes: "When states live at peace with one another and are involved in diplomatic relations and exchange money, goods and visitors with them they are, in effect, in compliance with important norms of the law of nations."[5]

Obviously, the international legal order cannot rest solely on voluntary compliance. Some enforcement procedures will be necessary to ensure accountability for those who willfully disregard the law. By the same token, legal compliance cannot be based solely on force. If most people oppose a law, there would never be sufficient force to ensure compliance. If the law is to be effective, most of a society's population must accept the laws and the law-making institutions as legitimate. Only significant voluntary support can ensure widespread compliance. In the United States, for example, most citizens obey traffic lights and complete annual federal and state income tax reports, not because they fear prosecution, but because they are in the habit of complying with the law. They recognize that compliance with government is not only in their self-interest but is essential for maintaining community life. If most citizens decided to disregard traffic laws and federal and state income tax statutes, government would be unable to hire sufficient law enforcement personnel to ensure compliance.

Thus, if international law is to provide an effective body of rules that regulate states' behavior, international law will have to be viewed as legitimate and backed by some sanctions. But unlike the domestic legal order, where the coercive authority of the state is used to ensure obedience, compliance with international law is not enforced through institutions but rather through the individual and collective actions of states.

Notes

1 For an overview of Austin's positivist conception of the law, see John Austin, *The Province of Jurisprudence Determined,* 2nd ed. (New York: B. Franklin, 1970). Reprint of 1861–1863 edition.

2 George F. Will, "The Perils of Legality," *Newsweek,* February 27, 1984, p. 84.

3 Roger Fisher, *International Conflict for Beginners* (New York: Harper & Row, 1969), pp. 151–177.

4 Louis Henkin, *How Nations Behave: Law and Foreign Policy,* 2nd ed. (New York: Columbia University Press, 1978), p. 28.

5 Hedley Bull, *The Anarchical Society: A Study of Order in World Politics* (New York: Columbia University Press, 1977), p. 137.

Enforcing International Law

Because no authoritative institutions exist in the international community to make and enforce legal rules, compliance with international law is ultimately dependent on sanctions, or enforcement procedures, carried out individually or multilaterally by states. Sanctions are of two types—legal and extralegal. Legal enforcement involves law-based measures that foster compliance with international legal rules. Extralegal actions, by contrast, resort to social, political, and economic actions to foster compliance with the law.

Legal measures can be approved by authorized international organizations, such as the United Nations or a regional organization like the Organization of American States or the African Union, and carried out multilaterally by member states. For example, in the 1970s and 1980s the United Nations instituted an arms embargo and economic sanctions against South Africa in order to encourage an end to the racially discriminatory system known as apartheid. A more recent example of collective enforcement action is the comprehensive economic sanctions imposed on Iraq in the 1990s after it failed to comply with Security Council resolutions demanding accountability for its WMD programs.

Legal sanctions may also be carried out individually by a state that is a victim of an illegal act. Although the UN Charter provides some measures for collective enforcement of international law, the chief legal sanctions in the international community are based on individual action, commonly defined as self-help. According to the *self-help principle,* an injured state may use its resources, including force, to redress a wrong it has suffered. Legal self-help measures used by states include public condemnation, rupture of diplomatic relations, economic sanctions, arms embargoes, halting the transfer of military arms, and trade sanctions.

Lawyers generally classify such actions either as a retortion or a reprisal. A *retortion* is an unfriendly but lawful act that seeks to penalize a state for committing an unfriendly or illegal act. For example, after Hamas won the 2006 parliamentary elections in the Palestinian Territories and assumed leadership of the Palestinian Authority, the United States halted all economic assistance to Hamas. It did so because Hamas refused to renounce terrorism and to acknowledge Israel's right to exist. A *reprisal,* by contrast, is normally an illegal act that is rendered legal by a prior illegal act. For example, when the Clinton administration determined that Iraq was behind the attempted assassination of former president George Bush during a ceremonial visit to Kuwait in April 1993, it retaliated with a missile attack on Iraq's intelligence headquarters in downtown Baghdad. And when it became clear that Al Qaeda was behind the 1998 bombings of the U.S. embassies in Nairobi, Kenya, and Dar es Salaam, Tanzania, the U.S. government responded with missile attacks on selected Al Qaeda targets in Afghanistan and Sudan.

Extralegal measures are perhaps even more effective than legal sanctions in fostering compliance with international law. This is because the institutions of global society are weak and at times ineffective. Some of the most important *extralegal sanctions* include habits of compliance, legal reciprocity, public opinion, and the desire for order and predictability. The habit of voluntarily obeying law, the foundation of all domestic and international law, provides the basis for national self-restraint. Karl Deutsch once observed that although the habits of voluntary compliance are an invisible partner of government, they do the bulk of the government's work by channeling the behavior of people. A political community is much like an iceberg, with the visible one-ninth representing the work of government and the submerged, invisible eight-ninths representing customs, habits, and voluntary compliance with community rules.[8] Because there is no international police force to enforce international law, the practice of national self-restraint, based on the habits of voluntary compliance, is the bedrock of effective international law.

Reciprocity is also a significant extralegal sanction. Governments often accept legal obligations because their own self-interest is achieved if other states abide by similar rules. The origins of international law developed out of the principle of reciprocity: States accepted certain rules when other states did the same. Some of the most fundamental norms of international law, such as diplomatic immunity, respect for the sovereignty and territorial independence of states, and the protection of civilians, women, and children in wartime, evolved from reciprocal practices. The reluctance to use chemical weapons has similarly been rooted in the fear of reciprocity. For example, it is commonly assumed that the Nazis' refusal to use chemical weapons in World War II was based on the fear of Allied retaliation in kind. And more recently in the 1991 Gulf War, Iraq's decision not to use its chemical capabilities, even when facing a major military defeat, was no doubt grounded in the fear of unacceptable retaliation.

International public opinion is a third important extralegal sanction. Because world public opinion is rarely coherent and well defined, especially on complex problems in international relations, its major contribution to international legal compliance is to judge the behavior of states. World public opinion might not define or clarify law, but it is a potent political force in world politics. During the Cuban Missile Crisis of 1962, Robert Kennedy, the brother of the president, attributed the decision not to intervene in Cuba to the potential loss of the U.S. international reputation.[9]

The fourth extralegal factor contributing to compliance is states' desire for international stability and order. A society of states is possible only if member states themselves devise and follow binding norms. Because law constrains behavior, it contributes both to the stability and order of the international community. J. L. Brierly, a noted scholar of international law, makes this claim as follows: "The ultimate explanation of the binding force of all law is that man, whether he is a single individual or whether he is associated with other men in a state, is constrained, in so far [sic] as he is a reasonable being, to believe that order and not chaos is the governing principle of the world in which he has to live."[10]

In sum, even though international legal institutions are underdeveloped, international law nevertheless helps to regulate the behavior of states, thereby fostering global order and predictable international relations. Those who criticize international law because of its weak enforcement procedures are of course correct, but those who call attention to the widespread state conformity with the rules of international law are also correct. We are thus drawn to the conclusion, articulated by political scientist Hedley Bull, that "international law is a social reality to the extent that there is a very substantial degree of conformity to its rules; but it does not follow from this that international law is a powerful agent or motive force in world politics."[11]

Key Principles of the International Legal Order

When the nation-state emerged in the mid-seventeenth century, the fundamental rule of the nascent global society was the sovereignty of states. Although states were independent and equal in the new Westphalian order, they nevertheless cooperated with other states in order to maximize their national security and economic interests. They did so through covenants, treaties, informal alliances, tacit agreements, and networks of communication and cooperation. Although a significant body of international law emerged during the classical Westphalian era, its application and implementation remained woefully inadequate because compliance was largely up to each state. Antonio Cassese terms this individualistic and autonomous perspective on international law the "laissez-faire approach."[12] This decentralized perspective of international law became more structured with the creation of the United Nations in 1945.[13] Although the international order was still rooted in the sovereign equality of states, the new organization reduced states' freedom of action by establishing legal principles that structure international relations. The fundamental goal of the new international organization was to foster peace and security by facilitating peaceful conflict resolution and by increasing the costs of aggression.

Most states have a written constitution that specifies the fundamental principles for governing society. Although the United Nations is not a world government, the organization's charter can be regarded as the constitution of the world, establishing legal principles for the functioning of the international community. Even though it is beyond the scope of this primer to describe and assess the United Nations, it is useful to highlight the organization's most important goals and its basic legal principles governing contemporary IR. In this section I sketch some of the major aims of the UN and then briefly describe the nature and role of six of the organization's key principles.

The UN Charter begins with a Preamble, a part of which declares:

WE THE PEOPLES OF THE UNITED NATIONS DETERMINED
> to save succeeding generations from the scourge of war . . .
> to reaffirm faith in fundamental human rights, in the dignity and worth of the human person, in the equal rights of men and women and of nations large and small, and

to establish conditions under which justice and respect for the obligations arising from treaties and other sources of international law can be maintained, and

to promote social progress and better standards of life in larger freedom.

Article 1 of the Charter then states three basic purposes of the organization: 1) to maintain peace and security, 2) to develop friendly relations based on the principle of equal rights and self-determination of peoples, and 3) to foster international cooperation on economic, social, cultural, or humanitarian issues and to promote human rights. In pursuing the peacekeeping goal, the Charter says that the UN must be prepared to take collective action to prevent and remove threats to peace, to suppress acts of aggression, and to help resolve disputes in a peaceful manner that is in conformity with "principles of justice and international law." In effect, the aim of the UN system is to foster a more peaceful and cooperative international system by pooling the resources of member states to prevent aggression and to promote peaceful conflict resolution. As noted above, the UN Charter does not seek to alter the Westphalian roots of the international system; rather, it builds on the principle of state sovereignty, structuring collective action of member states in the service of international peace and security.

The legal system of the United Nations is based on several core Westphalian principles. These include: sovereign equality, the right of political autonomy, nonintervention, peaceful settlement of disputes, protection of human rights, and the prohibition against the threat or use of force. Because some of these have been discussed earlier, I limit my discussion to three principles: sovereign equality, political autonomy, and protection of human rights.

⚋ P 7.1: States Are Sovereign and Fundamentally Equal

The foundation of the UN system is rooted in the principle of sovereign equality (Art. 2.1). For the founders of the United Nations, sovereignty was a symbol of liberty in the international community, comparable to democratic rule in domestic society. Because traditional international relations were based on the sovereign independence of states, the international law that emerged from the Westphalian order was based on this right and was affirmed through formal equality in law. As noted earlier (P 2.4), this principle asserts that all member states, regardless of their power, size, or wealth, are inherently equal and entitled to formal equality. This principle is enshrined in the UN General Assembly, where every state is entitled to one vote, as well as in the International Court of Justice, where the settlement of legal disputes is based on the principle of equal and fair treatment of state antagonists. Just as people's inherent dignity is affirmed through the claim of human equality, so, too, the sovereignty of member states is manifest through the norm of juridical equality. Cassese writes: "sovereign equality constitutes the linchpin of the whole body of international legal standards, the fundamental premise on which all international relations rest."[14]

ᐃ P 7.2—States Are Entitled to Political Independence and Territorial Integrity

Earlier I suggested that the major players of the IR game are sovereign states. Legally, this means that each state is entitled to political independence and is ruled by a government that maintains supreme authority over its internal affairs (P 2.1 and 2.5). It also means that states must respect the governmental autonomy and territorial boundaries of other states by not interfering in their internal affairs (P 2.2). A state's right to autonomy does not mean that a state can use its freedom irresponsibly. Just as personal freedom can be limited in domestic society when it leads to others' harm, so sovereignty implies responsibilities both domestically and internationally. Domestically, states are responsible for protecting the human rights of their people, and internationally, they are obliged to fulfill the international obligations of global society's member states. In recent years one of the most significant modifications in international law has begun to unfold with the recognition that sovereignty involves not simply a state's right to political autonomy but also a responsibility to protect human rights. I discuss this responsibility later (R 7.3).

Because states are entitled to political independence, they have a right to use force to protect their autonomy. Just as individuals have an inherent right to defend themselves from attack, so a state has a comparable right to use all necessary force to repulse a direct or indirect armed attack on its territory. Although war was traditionally accepted as a means of resolving disputes and acquiring territory, this ceased to be the case in the early twentieth century. And with the emergence of the UN system, international war is no longer considered a legally significant concept, because war is contrary to the aims and purposes of the UN. Instead, international law focuses on threats to peace by state and non-state agents that involve armed actions.

Because international law has historically been concerned with states, the only armed force that is considered legally legitimate is that which is authorized by states. If political or terrorist groups carry out violence, such action can be addressed legally only if it is imputable to a state. This principle of state responsibility was illustrated with the 9/11 attacks on the United States. When the United States determined that Al Qaeda was responsible for the horrendous destruction in New York and Washington, D.C., it demanded that Afghanistan halt its support of this radical group and turn over its leaders, including Osama bin Laden. When the Taliban regime refused to do so, the United States attacked Afghanistan, toppling the regime.

Terrorism involving the possible use of weapons of mass destruction has posed a significant challenge to the international legal order. Because terrorist groups cannot be deterred by the threat of punishment, how should states protect themselves from possible attack? Two alternative strategies are preemptive attack and preventive war. Preemption is the use of force to thwart an imminent attack, and prevention is the resort to force to destroy an enemy's capability before it alters the balance of power. Although both preemptive and preventive force pose challenges to law, the first can be reconciled with law more easily than the latter, because in preemption, the action is taken to forestall an impending attack, whereas preventive war seeks to address conditions that might result in future aggression.

⚖ P 7.3—The Legitimacy of States Depends Partly on Upholding Human Rights

As noted previously, the UN Charter's Preamble reaffirms the priority of human dignity, expressed in the inherent equality and rights possessed by all persons. The Charter (Art. 1.3) also states that a major aim of the UN is to encourage "respect for human rights and for fundamental freedoms." Because no international convention on human rights existed in 1945, the development of international humanitarian law was a task that would be undertaken at a later date. The first major step taken in this effort was the adoption of the Universal Declaration of Human Rights by the UN General Assembly in 1948. Since then, numerous treaties have been adopted on such concerns as torture, genocide, refugees, racial discrimination, minorities, women, and children. Examples of important human rights conventions are listed in Table 7.2.

Besides expanding the scope of international human rights law, the international community has also extended jurisdiction over gross human rights abuses. According to this emerging claim—known as *universal jurisdiction*—any state, acting individually or collectively, has a right to prosecute egregious human rights crimes, such as torture, ethnic cleansing, secret killing, and genocide. Although the home state has the chief responsibility for ensuring legal accountability, when a state refuses to prosecute egregious offenses in its territory, other states may do so.[15] The growing acceptance of the *universality principle* is the result of a number of developments in the post–Cold War era, including the rise in human atrocities in failed or weak states and the perpetration of heinous crimes against civilians as warring ethnic, religious, and political groups have fought for increased political autonomy.

Table 7.2 Selected Human Rights Conventions

Year	Title
1926	Slavery Convention
1948	Convention on the Prevention and Punishment of the Crime of Genocide
1948	Convention for the Suppression of the Traffic in Persons and of the Exploitation of the Prostitution of Others
1951	Convention Relating to the Status of Refugees
1952	Convention on the Political Rights of Women
1954	Convention on the Status of Stateless Persons
1965	International Convention on the Elimination of All Forms of Racial Discrimination
1973	International Convention on the Suppression and the Punishment of the Crime of Apartheid
1979	Convention on the Elimination of All Forms of Discrimination against Women
1984	Convention against Torture and Other Cruel, Inhuman, and Degrading Treatment
1989	Convention on the Rights of the Child

The quest for international legal accountability builds on the World War II experience of the allies, who prosecuted German and Japanese leaders in the Nuremberg and Tokyo War Crimes Military Tribunals. In 1993, the Security Council established an international war crimes tribunal in The Hague in order to prosecute gross human rights crimes committed during the 1992–1994 Bosnian War. Subsequently, the Security Council established another international tribunal in order to prosecute the leaders of the Rwandan genocide of 1994. The quest for global accountability for human rights atrocities culminated in July 1998, when some 120 countries voted in favor of the Rome Treaty establishing the International Criminal Court (ICC). The ICC, which the United States continues to oppose, began functioning in 2002.

🕮 P 7.4—States Must Honor Legal Commitments

One of the most basic principles of international law is *pacta sunt servanda,* meaning that agreements must be faithfully observed. This norm is especially important because, as noted at the outset of this chapter, compliance with international law depends primarily on the voluntary actions of states. When states sign and ratify treaties, whether bilateral or multilateral, they bind themselves to fulfill the terms of these agreements. And when they fulfill their promises, they help generate social capital in the international community and thereby contribute to global solidarity. Only through promise keeping and the fulfillment of interstate agreements can the authority of the international legal order be sustained.

States are often reluctant to enter into bilateral and multilateral treaties and agreements because such accords circumscribe their behavior. But it is precisely the creation of boundaries and limitations that contributes to the rise in the predictability of state behavior, which makes social solidarity and trust possible. Because membership in the international community is important to the fulfillment of state interests, and because trust is essential to sustain any level of communal life, promise keeping is a foundational norm of the international community.

International Legal Rules

Having covered the key principles of the current international system, we now turn to more specific rules of international law. These rules govern the behavior of states and other actors in many different areas, including diplomatic rights and responsibilities, international organizations, jurisdiction over people, international criminal law, the global environment, and international human rights. There is even a significant body of international law covering the making and interpretation of treaties and other agreements.

In what follows, I examine some of the most influential legal rules structuring the contemporary IR game.

♟ R 7.1—States Must Not Threaten or Use Force

A major reason for creating the UN was to establish an international organization to help prevent international war. UN members are required to "refrain in their international relations from the threat or use of force" (Art. 2.4). The central assumption of the UN Charter is that if every member state abides by this rule, the international system will be stable and peaceful. Aggression is therefore an illegal act in the international system.

Of course, the UN Charter's authors recognized that not every state would pursue peaceful foreign relations, and thus they provided for two exceptions to this principle: First, states have an inherent right to use force in self-defense (Art. 51) and second, force may be utilized as a part of collective enforcement measures that are authorized by the Security Council in accordance with Chapter VII of the UN Charter. It is important to stress that this prohibition is limited in two ways. First, because the ban on force applies only to interstate conflicts, it does not restrict states in using coercive force against insurgents, terrorists, or other agents that would threaten the sovereignty of the state. Second, the ban does not apply to nonmilitary punitive measures, such as economic sanctions.

𐐚 R 7.2—States Must Not Intervene in the Internal Affairs of Other States

As noted earlier, a core principle of the contemporary global system is the principle of respecting the political autonomy of states (P 2.2). And as noted previously, the UN constitutional system similarly is also based on this foundational principle (P 7.2). Because states are sovereign and equal, they must honor the principle of *nonintervention*. Sovereignty is so basic to the international legal order that the United Nations itself is prohibited from intervening in the domestic affairs of member states (Art 2.7). As originally specified, the nonintervention principle applied first to direct armed aggression, but during the Cold War it was extended to indirect armed aggression in order to deal with threats from internationally supported subversion.

Because the IR game is based on the notion of sovereignty, a society of states requires that states honor each other's political independence and territorial integrity. Although the classical Westphalian system of independent states continues to define IR, the notion of sovereignty is under increasing challenge, leading some analysts to regard nonintervention as a secondary rule. In the postmodern order, states' freedom of action in global society is being increasingly constrained by the growing prominence of human rights, the increasing influence of IGOs and NGOs, and the continued expansion of global functional integration. In particular, globalization—facilitated by the increasing speed and volume of international flows of information, money, and goods and services— has made state boundaries more porous and state authority less decisive. Of course, the increasing pressures on state autonomy are not new. As Stephen Krasner has noted, sovereignty was never absolute. Indeed, from the beginning of the nation-state, sovereignty involved "organized hypocrisy," because states' political and legal autonomy were regularly compromised at both the domestic and international levels.[16]

𐐚 R 7.3—States May Violate Sovereignty in Exceptional Circumstances

Although nonintervention is a basic constitutive norm of international society, states have historically intervened in the affairs of other states. They have done so for a variety of reasons, including economic expansion, political control, security, and humanitarianism. Indeed, foreign intervention has been so common in global politics that one IR scholar writes that international affairs is "in no small part the history of intervention."[17] Although scholars have offered a number of reasons for disregarding the nonintervention norm,[18] in what follows, I explore two of the most widely accepted justifications for intervention—the protection of human rights and territorial security.

Undoubtedly the most morally compelling justification for foreign intervention is the protection of persons from genocide or other atrocities. Soon after the sovereignty norm was adopted, international legal scholars recognized that rulers could potentially institute unjust policies that would lead to human suffering. Because political rulers were given ultimate authority in order to carry out responsible government, scholars emphasized that sovereignty could not be used as a cover for injustice. This is why Swiss jurist Emmerich de Vattel claimed in the late seventeenth century that states could intervene to protect oppressed people.[19] Ever since Vattel made his argument, theorists, legal scholars, and diplomats have repeatedly made the claim that sovereignty can be overridden to protect human rights.

As noted in Chapter 5, the international community has increasingly accepted the notion that human rights should take precedence over sovereignty when the two norms are in conflict. This trade-off has been expressed in the *responsibility to protect (R2P) principle,* which was affirmed at the UN World Summit in 2005. According to R2P, because a major task of the state is to protect human rights, when a regime is unable or unwilling to protect rights, the international community assumes the responsibility to intervene to protect humans. In sum, when human rights (P 7.3) are compromised by the state, the defense of people must take precedence over the claim of sovereignty and the duty of nonintervention (P 7.2).

A second justification for violating the nonintervention principle is national security. When a state perceives a foreign threat, especially from a neighboring state, it may resort to coercive action, including military intervention. For example, when India intervened in East Pakistan (Bangladesh) in 1971 after Pakistan embarked on a war against the Bengali people, it did so because it believed that the war and the atrocities committed as part of that war posed a direct threat to the territorial integrity of the Indian state. And when Tanzania intervened in Uganda in 1978, it did so not because Idi Amin, Uganda's dictator, was abusing human rights but because his authoritarian rule posed a threat to the peace and stability of central Africa. And when the U.S. military intervened in Haiti in 1994, it did so to alter the domestic political conditions in Haiti and thereby reduce the number of people fleeing the island's repression. The U.S. intervention, which was backed by the UN Security Council, sought to restore power to the country's elected president, Jean-Bertrand Aristide, and to maintain order during the period of transition to civilian rule. Although the United States succeeded in its immediate goals, the long-term goals of creating a humane, responsible government have remained unfulfilled.

က R 7.4—States Must Resolve Disputes Peacefully

The peaceful settlement of disputes is a major purpose of the UN system. The UN Charter (Art. 2.3) obliges member states to settle their international disputes without resorting to coercive force. Peace is important not simply because it prevents violence and destruction but also because it helps establish a legitimate global order, without which global justice and economic prosperity are impossible. The UN Charter (Art. 33) encourages the disputing states to pursue pacific settlement directly through negotiation, mediation, arbitration, and other peaceful means. The Charter also stipulates that conflict resolution can be taken up indirectly by the United Nations itself. According to the Charter (Chapter VI), the Security Council can address disputes and other threats to peace by investigating the nature of the conflict and making recommendations to foster a peaceful resolution of the conflict. Because war always leads to destruction, economic loss, and human suffering, this rule is consistent with the fundamental values and aspirations of all peoples. Nevertheless, when vital interests are at stake and states are unable to resolve their disputes through peaceful negotiation, they might be tempted to resort to force.

က R 7.5—States Must Protect the Global Environment

In the 1970s, states began to recognize that the misuse of the earth's resources could lead to short-term harmful environmental effects and that the overuse of resources could result in deleterious long-term consequences for the world. In order to better address the need to protect the global environment, the General Assembly established in 1972 the UN Environmental Program (UNEP). UNEP, headquartered in Nairobi, has helped to develop principles and has encouraged policies that contribute to sustainable development. In particular, UNEP has spearheaded numerous investigations, mobilized public concern about major global environmental challenges, and served as a catalyst for the development of numerous international environment accords. Undoubtedly, the most important international environmental conference was the 1992 Earth Summit in Rio de Janeiro, Brazil—formally called the UN Conference on Environment and Development (UNCED). The conference, the largest international conference ever held, drew officials from 172 countries, 115 heads of state, and some 15,000 representatives from thousands of environmental NGOs. The summit resulted in the signing of

Table 7.3 Selected Global Environmental Conventions

Year	Title
1973	Convention on International Trade in Endangered Species of Wild Fauna and Flora
1982	Law of the Sea Convention
1985	Vienna Convention for the Protection of the Ozone Layer
1987	Montreal Protocol on Substances That Deplete the Ozone Layer
1989	Basel Convention on the Control of Transboundary Movements of Hazardous Wastes and Their Disposal
1992	Convention on Biological Diversity
1992	Framework Convention on Climate Change
1998	Kyoto Protocol (Conference of the Parties to the Framework Convention on Climate Change)

treaties on climate change and biodiversity and the adoption by consensus of three nonbinding documents—a declaration on the environment and development, a statement on forest principles, and "Agenda 21," which set forth principles for sustainable economic development.

It is estimated that the international community has adopted more than 150 treaties since the UN began addressing global environmental protection in the early 1970s. Some of the major environmental treaties are included in Table 7.3.

Despite the proliferation of legal environmental conventions and the growing significance of global environmental protection, international environmental law remains comparatively undeveloped. This is because of the complexity of some of the challenges and the inadequacy of monitoring and enforcement procedures. Indeed, some of the most important initiatives achieved to date on global environmental protection are expressed in guidelines, declarations, principles, and recommendations—what scholars refer to as "soft law," distinguishing it from the hard law that imposes specific binding obligations.

Conclusion

Although legal institutions are underdeveloped when compared with those in domestic society, international law nevertheless plays an important role in structuring international relations. As I have shown here, the architecture of the IR game is based partly on legal principles that define rights and responsibilities of member states. The following are some of the most important of these:

P 7.1—States Are Sovereign and Fundamentally Equal
P 7.2—States Are Entitled to Political Independence and Territorial
     Integrity
P 7.3—The Legitimacy of States Depends Partly on Upholding
     Human Rights
P 7.4—States Must Honor Legal Commitments

In addition, a large body of international law has emerged over the past several hundred years. Such law imposes specific duties and responsibilities on states and other actors in a variety of areas, including diplomacy, force, jurisdiction over the sea and outer space, human rights, and the global environment. I illustrated the nature and role of such law by examining the following five legal rules:

R 7.1—States Must Not Threaten or Use Force
R 7.2—States Must Not Intervene in the Internal Affairs of
     Other States
R 7.3—States May Violate Sovereignty in Exceptional Circumstances
R 7.4—States Must Settle Disputes Peacefully
R 7.5—States Must Protect the Global Environment

States are likely to be more successful in the IR game if they follow these rules.

RECOMMENDED READINGS

Cassese, Antonio. *International Law* (Oxford: Oxford University Press, 2001).

Forsythe, David P. *Human Rights in International Relations,* 2nd ed. (Cambridge: Cambridge University Press, 2006).

Henkin, Louis. *How Nations Behave: Law and Foreign Policy,* 2nd ed. (New York: Columbia University Press, 1978).

Kaul, Inge, Isabelle Grunberg, and Marc A. Stern, eds. *Global Public Goods: International Cooperation in the 21st Century* (New York: Oxford University Press, 1999).

Singer, Peter. *One World: The Ethics of Globalization,* 2nd ed. (New Haven, CT: Yale University Press, 2002).

von Glahn, Gerhard, and James Larry Taulbee. *Law among Nations: An Introduction to Public International Law,* 8th ed. (New York: Pearson Longman, 2007).

EIGHT

Moral Rules of the IR Game

FROM APRIL TO JULY 1994, Rwanda experienced one of the most destructive mass atrocities in history, resulting in the death of some eight hundred thousand persons. The genocide began on April 6 and continued until the Hutu regime was toppled in mid-July.[1] During this period of about one hundred days, the Hutu-dominated government and Hutu extremists carried out a planned campaign of mass extermination of Tutsis. Although the genocide was planned at the national and regional levels, it was implemented locally by political, military, and civic leaders and trained militia (*interahamwe*) and claimed more lives in less time than any other mass atrocity in recorded history.[2] The killing came to a halt only when the Tutsi rebel force defeated Hutu extremists.

When mass atrocities occur in a small and impoverished country like Rwanda, who is responsible? If a government is unwilling or unable to halt the society-wide killing, must neighboring states and major powers intervene to halt genocide? Are international organizations like the United Nations and the African Union responsible? Because moral rights and duties of states depend on how the international community is conceived, when atrocities occur, such as those in the Rwandan genocide, fundamental questions arise about the nature and scope of international responsibility. Is global society an anarchical society where each member state is responsible only for its own national concerns, or is it a global moral community where the safety, prosperity, and human dignity of all peoples matter? If the world is rooted in a shared political morality, what is the scope and content of the world's international political morality?

Although moral values are an inescapable part of human life, scholars and public officials have often been reluctant to acknowledge the role of moral values in IR. The neglect of moral values and ethical analysis in global politics is clearly evident in the IR literature, which has historically given precedence to power over justice. In his account of the Peloponnesian Wars of the fifth century B.C., Thucydides suggests that international relations are primarily determined by power and security. Although Thucydides acknowledges that moral values can influence the thoughts and actions of statesmen, he observes that when leaders must choose between security and the general welfare, power and justice, the former takes precedence over the latter. "The strong do what they have to do," he writes, "and the weak have to accept."[3] Ever since Thucydides penned his powerful account of the systemic conflict between Athens and Sparta, political realism has served as the dominant perspective to assess international relations.

Realists assert that the international community is a realm of power and necessity, not morality and choice. Because no central authority exists to resolve disputes, some realists claim that the overriding concern of states is security and material well-being. According to George Kennan, a leading observer of U.S. diplomacy, the chief responsibility of a statesman is to secure the vital interests of states—a task he claims has no moral content. He writes, "Government is an agent, not a principal. Its primary obligation is to the interests of national society it represents . . . its military security, the integrity of its political life and the well-being of its people. These needs have no moral quality. They are the unavoidable necessities of national existence and therefore are subject to classification neither as 'good' or [sic] 'bad.'"[4] Kennan's view that foreign policy is essentially an amoral enterprise is based on the dubious claim that the core national interests (security, political independence, and economic prosperity) have no moral quality. But why should this be the case? Are not the legitimate goals of people rooted in shared moral values, including decency, honesty, fairness, and promise keeping? As Arnold Wolfers has wisely noted, international relations are not beyond the scope of morality but are themselves based on moral norms.[5]

Competitive games also involve moral norms, including fair play, sound sportsmanship, and the impartial interpretation and application of rules. When a player commits a flagrant foul, say, in soccer or football, the opposing team is either given a free kick (soccer) or the ball is advanced fifteen yards toward the end zone. In extreme cases, a player can be ejected from the game. Similarly, the use of illegal drugs to enhance an athlete's endurance in cycling and strength in baseball and football is also regarded as morally unacceptable because such action impairs the fairness and honesty required of competitive sports. Thus, when athletes are identified as having taken illegal drugs, they may be sanctioned by sporting authorities and even disqualified of prior titles. Like competitive games, global politics is based on moral values that ensure its integrity.

The aim of this chapter is to examine the moral principles and rules governing the IR game. This is a challenging and highly contested area of IR—challenging because identifying the nature and role of moral norms is difficult, and contested because many scholars and decision makers have regarded foreign affairs as a realm of power and necessity rather than of moral choice. The chapter has three major parts. In the first part I explore the nature of moral values and the role of ethical reasoning and then address the challenge posed by cultural pluralism in global society. The second part describes and assesses the role of political morality in the conduct of foreign policy. Specifically, I illuminate core principles and rules that structure the moral reasoning of government leaders in developing and implementing foreign policy. In the final section I describe and assess the role of moral values governing the international community itself. Whereas section two focuses on international justice, the final section is concerned with justice of the global society itself.

The Nature and Role of International Political Morality

Morality versus Ethics

The word *morality* comes from the Latin *mores,* meaning custom or habit. It typically describes what is good or right. The term *ethics* comes from the Greek *ethos,* meaning custom or common practice. Because both terms have a common root meaning, they are often used interchangeably. Strictly speaking, however, morality refers to values and beliefs about what is right and wrong, and ethics refers to the examination, justification, and application of morality.

Moral norms have three features. First, they command universal allegiance. This means that morality is binding on all peoples in all societies. Immanuel Kant articulated this requirement in his famous "categorical imperative," which requires that people treat others as an end (i.e., having inherent value) and that they act in accordance with norms as if they are valid for others. Second, morality demands impartiality. Because people are tempted to clothe and advance self-interest through moral rhetoric, authentic morality is best applied through dispassion and disinterest. Finally, morality is characterized by self-enforcement. Unlike law, which is enforced by government, morality is applied primarily through the voluntary actions of people. Compliance with moral obligations is rooted in the beliefs and values that people hold.

Personal morality and political morality are related but not the same. The former entails norms that are applicable to the conduct of individuals in their personal or private relations. The Ten Commandments is an example of such morality. Political morality, by contrast, involves norms that are applicable to the life of collectives. Examples of such moral norms include the right of political self-determination, the right of political independence, and the right of self-defense. Because of the different nature and role of personal and political morality, Lea Brilmayer writes, "the prohibitions found in interpersonal morality cannot be mechanically transplanted into a code of conduct for public officials."[6]

Ethics involves choosing or doing that which is good and avoiding that which is evil. Ethical decision making is difficult because decisions rarely involve simple moral verdicts. Rather, most issues, especially in domestic and international politics, involve judgments between competing moral values. Thus, in seeking to maximize the good, decision makers must carry the complex task of identifying relevant moral values, assessing the problem in light of those norms, developing alternatives actions, and finally selecting the preferred policy—the one that occasions the least harm and advances the most good.

The Problem of Cultural Relativism

Some IR observers have argued that because international society is composed of different societies, each with its own religion, culture, and social customs, a universal political morality is impossible. Because each society has its own values and customs, the only moral norms in international society are the diverse, culturally specific values of each society. The existence of cultural pluralism has led many thinkers to conclude that there is, and can be, no international political morality. Sir Harold Nicolson, the noted British diplomat, for example, observes, "there does not exist such a thing as international morality."[7] And former U.S. Secretary of State Dean Acheson declared, "what passes for ethical standards for governmental politics in foreign affairs is a collection of moralisms, maxims, and slogans, which neither help nor guide" decision making.[8]

Although competing moralities can impair the development of moral consensus and call into question the role of moral norms in international politics, they do not necessarily substantiate the cynic's conviction that morality is nothing more than the subjective preferences of each society, especially those with power. Nor do they support the skeptic's belief that morality is applicable to private life but not to public affairs. To begin with, morality is concerned with what "ought" to be, not with what "is." Because the diversity of cultural norms is a description of the world rather than an assignation of moral values, the prevalence of cultural pluralism does not threaten morality itself. Moreover, the moral pluralism that does exist generally is concerned with secondary norms, not basic principles. Thus, although people might hold different beliefs about, say, gender roles, criminal justice procedures, or policies of distributive justice, there is general widespread commitment to general principles like truth, promise keeping, and justice and to basic norms like human dignity, freedom from torture, and freedom of conscience. Michael Walzer calls this shared morality "minimal" to distinguish it from the more developed "maximal" morality found in each society. Moral minimalism is a "thin" morality not because it is unimportant or makes limited demands on people, but because its claims are general and diffuse across borders.[9] Because of this shared minimal or "thin" morality, Walzer claims that human beings from different societies "can acknowledge each other's different ways, respond to each other's cries for help, learn from each other and march (sometimes) in each other's parades."[10]

The strongest evidence for the existence of international political morality is the broad, demonstrable international consensus about the inherent dignity of human beings—a dignity that is affirmed by such human rights norms as the priority of religious freedom, the fundamental equality of persons, the prohibition against torture, civilian immunity in wartime, and the condemnation of racial, ethnic, and religious discrimination. This agreement on international morality has been repeatedly expressed in the actions and declarations of states and has been codified into multilateral treaties and conventions comprising a large and influential body of international humanitarian law.

In her illuminating study on global order titled *Code of Peace*, Dorothy Jones argues that the international community is based on an ethical framework—a "code of peace" as she terms it—that states have accepted as normative and legally binding in their international relations.[11] These norms are not based on states' behavior but rather are rooted in the shared doctrines and legal and moral principles embodied in the many treaties, conventions, accords, and declarations that states have accepted as binding. According to Jones, the "code of peace" involves the following nine tenets:

1. Sovereign equality of states
2. Territorial integrity and political independence of states
3. Equal rights and self-determination of peoples
4. Nonintervention in the internal affairs of states
5. Peaceful settlement of disputes between states
6. Abstention from the threat or use of force
7. Fulfillment in good faith of international obligations
8. Cooperation with other states
9. Respect for human rights and fundamental freedoms.[12]

Because this code specifies the acceptable behavioral norms of the international society of states, it provides not only a set of behavioral regulations but also an ethical structure. The code is ethical because it establishes binding moral rules on states that, if fulfilled, have the potential to foster peace and justice in global society.

Three Ethical Traditions

If we assume that international politics, like domestic politics, is influenced partly by moral norms, then our next task is to inquire how thinkers and decision makers have tried to integrate moral norms with global issues in general and with foreign policy in particular. Historically, the integration of political morality with global affairs has been expressed in three major approaches: moral skepticism, communitarianism, and cosmopolitanism. Whereas the first approach circumscribes the role of morality, the other two give a prominent role to moral values but apply them in radically different ways.

Moral skepticism, advocated by such thinkers as Hans Morgenthau and George F. Kennan, assumes that moral values have a limited role in international affairs. For moral skeptics, morality applies primarily to the private life of individuals rather than to collectives like organizations and states, because the necessities of world politics allow little room for moral judgment, especially when the survival of the state is at stake. Skeptics like Kennan claim that moral norms like truth telling, promise keeping, and the golden rule apply to individual life but not to government. He writes:

> Moral principles have their place in the heart of the individual and in the shaping of his own conduct, whether as a citizen or as a government official. . . . But when the individual's behavior passes through the machinery of political organization and merges with that of millions of other individuals to find its expression in the actions of a government, then it undergoes a general transmutation, and the same moral concepts are no longer relevant to it. A government is an agent, not a principle; and no more than any other agent may it attempt to be the conscience of its principal. In particular, it may not subject itself to those supreme laws of renunciation and self-sacrifice that represent the culmination of individual moral growth.[13]

Unlike cynics, who deny morality altogether, skeptics claim that moral values are central to human life but have limited impact on public affairs. In an influential essay titled "The Amorality of Foreign Affairs," Arthur Schlesinger Jr. argues that foreign policy should not be guided by moral norms, except in questions of last resort.[14] Because moral language can lead to moralism, fanaticism, inflexibility, and even utopianism—qualities that are inimical to orderly international relations—he argues foreign policy should be guided by prudential conceptions of the national interest. Schlesinger writes: "Saints can be pure, but statesmen must be responsible. As trustees for others, they must defend interests and compromise principles. In politics, practice and prudential judgment must have priority over moral verdicts."[15]

The *communitarian tradition* views the state as a moral agent, as a player that can be held collectively responsible for its actions. This perspective assumes that the quest for human dignity in international society is best secured within and through member states. To be sure, states vary in their capacity and commitment to pursue the domestic wellbeing of their people.[16] Indeed, a major source of global injustice has been the deliberate oppression and killing perpetrated by tyrannical regimes. Nevertheless, while recognizing that states have often been a source of great injustice, states are also the primary agents to secure human rights domestically and order and peace internationally. Communitarians recognize, however, that focusing solely on domestic order is not sufficient to ensure human dignity, because international war and global oppression can impede human rights and global order. Consequently, if global society is to be peaceful and just, states themselves must pursue behavior that is conducive to such ends. International political morality includes those norms that help structure the international behavior of states to ensure a just peace.

From a communitarian perspective, the quest for global peace and justice depends on the moral behavior of states. Just as individuals bear rights and responsibilities to one another within domestic society, states must fulfill mutual obligations to other states if a just peace is to be secured in global society. Examples of international political morality include such norms as self-defense, peaceful settlement of disputes, the sanctity of treaty obligations, nonintervention, and prohibition against aggression. A more specific illustration of communitarian political ethics is the just war theory, which sets forth moral rules for judging war (see Box 8.1 later in this chapter). In his classic *The Law of War and Peace,* Hugo Grotius, a seventeenth-century Dutch diplomat, argues that international society is based on fundamental legal and moral precepts. Even though states are sovereign, they are obliged to fulfill global legal and moral norms. According to Grotius, these norms are based on historical precedents, natural law, the Bible, and the collective decision of states. Even in wartime, states are not free to pursue victory at all costs, but must behave in accord with widely recognized rules of war. For Grotius, justice in the international community is possible only when states themselves fulfill their legal and moral obligations.[17]

The *cosmopolitan tradition,* by contrast, views global society as a unitary moral community.[18] While recognizing the reality of a decentralized, anarchic order, it claims that the international community, not its member states, is the primary bond of association. As a result, the welfare of people, and human rights in particular, takes moral precedence over the autonomy of states. From the cosmopolitan perspective, international society and its subsidiary institutions are obligated to serve and uphold the fundamental freedoms and rights of people. When member states fail to do so, they lose their moral legitimacy. Unlike the communitarian perspective, which assumes that state boundaries are morally significant, the cosmopolitan tradition does not regard sovereignty as morally sacrosanct. Philosopher Peter Singer captures the cosmopolitan perspective in the following statement: "National sovereignty has no intrinsic moral weight. What weight national sovereignty does have comes from the role that an international principle requiring respect for national sovereignty

plays, in normal circumstances, in promoting peaceful relationships between states. It is a secondary principle, a rule of thumb that sums up
the hard-won experience of many generations in avoiding war."[19]

In the cosmopolitan tradition, state sovereignty is not morally absolute. Whereas communitarianism asserts that human rights and global
justice are best secured through member states, cosmopolitanism assumes that the tasks of global justice and the protection of human rights
are ultimately the responsibility of the international community. Because
human dignity is fundamental, states are morally legitimate only to the
extent that they protect and secure human rights, promote the common
good, and secure collective goods. Thus, when gross human rights
abuses occur, foreign intervention, whether carried out individually or
collectively, is not only permissible but, in exceptional circumstances,
morally obligatory. Moreover, when states are unable or unwilling to protect the global environment (by threatening land and marine degradation, deforestation, resource depletion, loss of biodiversity, air pollution,
waste disposal, etc.), the claims of the international community take
precedence over the actions of recalcitrant states. For the cosmopolitan,
states have moral standing in the international community only when
they fulfill their moral obligations to their own people as well as to global
society itself.

In sum, both the communitarian and cosmopolitan traditions affirm
the role of international political morality, but they do so from different
perspectives. The communitarian perspective begins by viewing the world
as composed of sovereign states and seeks to pursue peace and justice
through the right actions of states. The cosmopolitan perspective, by contrast, views the world as a unitary and coherent moral community where
global welfare and individual human rights take precedence over national
interests. These two contrasting perspectives give rise to two distinct conceptions of justice—*international justice* for the communitarian and
world justice for the cosmopolitan. For the communitarian, justice is pursued and achieved through the transnational actions of member states.
For the cosmopolitan, on the other hand, justice is pursued by global society itself, with states playing an important but not decisive role. Indeed,
the quest for world justice might require challenging state actions and
overriding state sovereignty in defending global moral interests.

Because we have conceived of international relations in this study as
a game played chiefly by states, the quest for justice in global society will
necessarily depend on the behaviors and actions of states themselves as
they secure justice domestically and as they collaborate with other states
in securing peace and justice internationally. As a result, while acknowledging the contribution of cosmopolitan thinkers about global affairs,
our analysis focuses primarily on the quest for international justice from
the communitarian perspective—one that conceives of the world as a
weak international society of strong member states.

The Pursuit of Justice through States

Using the communitarian perspective, the quest for a peaceful and just world is best advanced through the right actions of member states. In particular, a just global peace is most likely to be advanced when the major players of the IR game behave in accordance with the principles and rules of international political morality. Because state officials and political realists tend to identify with the communitarian perspective, the emphasis on state behavior is the dominant perspective in IR and among some political philosophers. One leading theorist who has provided a compelling defense of this approach is John Rawls. In his noteworthy book *The Law of Peoples,* he offers a rigorous moral theory of how justice can be advanced based on the existing international system.[20]

Rawls is known for developing one of the most rigorous and influential theories of domestic justice. In *A Theory of Justice,* Rawls argues that if individuals were developing a theory of justice without knowing their own status in society (that is, based on impartiality, or what Rawls terms "the veil of ignorance"), they would be guided by two core principles. The first he calls Maximum Equal Liberty and the second Equal Opportunity and the Difference Principle. Rawls argues that the principle of liberty, which is affirmed through civil rights and constitutional norms, is fundamental because it ensures that individuals have the maximum freedom in domestic society to fulfill their wants and desires. His second principle suggests that social and economic benefits should be the result of fair competition and distributed so that all receive equal gain, unless differences helped those at the bottom of the social ladder. In effect, income inequalities are justified only to the extent that the poorest people also benefit from transactions. Ironically, Rawls applies his theory only to domestic society, not to states.[21]

In *The Law of Peoples,* Rawls seeks to uncover the principles that are most likely to advance a just international order based on "the political world as we see it," or what he terms a perspective of "realistic utopia."[22] His theory builds on the following premises: First, that peoples, not states, are the key actors. Unlike the traditional IR game, which focuses on the rights, duties, and interests of states, Rawls focuses on the institutions and moral character of societies. He does so in order to identify those political communities that are most effective in securing human rights. Second, a just international order is possible only among well-ordered societies. Such societies comprise two types of regimes: first, "liberal peoples"—constitutional, democratic regimes that protect and promote human rights domestically and fulfill international responsibilities—and second, "decent hierarchical peoples"—nondemocratic regimes that respect human rights and are nonaggressive in global society. Third, the world has societies that are not well ordered and are therefore incapable of contributing to international peace and justice.

These societies are of three types: "outlaw states"—societies that do not respect human rights, "burdened societies"—those that are incapable of meeting basic needs and protecting human rights because they lack the institutions, cultural values, resources, and human capital necessary for maintaining a decent, well-ordered society; and "benevolent absolutisms"—societies that protect many human rights but which do not allow their people to participate in political decision making.

Because liberal societies are thought to be reasonable and rational, Rawls claims that they will tend to work with other liberal societies in establishing "fair terms of political and social cooperation."[23] Such cooperative action is important because it illuminates the core moral principles governing the international community and thereby sets forth the structure of international justice. According to Rawls, the following eight principles characterize liberal societies:

1. Peoples are free and independent, and their freedom and independence are to be respected by other peoples.
2. Peoples are to observe treaties and undertakings.
3. Peoples are equal and are parties to the agreements that bind them.
4. Peoples are to observe a duty of nonintervention.
5. Peoples have the right of self-defense but no right to instigate war for reasons other than self-defense.
6. Peoples are to honor human rights.
7. Peoples are to observe certain specified restrictions in the conduct of war.
8. Peoples have a duty to assist other peoples living under unfavorable conditions that prevent their having a just or decent political and social regime.[24]

Rawls acknowledges that these norms are incomplete and that some of the rights—such as nonintervention and independence—might have to be circumscribed when dealing with autocratic, corrupt, and unstable societies. Although these norms are appropriate for decent, well-ordered communities, they might not apply fully to societies that are incapable or unwilling to protect human rights or to live peacefully with neighboring societies. While acknowledging the incompleteness of this list, as well as the possibility of exceptions to implementing some of its provision, Rawls claims that these principles constitute the basic framework of just international relations—or what he terms "the basic charter of the Law of Peoples."

I have sketched the rudiments of Rawls's theory because it illuminates the quest for international justice among distinct nations. Admittedly, Rawls focuses on peoples, not states, but he does so only to highlight that the quest for international peace and justice is dependent on the nature of the societies themselves. In particular, international justice can be advanced only if societies are themselves just—that is, if they are well ordered and protect human rights—and secondly, if they behave peacefully and fairly with other nations. In short, international justice can be secured only when two conditions are fulfilled: First, states are themselves well ordered and protect human rights, and second, states respect the autonomy of other states and cooperate to ensure a peaceful, stable, and prosperous international community.

Principles of International Justice

If states are to advance international justice they must be guided by moral principles that structure the decisions leaders make. Although we are chiefly concerned with the international behavior of states, peace and justice cannot be advanced within global society if societies themselves fail to protect human rights and foster a peaceful and prosperous social and economic life. Consequently, international political morality involves both domestic and international dimensions.

⟐ P 8.1—People Are Entitled to Basic Rights

This principal is the most fundamental moral claim in the IR game. It is foundational because the states and the international society of states are the instruments by which the rights and freedoms of people are affirmed. In earlier chapters I have stressed that human rights are a basic responsibility of states. In the previous chapter I argued that a major state duty was to promote and protect human rights (P 7.3). I suggested that, in view of the growing salience of international human rights, when states are unable or unwilling to secure basic rights for their people, foreign states might have a political responsibility to help protect them (R 5.9).

Human rights can be justified either from a legal (positivist) or moral (normative) perspective. Because this chapter is concerned with international political morality, we are concerned only with the claim that individuals are entitled to fundamental rights and freedoms by virtue of their inherent worth as human beings. The moral justification of human rights is grounded in core assumptions, including the following: 1) human rights are rooted in a transcendent moral order that can be apprehended by reason; 2) because people have inherent worth, they need to be treated always as ends, never as means; 3) because all persons have inherent worth, people are fundamentally equal; and 4) human rights are universal, applying to all persons regardless of their race, gender, age, ethnicity, or nationality. According to democratic theory, because government's legitimacy is rooted in its willingness and capacity to secure and protect individual human rights, the legitimacy of political society is ultimately dependent on its capacity to protect such rights.

⚲ P 8.2—States Are Presumptively Morally Legitimate

As noted in Chapter 3, states are the primary players of the IR game. Because the contemporary international legal order is based on the legitimacy of states, global politics—including the affairs the United Nations and its subsidiary organizations—are governed by the actions of states. Because states are the primary players in international society, we assume that states are presumptively morally legitimate.

This principle is consistent with the communitarian tradition discussed earlier. According to this perspective, the state is a significant moral actor in global society, securing human rights domestically and fostering order and justice internationally. For the communitarian, states are responsible for providing domestic justice within their territorial boundaries and for pursuing international justice through the fair and responsible actions in the world itself. The cosmopolitan tradition, by contrast, regards global society itself as the primary moral community. States are morally legitimate only insofar as they facilitate global governance, help develop global public goods, and help secure human rights. Because cosmopolitans regard the state as a second-level community, they do not presume the state to be a major legitimate actor in global society.

⚲ P 8.3—Human Rights Must Have Priority over Sovereignty

As I have stressed previously, borders are not absolute. When states are unwilling or unable to carry out their duties domestically or to fulfill legal and moral obligations internationally, they lose their moral legitimacy. The rise of weak and failed states—manifested by corruption, lawlessness, domestic civil strife, war, and genocide—has resulted in a growing recognition that sovereignty should not be allowed to protect gross human rights violations. Long ago, scholars claimed that foreign intervention was morally permissible when egregious injustices were being perpetrated in a foreign state. But in the modern era, as gross human rights have increased, more explicit criteria have been demanded about the international responsibility when genocide and other human atrocities occur. Although there is a fixed guideline for defining when or how sovereignty can be compromised to defend human rights, the international community has shifted in support of human protection. Thus, when a conflict arises between sovereignty and human rights, the latter takes precedence over the former in exceptional circumstances.

In 2001, the International Commission on Intervention and State Sovereignty (ICISS) issued a report, entitled "The Responsibility to Protect," which suggested that the idea of sovereignty should be reconceived.[25] Rather than viewing sovereignty as the right to independence and state control, the ICISS recommended that sovereignty should be viewed as "the duty to protect." Thus, when states can no longer fulfill this responsibility, ICISS recommended that the protection of human rights should be borne by the international community itself. According to the report, when societies are suffering from genocide, war crimes, ethnic cleansing, and crimes against humanity, "the principle of nonintervention yields to the international responsibility to protect."[26] At the UN World Summit in 2005, member states endorsed the *responsibility to protect* (R2P) *principle,* and in April 2006, the Security Council unanimously adopted Resolution 1674, which reaffirmed some of the principle's key provisions.

P 8.4—Foreign Policy Must Be Judged in Terms of Its Intentions and Outcomes

Historically, two major ethical strategies have influenced foreign policy decision making: ends-based thinking (or consequentialism) and rule-based thinking (or moral absolutism). The first strategy assumes that the ethics of a decision must be judged primarily by its consequences. Sociologist Peter Berger writes, "when it comes to politics, we get no moral Brownie points for good intentions; we will be judged by the results."[27] Rule-based action, by contrast, assumes that the ethics of decision making must be judged by the inherent rightness or moral intentions of an action. Because the rule-based perspective places a premium on moral duties and obligations, it is agent-centered, emphasizing the moral responsibilities of leaders, not the outcomes of decisions. Ends-based thinking is important because it reminds foreign policy decision makers that just outcomes are what matter. But rule-based analysis is also important because it guards against the pragmatism of consequentialism.

Although both consequentialism and moral absolutism offer important perspectives in developing ethical decision making, neither approach is sufficient. Indeed, both are essential in developing morally prudent foreign policies and just global political relations. Ideally, decision makers should rely on an ethical strategy that incorporates goals, means, and results into the development and assessment of political action. Such a tridimensional framework is useful in developing ethical action because it highlights the moral demands at the level of motives, methods, and consequences. Moreover, because moral action inevitably involves trade-offs among each of these three dimensions of political action, prudence is essential in translating moral ideals into effective action. Stanley Hoffmann has observed, "moral politics is an art of execution: principles unaccompanied by practical means or by an awareness of possible trade-offs remind one of Peguy's famous comment about Kant—his hands were pure, but he had no hands."[28] Thus, in the final analysis, international political action must be guided and judged by its overall results—a perspective that Max Weber called "the ethics of responsibility."

Moral Rules of International Justice

Using the moral principles outlined in the previous section, I now examine specific rules that provide a moral map for states' foreign policy decision making.

R 8.1—States Must Fulfill Commitments and Promises

In the previous chapter I noted that a basic rule of international law is the need to fulfill treaties and other international agreements (*pacta sunt servanda*). From a moral perspective, states must fulfill the treaties, formal agreements, and tacit accords to which they have assented, because promise keeping is fundamental to building communal trust. Without promise keeping, individual and collective behavior is unpredictable; moreover, without predictability there can be no social trust; and without trust, there can be no communal life or social solidarity. Morally, the fulfillment of commitments and promises is important because an international community is possible only if member states fulfill their obligations to each other.

R 8.2—States Are Entitled to Defend Themselves from Foreign Aggression

When a state is threatened or attacked, it has a moral right to protect its territory and its people from external coercion. Self-defense potentially involves three types of military response: defensive war, preemptive war, and preventive war. Defensive war responds to aggression by using military power to halt and redress military attack. Michael Walzer has argued that because aggression is an international crime, states have a right not only to repel the unjust and illegal military action, but to punish the agents of aggression as well.[29] Of the three types of force, defensive war is the most ethical alternative, because it seeks to redress wrongdoing after an attack. But the increasing threat from terrorist organizations with potential access to weapons of mass destruction has increased the moral legitimacy of the other types of war.

Preemptive war involves the use of military force when aggression is imminent. To preempt means to attack before an aggressor strikes. According to Walzer, a preemptive attack is morally justified when three conditions are fulfilled: the existence of an intention to injure, the undertaking of military preparations that increase the level of danger, and the need to act immediately because of the increased level of risk.[30] Following the 9/11 attack, the U.S. government developed a new National Security Strategy (NSS) in 2002 that explicitly asserted the "option of preemptive action" to confront the growing lethal threats from global terrorism. According to the NSS, "the greater the threat, the greater is the risk of inaction—and the more compelling the case for taking anticipatory action."[31]

Preventive war occurs when a state initiates military action to inhibit future military attack. Such action is generally undertaken in response to a growing imbalance of military power or to the development of greater military capabilities that could pose a future security threat. Unlike preemption, which is undertaken because of imminent danger, a preventive attack is undertaken to destroy an enemy's growing military capabilities. The goal of such action is to eliminate an enemy's ability to carry out aggression before it can mobilize that capability. This type of force was illustrated by Israel in 1981 when it bombed and destroyed an Iraqi nuclear reactor shortly before it was to become operational. Israel carried out the raid because it feared that the reactor would produce nuclear fuel that could be used in making a nuclear weapon.

The most developed moral theory of international relations is the *just war tradition,* which is highlighted in Box 8.1. According to this perspective, war is considered morally legitimate if its purposes and methods are just. Of the three types of war, defensive force is the strategy most easily reconciled with the principles of just war, and preventive war is the one that is most morally problematic because it undertakes military action largely on speculative grounds. This is so because, even with the best intelligence, determining an adversary's present and future intentions and capabilities is never certain.

≙ R 8.3—States Should Assist Foreign Nations in Need

As noted earlier, the primary responsibility of a state is to ensure the security and well-being of its people. Because states are members of a global society, they also bear subsidiary responsibilities toward other societies. Although humanitarian needs arise from a variety of factors, two sources that contribute greatly to human suffering in the modern world are humanitarian crises arising from either natural disasters or failed states that are unable to meet basic human needs. I first examine the nature of modern humanitarian crises and the primary ways in which

⨚   ⨚   ⨚

Box 8.1 Principles of the Just War Tradition

The just war tradition, which originated in the ancient world from Christian and secular sources, is composed of three parts: the justice of going to war (*jus ad bellum*), justice in war (*jus in bello*), and the justice after war has ceased (*jus post bellum*). The first two elements of the theory are the most developed, and the third represents a new and emerging dimension. The first specifies moral principles for judging when resort to war might be morally justified; the second specifies moral principles for judging how force should be used in war; and the third specifies the conditions required following war. The goal of the just war tradition is not to justify violence but rather to restrain it in the service of the common good.

Justice of War (*jus ad bellum*)

1. *Just cause:* The only legitimate justification for war is to deter aggression, to defend against unjust attack, to halt ethnic cleansing and genocide, or to right a grievous wrong.
2. *Competent authority:* Force is morally permissible only when it is authorized and carried out by legitimate authority for public purposes. Normally, this means that the only actors that are morally authorized to use force are states. Because nongovernmental groups or private individuals are not legitimate authority, their use of violence is immoral.
3. *Right intention:* A war is considered just only if its goal is the restoration of a just peace. The only legitimate reason for resorting to war is to defeat aggression and to redress the evil perpetrated by aggressors.
4. *Limited objectives:* A just war is one that pursues limited goals. Not only must the purposes of war be limited and conditional, but the goals and means must be proportionate to the ends being pursued. This means that the good to be realized by prosecuting a war must be commensurate with the probable evil resulting from war.

developed countries can assist societies in need. I then explore the role of governments in providing development assistance to foster economic growth.

Humanitarian crises are of two sorts—those caused by nature and those caused by misguided human action. Natural disasters—which are often brought about by earthquakes, typhoons, torrential rains, floods, tsunamis, or draught—can result in untold human suffering. This is es-

5. *Last resort:* Before a state resorts to war, it must exhaust all peaceful alternatives.
6. *Reasonable hope of success:* The use of force must have a reasonable chance of achieving the goals of a just peace. Inflicting harm as an act of vengeance is morally unacceptable.

Justice in War (*jus in bello*)

7. *Discrimination:* In war civilians must not be directly attacked. Because the aim of war is to defeat the enemy state, only military and political targets can be justified. Every effort must be made to discriminate between combatants and noncombatants. Indiscriminate mass destruction is immoral.
8. *Proportionality:* The destruction inflicted by military forces in war must be proportional to the goals being pursued. The aim should be to use the lowest level of violence to achieve the limited aims of a just peace.

Justice after War (*jus post bellum*)[1]

9. *Restoration of a just order:* Once war is over, the victor must restore order, help to rebuild the economy, reestablish political autonomy to allow self-government, and hold leaders accountable for past atrocities and egregious war crimes.

Notes

1 For a discussion of this emerging element of just war theory, see Louis Iasiello, "The Moral Responsibilities of Victors in War," *Naval War College Review* (Summer/Autumn 2004), 33–52, and Robert E. Williams Jr. and Dan Caldwell, "*Jus Post Bellum*: Just War Theory and the Principles of Just Peace," *International Studies Perspectives* 7 (2006), 309–320.

pecially the case when they occur in poor countries where infrastructure is inadequate and financial resources are limited. Developed countries can greatly assist in meeting the humanitarian needs arising from such crises by providing immediate medical and material aid, food and water, and logistical support. This type of aid was illustrated in the aftermath of the deadly December 2005 Asian tsunami that killed more than one hundred fifty thousand people and left hundreds of thousands of persons homeless and destitute. Foreign states, led by the United States, responded immediately with large quantities of food and water, financial aid, medical care, and most importantly, logistical support to help distribute resources. Without this foreign assistance hundreds of thousands of additional people would have perished.

The second type of humanitarian crisis is generally the result of conflicts instigated by governmental policies and antigovernmental actions. When domestic political conflicts become intractable, they can sometimes lead to war, genocide, and ethnic cleansing, involving widespread human rights atrocities. When genocide and ethnic cleansing occur, as was the case in Rwanda in 1994, and Bosnia in 1993–1995, the only way to halt the killing and the gross abuse of human rights abuses might be through foreign military intervention. Thus, whereas ecological disasters can be addressed through short-term relief, halting atrocities will involve not only more time but also a far more intrusive engagement in foreign societies. As noted earlier in the chapter, the rise of humanitarian disasters caused by political conflict has encouraged leaders and scholars to redefine the notion of sovereignty. Under the emerging conception, sovereignty is no longer simply the right of political independence but also the responsibility to care for people. Secretary General Kofi Annan captures this emerging conception when he says, "States are now widely understood to be instruments at the service of their peoples, and not vice versa."[32] Because protecting human rights is increasingly viewed as a shared responsibility of the international community, there is a growing acknowledgment that military force might be necessary to halt ethnic cleansing and genocide and that humanitarian intervention by one or more countries might be morally permissible.

Peacemaking and peacekeeping are difficult tasks in deeply divided societies. Although multilateral forces are generally successful in reestablishing order and maintaining social peace, if such military missions are to succeed in transferring political and military authority to indigenous forces, they must address and help resolve the fundamental political sources of unrest. Compared to peacekeeping, the task of restoring trust, fostering social and economic cooperation, and building political institutions is enormously complex and long term. The introduction of NATO peacekeepers in Bosnia in 1995 resulted in an immediate cessation of fighting. But the fact that NATO military forces continue to patrol the cities and countryside of Bosnia in 2007 suggests that the work of restoring community is far more elusive than meeting human needs in the aftermath of a natural disaster.

Sometimes, military victory might be the only way to settle a conflict and thereby create the order necessary to carry out political and economic reconstruction. But the cost of fighting a war can be horrific—as was demonstrated by the U.S. Civil War and by the 1994 genocide in

Rwanda. When the international community, and more particularly the leading states in the UN Security Council, failed to intervene in Rwanda to halt the mass killing of Tutsis, they effectively allowed the deadliest and most efficient genocide in history to run its course. The mass killings came to an end only when the Tutsi Rwanda Patriotic Front (RPF) defeated the Hutu military forces and militia in July 1994. By that time more than eight hundred thousand Tutsis and moderate Hutus had perished. But with their victory, the Tutsis gained control of the government, allowing them to restore public authority and rebuild the civic, political, and legal institutions. It is of course too early to judge the results of the current governmental initiatives. What is important to recognize, however, is that the military victory has allowed state building to occur—something that would have been difficult to achieve had UN peacekeeping forces been deployed when the killing began.

From a moral perspective, prosperous, well-governed nations should assist societies facing misfortune, human rights abuses, and poverty. They should do so not to ensure greater economic equality among states but to care for peoples suffering from disasters, war, and absolute poverty. Whereas cosmopolitanism calls for international affirmative action programs to redistribute resources from well-endowed societies to those that lack them, communitarianism seeks to care for human needs based on common moral precepts, such as charity, compassion, and the golden rule. In practice this means that a communitarian approach to foreign policy will seek to balance national interests and global interests and seek to promote well-governed, prosperous states so that they can effectively meet their domestic and international obligations as members of global society. Its aim is to foster international justice—justice among peaceful, productive states. Unlike cosmopolitanism, communitarians are more reluctant to support unilateral or multilateral foreign intervention in the belief that such action might undermine the quest for authentic self-rule. Rawls writes that the goal of assisting "burdened states" is to help them "become full members of the Society of Peoples and to be able to determine the path of their own future for themselves."[33]

Although states should ideally provide both humanitarian relief and peacemaking assistance, communitarians are likely to give moral priority to the former. There are several reasons for this. First, external relief aid can alleviate human suffering immediately, whereas halting war and building peace is a more difficult, long-term process. Second, relief aid can achieve its goals without compromising the sovereignty norm, whereas war termination and peace-building often can only be achieved if the sovereignty of the failing state is qualified, either voluntarily with the consent of the antagonists or involuntarily through military intervention. Finally, meeting immediate human needs through the transfer of resources, medical aid, and logistical support is normally a feasible task.

In contrast, building peace and fostering political reconciliation are enormously complex tasks. Although ending a war might be feasible when sufficient military forces are introduced, establishing the preconditions for a stable peace will inevitably entail cultural, political, and social reforms, which can only be achieved with time as greater trust is developed among antagonists. Thus, whereas the outcomes of relief aid are quite certain, the results of military intervention and nation building are likely to remain uncertain, if not elusive.

⚓ R 8.4—Developed States Should Help Foster the Economic Development of Poor Countries

Because cosmopolitans view the international system as a unitary moral order, significant economic inequalities among nations are morally unacceptable. Therefore, cosmopolitans place great emphasis on distributive justice, calling on the leading rich countries to transfer resources to poor nations. The aim of such transfers is to reduce inequalities among people. For communitarians, by contrast, inequalities are not necessarily evidence of injustice. Because their concern is international justice among states, their goal is to empower poor societies to become more prosperous. The responsibility to aid poor countries is not based on considerations of distributive justice but on the desire to help countries become more economically developed so that they can become more independent and self-reliant.

In *The Law of Peoples*, Rawls, who identifies with a communitarian perspective, argues that developed states ("well-ordered peoples") have a duty to assist poor countries ("burdened societies"). This duty arises not because there is an ethical responsibility to achieve a just distribution of resources but rather because it is morally desirable to "bring burdened societies . . . into the Society of well-ordered Peoples."[34] Thus, the moral reason why rich countries should help poor countries is that such aid, given out of compassion and charity, can help countries become more prosperous and more democratic and thereby become more fully integrated into the international community.

The difficulty in fostering development is well illustrated in the modern history of Haiti, one of the poorest, most corrupt, and politically fragile countries in the world. Despite receiving significant financial aid over the past three decades, Haiti has been unable to improve its peoples' standard of living. The economy has remained stagnant, crime and corruption are pervasive, legal and political institutions are weak, and government remains ineffective. Not surprisingly, Haiti ranks among the least developed countries in the world, ranking 154th among 177 countries on the human development index (HDI).[35]

⚑ R 8.5—States Have a Moral Responsibility to Protect the Global Commons

Because states share many global resources (the atmosphere, ocean waters, animal life, outer space, etc.), they have a common interest and moral duty to protect the earth's resources. The global commons can be defined as those global public goods that benefit all member states. Global "bads" are those conditions that arise from the misuse or overuse of resources that impair the quality of life for future generations. Global "bads" involve conditions such as the overuse of resources, land degradation, air pollution, improper waste disposal, marine degradation, and the loss of biodiversity. In Chapter 5, I observed that promoting and protecting global public goods demanded some enforcement mechanism because of the "free-rider" problem. Because public goods are available to all members of society, this problem arises from the propensity of community members to let others establish and maintain the good. As a result, if all members wait for others to pay for the collective good, it is likely that the collective good will never be realized.

The difficulty of providing and protecting a global public good is currently illustrated with the challenge of responding to the threat of *global warming*. According to the UN Intergovernmental Panel on Climate Change (IPCC), the earth has been getting warmer. The principal reason for this is that water vapor and human-made gases trap solar radiation by impeding the release of the sun's rays back into space. Although most of the so-called greenhouse effect is caused by nonhuman factors, air pollution from the burning of fossil fuels plays a key role in this process. When such fuels are burned, they result in a number of harmful by-products, including carbon dioxide, methane, nitrous oxide, and sulfur dioxide. Because most of the world's energy comes from the burning of fossil fuels,[36] combating global warming will necessarily involve a reduction in coal and petroleum consumption.

If we assume that the earth is getting warmer and that man-made air pollution is a major cause of this problem, how should states respond? Although traditional economic growth has relied on energy from fossil fuels, could modern growth be achieved with alternative sources of energy? And could alternative energy sources meet the world's energy demand without adversely affecting job creation? Because the rich, developed countries of the world are responsible for most of the world's pollution, should they bear the principal responsibility for cutting back on greenhouse emissions? More specifically, because the United States contributes more pollution per capita than any other nation, does it bear greater responsibility to reduce emissions?

The challenge, therefore, is how to balance the interests of individual nations with those of other states. To date the major international efforts to address the challenge of global warming have been through treaties. At the 1992 Earth Summit, some 166 countries signed the Climate Treaty that established a framework for reducing greenhouse gas emissions. Because the treaty did not establish specific targets, states made few changes. As a result, in 1997 states met in Kyoto, Japan, to develop a more authoritative global warming regime. The resulting Kyoto Protocol—essentially an addendum to the 1992 Climate Treaty—required developed nations to reduce their emissions by about 5 percent below their 1990 level no later than 2012.[37]

There can be little doubt that sustainable development is a widely shared goal. Morally, states need to be concerned not only with their own well-being but also with the well-being of other nations. Similarly, states must be concerned not only with their current living standards but also with those of future generations. Although global political morality on the environment might be a necessary foundation for collective action, the collective experience in addressing global warming suggests that moral values alone are unlikely to overcome the predisposition of people to give precedence to their current national concerns.

In sum, international political morality provides important norms that structure the decision making of states. But if difficult challenges like protecting the global commons are to be realized, more than moral suasion will be required. At a minimum, moral principles and rules will have to be supplemented with political and legal initiatives that ensure accountability among member states.

Conclusion

In a recent study on international law, Jack Goldsmith and Eric Posner write that "morality is so indeterminate and so contested, especially among states and peoples, that it can provide little guidance for international relations."[38] This chapter has challenged this perspective. Despite significant cultural pluralism among the world's countries, the international community is based on a substantial body of international political morality. Although this morality is "thin" in that it focuses chiefly on basic human rights and important duties and responsibilities of states, it nevertheless plays an important role in structuring the behavior of states. Just as moral values serve as the foundation of domestic societies, so, too, the shared moral values of the international community provide a basis for the political, economic, and legal relations of states. In short, the moral values of the international community might not provide a roadmap on foreign policy, but they do provide moral precepts that should structure states' problem solving and influence their decision making.

Because moral values can contribute to a more peaceful and just world, states would be well advised to incorporate the moral dimension into their decision making, paying particular attention to the following principles covered in this chapter:

P 8.1—People Are Entitled to Basic Rights
P 8.2—States Are Presumptively Morally Legitimate
P 8.3—Human Rights Must Have Priority over Sovereignty
P 8.4—Foreign Policy Must Be Judged in Terms of Its Intentions and Outcomes

States should also fulfill the following five rules of international political morality:

R 8.1—States Must Fulfill Commitments and Promises
R 8.2—States Are Entitled to Defend Themselves from Foreign Aggression
R 8.3—States Should Assist Foreign Nations in Need
R 8.4—Developed States Should Help Foster the Economic Development of Poor Countries
R 8.5—States Have a Moral Responsibility to Protect the Global Commons

RECOMMENDED READINGS

Amstutz, Mark. *International Ethics: Concepts, Theories, and Cases in Global Politics,* 2nd ed. (Lanham, MD: Rowman and Littlefield, 2005).

Caney, Simon. *Justice beyond Borders: A Global Political Theory* (New York: Oxford University Press, 2005).

Jones, Dorothy. *Code of Peace: Ethics and Security in the World of Warlord States* (Chicago: University of Chicago Press, 1992).

Rawls, John. *The Law of Peoples* (Cambridge, MA: Harvard University Press, 1999).

Robertson, Geoffrey. *Crimes against Humanity: The Struggle for Global Justice,* 3d ed. (New York: New Press, 2006).

Walzer, Michael. *Just and Unjust Wars: A Moral Argument with Historical Illustrations,* 4th ed. (New York: Basic Books, 2006).

PART THREE

Prospects for a New IR Game

NINE

The Future IR Game

WHAT WILL THE IR GAME LOOK LIKE IN 2050? Will the state-centric system continue to prevail, or will state authority diminish and be replaced by global governance? If global governance becomes more pervasive, what role will international organizations like the UN and the EU have in the international system? If globalization persists, will the future order be peaceful and harmonious, or will the society of states be characterized by increasing chaos and instability?

Because it is impossible to predict future global politics, I first explore some contemporary political and economic dynamics that are influencing the evolving architecture of the international community and then sketch some possible futures based on alternative assumptions. In the first part, I focus on two powerful forces—globalization resulting from increasing international integration, and fragmentation resulting from the growing demand for political identity rooted in culture, religion, or ethnicity. I next assess a second major contemporary tension, the conflict between state sovereignty and globalism, between the desire for national political and economic autonomy and the quest for a more peaceful, harmonious, and prosperous world through a network of expanding global institutions. In the final section, I present three different models of the future political world. These models are based on realism and idealism/institutionalism, the dominant IR paradigms sketched in Chapter 5, and the postmodern perspective associated with the emergence of a post-Westphalian global order.

Globalization versus Fragmentation

Thomas Friedman uses the metaphors of "the Lexus" and "the olive tree" to contrast the tension between modernity resulting from global technological, informational, and economic integration and the demands for stronger ethnic and cultural bonds rooted in one's locality.[1] Although global integration has resulted in increasing economic comfort for many, globalization has also led to increasing demands for deeper, more meaningful contact with one's local community. Modernization and international economic integration might result in better health care, more comfortable living conditions, and increasing opportunities to satisfy human desires, but economic development itself does not ensure human dignity. People also long for a meaningful life rooted in communal relationships and shared values that define what and where home is. "Olive trees" are important because they provide the values, roots, and social ties to family, community, and nation. Friedman explains the importance of being anchored to a specific people, culture, or community as follows:

> Olive trees are what give us the warmth of family, the joy of individuality, the intimacy of personal rituals, the depth of private relationships, as well as the confidence and security to reach out and encounter others. We fight so intensely at times over our olive trees because, at their best, they provide the feelings of self-esteem and belonging that are as essential for human survival as food in the belly. Indeed, one reason that the nation-state will never disappear, even if it does weaken, is because it is the ultimate olive tree—the ultimate expression of whom we belong to—linguistically, geographically and historically.[2]

Because globalization poses a major threat to people's local identity, Friedman thinks that societies must learn to balance the forces of modernization with the demands of cultural and social identity. There is no simple formula to achieve this balance. Individuals and nations must each determine how best to modernize while protecting their sense of belonging and communal affinities. Friedman writes: "A country without healthy olive trees will never feel rooted or secure enough to open up fully to the world and reach out into it. But a country that is only olive trees, that is only roots, and has no Lexus, will never go, or grow, very far. Keeping the two in balance is a constant struggle."[3]

Benjamin Barber provides a more pessimistic assessment of the contemporary forces of integration and disintegration. Barber—who characterizes the forces of globalization and international integration as "McWorld" and the forces of disintegration as "Jihad"—argues that the tension between global unity and disunity will likely persist.[4] But whereas Friedman views globalization and communalism as beneficiary processes that can improve the quality of life, Barber sees McWorld and Jihad as destructive because they undermine the state and threaten civil liberty. Rather than fostering greater democratic participation, these two forces weaken democratic institutions and undermine responsible citizenship. Barber writes:

> Jihad forges communities of blood rooted in exclusion and hatred, communities that slight democracy in favor of tyrannical paternalism or consensual tribalism. McWorld forges global markets rooted in consumption and profit, leaving to an untrustworthy, if not altogether fictitious, invisible hand issues of public interest and common good that

once might have been nurtured by democratic citizenries and their watchful governments. Such governments, intimidated by market ideology, are actually pulling back at the very moment they ought to be aggressively intervening.[5]

Thus, whereas Friedman views globalization as a progressive force that can improve the quality of life for all peoples, Barber sees McWorld as a rapacious, materialistic process that fosters crude consumerism and undermines social solidarity. And whereas Friedman views local customs and traditions as essentially benign and necessary in forging stable and humane societies, Barber views the forces of identity politics, localism, and tribalism as destructive. Far from strengthening democratic governance, the quest for self-determination in the modern world is harmful because it leads to the fragmentation of existing states through "ethnic membership enhanced via national dismemberment."[6]

Although both globalism and tribalism are evident in the modern world, scholars differ in their opinions of the relative influence and effect of each. Optimists about modernization tend to regard globalization as inevitable and triumphant, while skeptics view the growing international economic integration as not only problematic but also as the source of increasing cultural and social divisions within and among nations. Indeed, some scholars view modernization as responsible for increasing the scope and intensity of the politics of identity, which has become a major source of political fragmentation and social disintegration in the post–Cold War world.

Integration

There can be little doubt that economic globalization has been a potent force in shaping the post–Cold War world. As noted earlier, globalization has been manifest in two extraordinary revolutions—one in communications and the other in trade and travel. The first, a result of modern information technology, has resulted in global information networks that have transformed international business, global capital markets, the media, advocacy networks, and other related social and economic activities. At the Seattle World Trade Organization (WTO) summit in December 1999, fifteen hundred NGOs relied on the Internet to mobilize and structure international opposition to global trade. Similarly, following the 2004 South Asia tsunami that devastated coastal regions in Thailand, Indonesia, and Sri Lanka, governments and humanitarian NGOs relied on modern technology to coordinate the mobilization of aid and the allocation of humanitarian assistance. And when war between Israel and Lebanon broke out in mid-2006 (after Hezbollah terrorists killed several soldiers and captured two), modern communications technology

made possible televised broadcasts of "real-time" Hezbollah missile attacks on Israeli cities and villages and Israeli bombing of Lebanon's highways and airports and raids on southern Beirut.

The second major transformation brought about by globalization has
been in economic life. This has been especially evident with the dramatic rise in international production and global trade. The former has
been facilitated by the increasing reliance on multinational components
and labor in the production of goods and services. This means that industrial goods like cars, refrigerators, and televisions are made with components from several countries and are assembled in still one or more
other countries. Services similarly can involve labor from two or more
countries. A telephone company located in the United States might out-
source its billing or long-distance service to a firm in a foreign country,
so that an order for a product or service by a Chicago customer is taken
by a person eight thousand miles away—say, in Pakistan or India. International trade has also greatly increased through revolutions in transport. Although the use of air cargo has dramatically reduced the time
involved in shipping perishable goods (e.g., flowers, fresh fish), the most
significant revolution has been in global shipping. As a result of the use
of sealed containers, producers can now ship products from the interior
of a country to distant regions in foreign countries without opening a
large, sealed container. Prior to the development of containers, shipping
was inefficient and costly because goods had to be individually loaded
and unloaded onto ships, trains, and trucks. Now, containers provide a
universal standard for the shipping of goods, thereby consolidating
global transport and greatly reducing costs.[7]

In his most recent book, *The World Is Flat,* Thomas Friedman argues
that the global dispersion of information, skills, technology, and capital
has greatly decreased the economic advantages that advanced countries
once had over emerging economies.[8] Whereas the development and production of goods during the industrial era were typically carried out
within a single country, in the globalized world the design and production of goods and services usually involve numerous countries. The research and design of a product might originate in one or more countries,
the manufacture of product components might similarly involve multiple
countries, with assembly being undertaken in still another. In such a
world, what matters is not where a good or service is made but rather the
relative quality and cost of a good or service. As a result, producers are
continually seeking the most efficient way of designing, producing, and
marketing goods and services. And because a growing number of emerging economies have significant labor pools of well-educated, highly
trained workers, it is not surprising that many firms have begun to out-
source labor services of computer programmers, trained scientists, engi-
neers, and other professionals at substantially lower costs than in their
own countries.

Fragmentation

Despite the significant integration facilitated by economic globalization and the revolution in information technology, the world has not become a more peaceful and harmonious community. Indeed, the post–Cold War era has witnessed increasing factionalism and tribalism within and among cultures as people seek deeper meaning and a stronger sense of belonging through their ethnic, religious, and cultural traditions. Because modern capitalism increases the economic aspirations of people and makes available new goods and services (e.g., the cell phone, television, motorized transport), it can threaten traditional culture. And because modern science and technology challenge local customs maintained by isolation, the spread of modernity challenges the values, patterns of behavior, and sources of identity in traditional societies. Not surprisingly, the spread of modernity through globalization has spawned increasing opposition to secularism, consumerism, and commercialism. To a significant degree, Islamic fundamentalism has increased its global influence as a result of its opposition to Western secular, commercial, and political values.

In the early 1990s, Samuel Huntington argued that future international conflict would not be ideological, as it had been during the Cold War, but would be based on cultural and religious sources—or what he termed a "clash of civilizations." Huntington wrote: "It is my hypothesis that the fundamental source of conflict in this new world will not be primarily ideological or primarily economic. The great divisions among humankind and the dominating source of conflict will be cultural. Nation-states will remain the most powerful actors in world affairs, but the principal conflicts of global politics will occur between nations and groups of different civilizations."[9] According to Huntington, because the world was divided into eight major civilizations, future global conflict would be primarily centered between and within these different civilizations. Moreover, because cultural conflicts over blood and belonging were more intractable and less amenable to compromise than political conflicts, international conflict resolution in the future would be far more challenging than it had been during the Cold War.

Although Huntington's notion of civilization was unnecessarily static,[10] his overall insight that future conflict would become more cultural has proved valid. Indeed, virtually all the major international conflicts of the 1990s and the new millennium have been religious, ethnic, or cultural in nature. Examples of ethnoreligious conflicts include the Bosnian War of the early 1990s, the Kosovo War of 1999, and the civil conflict between Al Qaeda and other Muslim fanatics and Western democratic societies. The ongoing Iraqi war in 2004–2006 involving Sunni insurgents and Shia militia similarly demonstrates the difficulty of consolidating political authority when cultural and religious groups refuse to collaborate in establishing and maintaining a multiethnic, pluralistic political regime.

It is important to stress that the processes of global modernization are fomenting integration and fragmentation simultaneously. Jihad and McWorld are not two separate, unrelated developments but different sides of the same coin. IR scholar James Rosenau has developed the concept "fragmegration" to capture globalization's dualistic dynamic of integration and fragmentation.[11] What makes global governance in the modern world challenging, according to Rosenau, is that contemporary global change is fostering both greater localization and decentralization as well as greater centralization and interconnectedness. This dualistic process has not only resulted in growing challenges in confronting global issues but it has simultaneously created challenges at the domestic level as well. Rosenau writes: "What is remote today is also in our backyards; what was distant is now also proximate, and the prevalence of these distant proximities underlies the messiness that sets our time apart from pervious generations."[12]

Sovereignty versus Globalism

A second dimension that will likely define the future IR game is the evolution of state sovereignty. As I noted in Chapter 2, important transformations are under way in the Westphalian order. The emerging postmodern system, which is evolving from the classical order, is characterized by a decline in sovereignty, a growth in fragile states, a loss of governmental authority, and a decline in military power. How well the future world will be able to maintain peace, protect human rights, foster sustainable development, and protect the global commons will depend on the quality and capacity of states as well as on the quality and capacity of global institutions. Two factors are likely to pose major challenges to the future international community: 1) the capacity of states in meeting domestic human needs as well as in fulfilling their international responsibilities, and 2) the capacity of global institutions to fill the vacuum created by the decline in state sovereignty and the rise of fragile states.

The Strength of States

Stable, peaceful international relations presuppose strong, coherent sovereign states. When states are fragile and do not have the authority to fulfill domestic and international responsibilities, the maintenance of international order and the promotion of global economic prosperity are likely to become a daunting challenge. Thus, when brutal civil wars and genocide threaten human values or when terrorist groups threaten regional security, who is responsible for ensuring global order and for rescuing people from unjustified suffering? Historically, states have become players in the IR game when they have succeeded in making and sustaining the claim of self-determination. But military success in a civil war does not ensure successful governance. As a result, some groups might succeed in claiming sovereignty, but they might be ill-equipped to carry out the domestic and international responsibilities of statehood. But the UN legal order does not differentiate between strong states and weak states or between those that pursue humane policies and those that do not. Indeed, so long as a state does not threaten other states, it has a presumptive legal right to rule within its territory. Of course, this failure to differentiate between strong and weak states is a major shortcoming of the state-centric UN system.

As noted earlier, the post–Cold War has witnessed an increase in the number of fragile and failed states. The major problems of the contemporary international system are no longer aggression and interstate wars, but rather the proliferation of *fragile* and *failed* states. Fragile states are a threat to world order not only because they are incapable of providing domestic order and protecting human rights, but also because they serve as a breeding ground for regional political chaos and international aggression. According to K. J. Holsti, the major problem in contemporary society is not international aggression but rather "the collapse of states, humanitarian emergencies, state terror against segments of local populations, civil wars of various types, and international terrorist organizations."[13]

State failure is expressed by increasing ethnic violence, tribal wars, criminality, lawlessness, corruption, ecological degradation, and humanitarian crises. Some post–Cold War examples of state failure include:

⚉ The Bosnian and Kosovo wars in the aftermath of the collapse of the former Yugoslavia. Order is being maintained in these two territories only because NATO maintains substantial military forces in both areas.

⚉ In Rwanda in 1994, the ruling Hutus, fearing a return to power of the Tutsis, carried out the deadliest genocide in history—resulting in the death of more than eight hundred thousand persons in one hundred days. The killing came to a halt only when the Tutsi liberation force (the Rwanda Patriotic Front, or RPF) defeated the Hutu armed forces and militia.

⚉ Despite significant infusions of foreign aid and the forceful restoration of its elected president, Jean-Bertrand Aristide, in 1994, Haiti remains a failed state. The country has high levels of crime, corruption, lawlessness, poverty, and unemployment, and there is little prospect for constituting constitutional government in the foreseeable future.

🀂 The longtime dictator of the Democratic Republic of Congo (DRC), Mobutu Sese Seko (originally Joseph Mobutu), was forced from office by Laurent Kabila in 1997. The sudden change in government precipitated a vicious internal war among political groups, armed gangs, regional warlords, and foreign soldiers. It is estimated that more than three million people died during the five-year civil war, most from starvation and disease. Domestic order has been maintained in recent years through a fourteen-thousand-member UN peacekeeping force.

🀂 During the 1990s political and tribal factions carried out vicious fighting in Côte d'Ivoire, Liberia, and Sierra Leone. These wars, which were fueled partly with mineral wealth and conscripted tens of thousands of child soldiers, destroyed whatever meager infrastructure these countries had before the fighting began. Even though the wars are over, the countries remain fragile. In 2006, the UN still maintained major peacekeeping missions in the Ivory Coast (11,000) and Liberia (18,000).

The major source of modern humanitarian crises arising from civil strife, genocide, and war is the absence of responsible state government. When major crises emerge in fragile states, the international community can respond in one of three ways. First, powerful member states can impose a settlement, as NATO countries did when they forced Serb military and police forces from Kosovo in 1999. Second, the Security Council can adopt a resolution that authorizes a multinational peacemaking initiative (under Chapter VIII), as was done in 1999 to address severe violence in East Timor. Once the UN peacekeepers restored political order, they created sufficient stability to allow for elections and to permit East Timor to become a politically independent state. Third, the international community can do nothing, thereby allowing the conflict to be resolved solely by indigenous political and security forces. This was the case in Rwanda in 1994, when the genocide ended only after Tutsi military forces had defeated the Hutu armed forces and militia.

Although international organizations can help maintain order and resolve international disputes, it is less clear how effective external actors are in facilitating conflict resolution among different ethnic, religious, cultural, and political groups. To a significant degree, the ability to resolve domestic religious and ethnic conflicts like the Bosnian war or the Israeli–Palestinian conflict, will depend on how people conceive of their identity. If, as one scholar claims, "identity is becoming less tied to territory,"[14] then perhaps local territorial disputes could become less prominent in the future. Although nationalism and territorial identity might be receding among progressive communities in Western Europe, this is not the case for a large sector of the world's people, who continue to support a close affinity between land and identity. Indeed, most of the post–Cold

War conflicts in areas such as Bosnia, Kosovo, Lebanon, the Holy Land, Iraq, and Rwanda emerged in response to groups demanding political recognition rooted in territorial claims. Even in progressive Norway, when its citizens were given an opportunity to join the EU, they refused to give up their political autonomy and identity for economic benefits arising from closer economic integration.

The Efficacy of Global Governance

A second factor that will affect the future world order is whether global institutions can supply effective conflict resolution, foster sustainable development, and provide sound management of global resources. Additionally, the capacity of global institutions is likely to be challenged by the need to fill the vacuum of authority created by failed states and the decline of state sovereignty. To date, the record of the United Nations, the leading international organization, in fostering peace, protecting human rights, and fostering sustainable development has not been encouraging. Because the United Nations and its sister institutions remain wedded to the state-centric Westphalian order, the ability of the UN to advance global interests depends on the capacity and willingness of member states, especially the major powers, to cooperate in advancing shared concerns. And even where common interests are strongly shared—such as protecting human rights, deterring genocide, reducing absolute poverty, and protecting the global environment—collective action is often difficult. Indeed, the role of the UN is often nonexistent (such as halting atrocities in Darfur, Sudan, in 2004–2006), ineffective (such as restoring a just peace in Bosnia, Kosovo, and East Timor), or too late (such as halting the 1994 Rwanda genocide with an expanded UN peacekeeping mission).

With the exception of the twenty-seven-member European Union, general purpose regional organizations continue to play a modest role in promoting international conflict resolution and prosperity and managing shared social and economic concerns. In great part this is because of the limited independent authority of such organizations. The Organization of American States, like the UN, can act only where a substantial consensus exists among its member states. In contrast to the relative weakness of general-purpose international organizations, specialized international organizations tend to play a much more important role in addressing shared global concerns. Organizations like the International Monetary Fund, the World Bank, the World Trade Organization, and the World Health Organization are effective not only because their tasks and responsibilities are specific but also because their decision-making procedures are well institutionalized. Thus, in view of the limited authority of existing state-based international organizations, the challenge in building a more stable and just world is how to strengthen global governance. Such a process will necessarily involve strengthening international organizations, but it will also necessitate strengthening NGOs and global networks.

Several factors are likely to impair the institutionalization of global governance. One impediment is the lack of democratic legitimacy of international organizations. Because global institutions are not constituted through democratic elections and they do not follow democratic decision making, they suffer from a democratic deficit.[15] Ordinarily, IGOs represent states and more particularly the policies and wants of governments. The Security Council, WTO, and IMF, for example, all make decisions based upon the (weighted) will of states. NGOs similarly suffer from limited democratic legitimacy, because they arise not from democratic contestation but from pursuit of specific global concerns and ideals by a group of like-minded citizens. Like domestic political interest groups, transnational NGOs typically arise because concerned citizens seek to reform domestic or international conditions by mobilizing public support for a particular cause. Although NGOs are a part of democratic politics, successful public policy need not be based on democratic legitimacy. Indeed, some groups owe their global influence to exceptional organization and ample funding rather than to widespread public support.

Another barrier to global governance lies in the fragile ties between decision makers and citizens. Robust governance presupposes a high level of *social capital*—that is, a high level of voluntary cooperation because people have significant trust and share many values and goals.[16] Typically, as the size of a community expands and as ethnic, cultural, linguistic, and religious differences increase, the bonds of trust and cooperation become more tenuous. Not only do the bonds among people become more fragile as communal authority is extended from the locality to the state and onto the world, but the bonds between people and political institutions are similarly compromised. Thus, whereas a vigorous civic engagement is possible at the local and state levels, it becomes much more difficult at the regional and global levels.[17]

A third obstacle to global governance is the limitation of centralized decision making. Central authority is of course indispensable for effective conflict resolution and the maintenance of global order. But if government is to be a positive, creative force in the international community, it must empower citizens, foster "creative destruction" in economic life, encourage group initiatives in public life, and facilitate institutional change to respond to new global challenges. And it can only do so if global institutions are effective, yet not intrusive. In his analysis of state-building, Francis Fukuyama distinguishes between the strength and the scope of governance. He argues that although strong government is essential in facilitating a humane and productive society, a government that limits its scope of responsibilities is also important.[18] Historically, however, the strengthening of the state has often been associated with centralized decision making. Social scientists, however, now recognize that excessive centralization can impair effective decision making. Nobel laureate Amartya Sen has argued that freedom is not only a necessary goal, but also an indispensable means for constituting an effective state and for creative problem solving. He illustrates the priority of freedom by arguing that free societies are better able to prevent and respond to famines than authoritarian or totalitarian regimes. This is so not because free societies can produce more food but because they disseminate information more efficiently and effectively.[19] Thus, the challenge in strengthening global institutions is how to make such institutions more effective without necessarily expanding the scope of responsibility—how, in other words, to foster strong institutions that facilitate decentralized decision making.

Finally, developing strong and effective global governance is likely to remain a daunting challenge because of the diversity of worldviews and values among the world's countries. Given the absence of shared political ideals and values, developing and sustaining cooperation and trust (social capital) are likely to be difficult. Moreover, given the world's cultural diversity, strengthening transnational nongovernmental associations, international networks, and other institutions of global civil society will also present formidable challenges. Indeed, if Huntington's claim about the basis of future international conflict is correct, global cultural diversity is likely to be a breeding ground for conflict rather than a basis for strengthening trust and building global civil society.

IR scholars tend to agree that the international community is undergoing important changes, but there is little agreement about the likely future role of global institutions. Although the state might be shrinking and governmental authority might be declining in many countries, the loss of sovereignty has not necessarily led to stronger international institutions. Global governance has proliferated as it has taken on a wide range of transnational issues and concerns. But if global governance has assumed an increasing range of activities, this has not led to stronger, more authoritative institutions.

Given the fragility of international institutions, the strengthening of global governance will most likely continue to depend on the collective decisions of states themselves, especially from the dominant states in the international community. Because the United States remains the most powerful country in the world, it will necessarily play a critical role in either supporting or impeding global governance. IR scholar Michael Mandelbaum has gone so far as to claim that the United States has been serving as the "world's government" by providing global goods to the international community.[20]

Because U.S. dominance is unlikely to be sustained indefinitely, global governance will likely emerge from a collective effort between the United States and other major powers. In the short term, these states will include the other members of the Security Council (Britain, China, France, and Russia) along with Germany and Japan. In the longer term, a number of emerging economies are likely to play a much more important role in global politics. China and India—the two most populous states in the world and whose economies have been growing at 7 to 10 percent annually since the end of the Cold War—will likely become the most influential countries in the international system after the United States. One study has estimated that by 2040 five emerging countries (Brazil, China, India, Mexico, and Russia) will rank among the top ten economic powers.[21] If this projection is fulfilled, Brazil and Mexico would also become key players in global governance.

Three Models of the Future

Earlier I stressed that globalization had resulted in social, political, and economic developments that were challenging the architecture of the classical Westphalian IR game. As a result, a postmodern system had begun to emerge—one that involved less force in settling global disputes, a rising role for nonstate players, a more influential role of global governance, and an expanding concern for transnational concerns. Although I noted that the world currently is state-centric, the global forces of integration and fragmentation are transforming the structure of the current world order.

Because it is impossible to anticipate how the dual forces of integration and fragmentation are likely to evolve in the world, I explore in what follows three alternative futures. The first two models are derived from the realist and idealist paradigm presented in Chapter 5. The realist model represents a continuation of the classical world order but with important changes in both the state as well as global institutions. The idealist/institutionalist model, by contrast, represents a system where state authority has diminished and the role of global governance has greatly expanded. The third model, which I term postmodern, assumes that the future world order will involve a radical departure from the classical IR game.

The Realist Model

From a realist perspective, the international community of 2050 will remain fundamentally Westphalian in structure. Although important changes will continue to affect the number and capacity of states, the IR game will remain rooted in a state-centric order. States will continue to be the major determinant of IR, with major players defining the rules

and institutions in global society. International law and international organizations, which will remain based on sovereign states, will continue
to have modest influence in the international system. To be sure, global
institutions will continue to proliferate, but their authority will remain
limited. Global governance will continue to be determined by the individual and collective action of states. The United Nations will continue
to play an important function in global peacekeeping, but its influence
will diminish because of its failure to adapt to the changing conditions of
the postmodern world. In particular, membership on the Security Council will continue to reflect the past world order rather than power patterns in 2050. As a result, the most important global institutions will be
regional and specialized agencies rather than international organizations
like the UN and the WTO.

Several other features will characterize the future realist game. To
begin with, the international community will increase by five to ten
countries, and if the demand for political self-determination persists in
fragile, multinational countries, the number of new countries could increase by twice that number. Thus, if ethnic, religious, and cultural fragmentation continue, the international community could increase to
more than two hundred twenty member states. Although these new
states will contribute to the complexity of global politics, the major challenge posed by the new states will arise not from their number but from
their frailty. With few exceptions, the new states will have limited resources to meet people's basic needs and have little authority to sustain
the rule of law. The international community will therefore be faced with
many deeply divided states, where violence, corruption, poverty, and humanitarian crises are prevalent. Despite the expansion of global governance, the international community will not have the political will to
meet all the needs of failed states.

Second, globalization will continue to expand among most countries
but especially among high-income countries. For most peoples, the benefits from increased global interaction will clearly outweigh the costs of
increased materialism, economic inequality, and the threat posed to local
traditions by global norms. China's dramatic economic expansion will
continue to inspire other emerging nations to emulate their outward-
looking economic policies. At the same time, radical religious movements will continue to oppose modern economic growth, preferring
instead to advocate theocratic political regimes.

Third, the number of democratic nations will rise from about eighty
countries to more than one hundred twenty. The expansion of democratic
government will result, in turn, in a significant improvement in human
rights. Despite the noteworthy expansion in freedom, however, many
partly democratic societies will remain fragile. As a result, the consolidation of democratic governance will demand the further strengthening of

legal and political institutions. In particular, major democratic nations will have to assist transitional democratic regimes if democracy is to be institutionalized in such fragile societies.

Fourth, the future world will be stable and largely peaceful. Interstate wars, especially among major players, will have become improbable.[22] To be sure, armed conflicts will persist in the international community, but such conflict will be found almost exclusively within weak, fragile states. As a result, the world will be divided between a "zone of peace" and a "zone of turmoil."[23] The first zone, the core, will be composed of some one hundred twenty developed, mostly prosperous, and mostly democratic states; the second zone, the periphery, will consist of some sixty to eighty fragile, undemocratic, and relatively poor countries. The primary threat to international peace will come from wars in collapsed states and from the acquisition of weapons of mass destruction (WMD) by autocratic regimes. In spite of the dangers arising from the zone of turmoil, the core, led by the United States, will nevertheless be able to contain the dangers arising from the fragile periphery.

Finally, contrary to predictions of environmental decline, the global commons will not experience an overall deterioration. Some problems, including waste disposal and global warming, will become more serious. But other environmental conditions—such as the protection of the atmosphere, renewal of forests, water conservation, and the protection of endangered species—will remain either stable or improve. Although treaties will contribute to an awareness of global environmental concerns, the primary cause of environmental protection will be the self-interested actions of states, not the promulgation and enforcement of international conventions.

The Idealist-Institutionalist Model

From the idealist/institutionalist perspective, the IR game would continue to function much as it is in the current world, except that cooperation would be greatly increased by the further institutionalization of global networks. Whereas the realist future continues to be directed by the collective actions of states, global governance in the idealist world would be supplemented by an expanded and enhanced international civil society. Because civil society normally refers to those nongovernmental, mediating institutions that connect government to citizens, *international civil society* can be conceived as a collection of transnational nongovernmental associations, professional organizations, advocacy networks, social movements, and religious organizations that foster coordination and cooperation among state and nonstate actors.

The idealist-institutional future world will be characterized by a number of distinctive features. First, although states will continue to be major players in the international community, transnational NGOs, global coalitions, policy advocacy networks, and other nonstate actors will also play a more important role in global affairs. The influence of these other actors will be due primarily to their ability to fill the vacuum of authority resulting from the decline in state sovereignty. Even though the number of weak and fragile states will rise, human suffering and international instability from failed states will be partially contained by the expanding assistance provided by official and private humanitarian organizations.

Second, global governance will expand as governmental and nongovernmental institutions emerge to address global problems and to facilitate transnational cooperation. In addition, the growth of global NGOs will facilitate more efficient transnational flows of goods, services, and knowledge. The United Nations will continue to play an important role in peacekeeping operations, but it will have limited success in rescuing failed states, preventing internal wars, or resolving humanitarian crises. Indeed, the most significant achievements in global governance will be realized through regional and specialized organizations rather than through global institutions. The shift toward regional and specialized organizations will be a result of the growing challenges in achieving global accords. This problem was especially evident in the increasing challenge in pursuing global trade liberalization. As a result, leading states began pursuing this goal through bilateral and regional accords rather than through the WTO. It has been estimated that by 2006 the number of bilateral and regional trade accords had reached two hundred fifty, or roughly double the number of a decade before.[24]

Third, globalization will continue to foster increased economic, financial, technological, and informational integration across national boundaries. Although such integration will exacerbate economic inequalities within and among states, it will also continue to improve the standard of living for rich and poor societies alike. Additionally, globalization will not only increase the efficient flow of goods, services, and information, but it will also spawn a global consciousness that contributes to increases in the salience of global concerns. This increased global solidarity will strengthen international law and international organizations, but it will also help restrain nationalism and contain ethnic fragmentation.

Fourth, the number of democracies will continue to proliferate, rising to more than one hundred twenty. The continued expansion of democratic governance will, in turn, contribute to further improvements in global human rights. Additionally, the expanding role of global civil society—made possible by the growth in transnational NGOs, multinational businesses, coalitions of professional groups, and other nongovernmental associations—will strengthen human rights protection by creating intermediary institutions that can serve as a buffer between people and state, citizen and government. Finally, the International Criminal Court and regional criminal tribunals will gain increasing legitimacy and become more important in prosecuting military and political leaders responsible for genocide or other atrocities.

Fifth, the world will be increasingly peaceful. The major source of this stability and prosperity will be the 100–120 developed and emerging democratic countries that comprise the zone of peace. These states, supported by increasingly effective global institutions, will play a decisive role in propagating values and interests that are conducive to a humane world. The values and interests will be increasingly codified in international conventions and will be supported by international governmental and nongovernmental actors. The fragile states in the periphery will of course affect regional and global order. But given their increasing influence, global institutions will be able to contain the harmful effects arising from local ethnic and religious fragmentation and from the spread of WMD not only to fragile states but to terrorist groups and radical political movements.

Sixth, despite significant industrial expansion in the emerging economies, the international community will achieve significant gains in protecting the global environment. These achievements will be largely attributable to the growing body of international environmental law. The success in conserving resources, reducing harmful pollutants, and protecting endangered species will also be a result of the growing public support for environmental conservation among elites in economically developed nations. The one area where there will be limited progress is in confronting the harmful effects from the burning of fossil fuels. Because of the rising world demand for energy, and because fossil fuels will continue as the primary source of the world's energy, little progress will have been achieved in the reduction of harmful greenhouse gas emissions. To be sure, significant technological innovations will make possible a more efficient generation of energy, but the demand for oil and coal will outstrip conservation initiatives from technological innovations or from alternative energy sources.

The Postmodern Model

The postmodern model represents a significant departure from the classical IR game. In this model states are no longer the major players in global society. Similarly, state-based IGOs, such as the WTO, IMF or the UN, no longer dominate global politics or play the decisive role in resolving international disputes or in fostering global economic prosperity. Instead, IR is increasingly directed by a variety of nonstate actors including regional organizations, ethnic associations, religious groups, worker's movements, NGOs, transnational networks, advocacy groups, and other similar collectives. To a significant degree, the ascendance of these new players is a result of the vacuum of political authority within states—a vacuum created by the growing fragmentation within existing societies. Although the force of fragmentation is, as noted earlier in this chapter, a direct by-product of the process of globalization, to a significant degree the loss of domestic solidarity is a result of the shift in communal identity from ideological beliefs to cultural, ethnic, and religious commitments.

The postmodern future will be characterized by several distinctive features. First, this model assumes that the world in 2050 will have many more states, as ethnic and religious minorities demand self-rule from existing countries. These thirty to fifty new states, however, will be small and politically fragile. They will have limited capacity to meet domestic responsibilities toward their own people and even less capacity to fulfill international obligations toward global society. Thus, a salient trait of the postmodern game will be the growing weakness of member states to play the IR game.

A second related feature of this postmodern world is the dramatic loss of political authority by states and the growing influence of nonstate actors. Unlike states, which historically had sovereign authority within their territorial boundaries, the new actors—NGOs, religious movements, regional organizations, ethnic groups, global networks, and related institutions—will fill the vacuum of authority created by the growing number of fragile states. Whereas traditional states enjoyed a monopoly of force, the new actors will not be based on coercive force. Rather, their authority will be rooted in voluntary cooperation based on shared interests. As with international law, which is based on voluntary compliance, the capacity of global governance will derive from persuasion, modeling, and the "soft power" of inducement.

Thirdly, the postmodern world of 2050 will be characterized by an increasingly interdependent world. The effect of globalization will be felt most deeply in the prosperous societies of the world, but it will also extend to all poor countries as well, although its impact will be limited primarily to urban areas. Nonetheless, the forces of integration will likely be undermined by even stronger forces of fragmentation. As a result, rather than spreading peace and prosperity, modernization will foster an antiglobalization that gives precedence to local traditions, traditional social patterns, and religious values over secular, universal norms.

A fourth trait of the postmodern world will be the growth of democracies, rising to more than one hundred forty of the world's two hundred forty countries. But the growth in democracy will involve the expansion of fragile illiberal political systems that demand only periodic election of government leaders and provide limited protection of human rights. Given the increasing frailty and fragmentation of most societies, institutionalization of constitutional norms will be difficult. Thus although democratic values and institutions continue to proliferate in global society, the number of liberal democratic regimes will remain at about one hundred countries, as it was at the beginning of the new millennium.

Fifth, the postmodern world will be characterized by increasing instability. Because states and IGOs will be less influential in world politics and because nonstate actors will not fill the vacuum of authority left by states, global governance will remain fragile and largely ineffective. Although the institutions of postmodern governance will be pervasive, they will have limited capacity to resolve domestic and transnational conflicts. The instability of the postmodern world will not arise from major interstate conflicts; rather, it will derive from small-scale collective violence by private groups, terrorist organizations, and religious fundamentalist groups.

Finally, the postmodern world will be characterized by further environmental degradation. Because the institutions of the postmodern order will have limited authority, they will remain largely ineffective in fostering sustainable development, protecting endangered species, reducing air and water pollution, and managing the use of scare resources. Thus, even though the postmodern world will involve far greater interdependence and global integration than the classical model, the new system will be less effective in protecting the global commons. Because most global environmental accords will have been achieved through interstate negotiations and have culminated in binding treaties, the decline of state authority will undermine the efficacy of the major environmental treaties. The proliferation of nonstate actors will not lead to an increased capacity to regulate the global commons.

Box 9.1 compares some of the salient features of the realist, idealist, and postmodern models examined above. Each model represents a different way of conceiving the IR game. Since the nature and role of players and international institutions differ in each of the models, the strategies for playing the IR game are also different. Similarly, although many of the fundamental principles and rules remain largely the same for each of the models, their interpretation and application likely will vary considerably. Not surprisingly, states following the traditional Westphalian game of realism will tend to be more reticent in ceding political autonomy, and idealists will be more willing to forge legal and political institutions that foster and protect global goods. Because the postmodern model represents the most radical departure from the traditional realist game, it is difficult to conceive how the pursuit of order, justice, human rights, and economic prosperity can be advanced within global society. In the realist and idealist models, that task is in the hands of states. In the postmodern model, however, the loss of state authority means that states will play a limited role in fostering and protecting global goods. And to the extent that citizens, groups, and organizations spearhead the cause of a just global order, the responsibility for global order and well-being will fall increasingly on NGOs and the mediating institutions of civil society.

The distinctive logic of each of the alternative IR models can be illustrated from the contemporary world of athletic competition. For example,

♟   ♟   ♟

Box 9.1 Comparison of Three Models
of the Future IR Game

Realist Future	*Idealist Future*	*Postmodern Future*
Role of States		
5–10 new states	10–20 new states	30–50 more fragile states
Many states are strong; some are weak	Many states are strong; some are weak	Most states are weak, with little authority
Nonstate Actors		
NGOs are more numerous and influential	NGOs are more numerous and more influential	NGOs, religious movements, regional organizations, ethnic global networks are increasingly influential
Global Governance		
Moderately weak	Moderately strong	Strong in developed regions, but weak among developing societies
States are main actors	States and nonstate actors cooperate in decision making	Nonstate actors are the major actors; IGOs are important
Globalization		
Greater global integration	Greater global integration	Greater global integration
Some fragmentation	Some fragmentation	Significant fragmentation
Greater international cooperation	Significant international cooperation	Significant cooperation in zone of peace and prosperity
Status of Democracy		
Significant democratization	Significant democratization	Increased illiberal democracy
More than 125 countries are democratic	More than 125 countries are democratic	Societal fragmentation impedes democratic governance
Most societies are coherent	Most societies are coherent	Most societies are deeply divided

(continues)

BOX 9.1 continued

Global Order

International system is stable	International system is stable	World is less stable
Developed states comprise a zone of peace and prosperity	Developed states comprise a growing zone of peace and prosperity	Zone of turmoil in developing areas is increasing because of small-scale wars within and among nations

Global Commons

Some protection of global environment	Significant protection of global environment	Uneven protection of global environment, with developed regions providing most protection

≜   ≜   ≜

the realist model, which represents the autonomy of cultural and political communities, is represented by team sports based on national identity. Such competition is best exemplified in quadrennial World Cup soccer— a contest between the world's best national teams. At the other extreme is the postmodern model, where universal, cosmopolitan values supersede national or ethnic identity. In such games or sporting contests, all that matters is excellence—expressed in a person's or team's standing. The Tour de France, the most important cycling competition in the world, represents this type of sporting event.[25] As with most cycling races, riders participate in teams and work collectively to maximize victory for their top cyclist. Finally, the idealist model represents an intermediate position between the nationalism of realism and the cosmopolitanism of the postmodern model. In the idealist model, individual and team excellence are combined with the celebration of soft nationalism. The quadrennial Olympic Games, which involve national competition in a variety of sporting events, represent this idealist vision of athletic competition.[26] The games fit the idealist model because individual and team achievement are celebrated under the banner of athletes' national identity.

Conclusion

Public officials and scholars cannot predict the future. They do not know the future of globalization, or the fate of the United Nations, or the number of new states in the postmodern world of 2050. Moreover, nobody knows how religious and ethnic forces will affect the demands of self-determination among minorities. Perhaps the forces of integration will triumph over the forces of fragmentation. Or perhaps civil conflict will give way to stronger global integration supported by a robust transnational civil society. However the future unfolds, it is clear that the creation and sustenance of a more stable, prosperous, and just international community will require the persistent and informed work of civic and political leaders. In particular, it will necessitate creative political leadership to ensure that a balance is maintained between the quest for international peace and prosperity and communal well-being, global integration, and local identity.

RECOMMENDED READINGS

Cusimano Love, Maryann, ed. *Beyond Sovereignty: Issues for a Global Agenda,* 3d ed. (Belmont, CA: Thompson/Wadsworth, 2007).

Fukuyama, Francis. *State-Building: Governance and World Order in the 21st Century* (Ithaca, NY: Cornell University Press, 2004).

Huntington, Samuel P. *The Clash of Civilizations and the Making of World Order* (New York: Simon and Schuster, 1996).

Mueller, John. *The Remnants of War* (Ithaca, NY: Cornell University Press, 2004).

Nye, Joseph S., Jr. *Power in the Global Information Age: From Realism to Globalization* (London: Routledge, 2004).

Notes

NOTES TO CHAPTER ONE

1 For a discussion of the role of ideas in foreign policy, see Judith Goldstein and Robert O. Keohane, eds., *Ideas and Foreign Policy: Beliefs, Institutions and Political Change* (Ithaca, NY: Cornell University Press, 1993).

2 Daniel Philpott, *Revolutions in Sovereignty: How Ideas Shaped Modern International Relations* (Princeton, NJ: Princeton University Press, 2001), 49.

3 Philpott, *Revolutions in Sovereignty,* 47.

4 Since collective goods are freely available to all once they are established, the creation of such goods is often difficult to establish because of the so-called free-rider problem. This problem arises because actors will delay contributing to the creation of a public good, knowing that after a good is established by others it can be enjoyed by all.

5 Michael Mandelbaum, *The Ideas That Conquered the World: Peace, Democracy, and Free Markets in the Twenty-first Century* (New York: Public Affairs, 2002).

6 For an overview of constructivism, see Friedrich V. Kratochwil, *Rules, Norms, and Decisions: On the Conditions of Practical and Legal Reasoning in International Relations and Domestic Affairs* (Cambridge: Cambridge University Press, 1989); Richard K. Ashley, "The Poverty of Neorealism," *International Organization* 38 (Spring 1984): 225–286; and Alexander Wendt, "Anarchy Is What States Make of It: The Social Construction of Power Politics," *International Organization* 46 (Spring 1992): 391–425.

7 Raymond Cohen, *International Politics: The Rules of the Game* (New York: Longman, 1981), 6.

8 This distinction is based on John Rawls's analysis. See John Rawls, "Two Concepts of Rules," *Philosophical Review* 64 (1955): 3–32.

9 Hedley Bull, *The Anarchical Society: A Study of Order in World Politics* (New York: Columbia University Press, 1977), 13.

10 K. J. Holsti, *Taming the Sovereigns: Institutional Change in International Politics* (Cambridge: Cambridge University Press, 2004), 318.

11 Condoleezza Rice, "Promoting the National Interest," *Foreign Affairs* 79 (January/February 2000): 60.

12 As I note in Chapter 3, governments vary greatly in their nature and capacity. Some, like the democratic states of Europe, are benevolent and humane, whereas others, like the dictatorships of Belarus and Zimbabwe, are corrupt and abusive. Still others are strong, like Chile and the Netherlands, and others, like

Congo and Haiti, are fragile and incapable of maintaining domestic order and providing essential public goods, such as education and basic health care.

13 To be sure, moral obligations can supersede a government's authority when it carries out actions that contravene a basic moral principle, such as the sanctity of life or the gross abuse of human rights.

14 Carl J. Friedrich, *Man and His Government* (New York: McGraw-Hill, 1963), 423.

NOTES TO CHAPTER TWO

1 Excerpts from Jean Bodin, "Six Books on the State," in William Ebenstein, *Great Political Thinkers: Plato to the Present,* 4th ed. (Hinsdale, IL: Dryden, 1969), 354–355.

2 For an excellent overview of the origin and impact of the idea of sovereignty on interstate relations, see Daniel Philpott, *Revolutions in Sovereignty: How Ideas Shaped Modern International Relations* (Princeton, NJ: Princeton University Press, 2001).

3 Quoted in Kelly Kate Pease and David P. Forsythe, "Human Rights, Humanitarian Intervention, and World Politics," *Human Rights Quarterly* 15 (1993): 292.

4 The UN Security Council can authorize a multinational peacemaking force to compel a state or to restore public order where authority is absent. But such a development is a rare occurrence in international affairs.

5 Roger Masters, "World Politics as a Primitive Political System," *World Politics* 16 (July 1964): 594–619.

6 Kenneth Waltz, *Theory of International Politics* (Reading, PA: Wesley, 1979), 118.

7 Ian Brownlie, *International Law and the Use of Force by States* (Oxford: Oxford University Press, 1963), 16.

8 Organization for Security and Co-operation, "Declaration on Principles Guiding Relations between Participating States," Final Act of the 1975 Summit, available at http://osce.org/docs/english/1990-1999/summits.

9 Ronald Inglehart, *Modernization and Postmodernization: Cultural, Economic, and Political Change in 43 Societies* (Princeton, NJ: Princeton University Press, 1997), 74–80.

10 For a discussion of the dangers of the new world order, see Robert Cooper, *The Breaking of Nations: Order and Chaos in the Twenty-First Century* (New York: Atlantic Monthly Press, 2003).

11 Quote from Tony Zinni, *The Battle for Peace,* in Michiko Kakutani, "The Fire This Time: A General's Report on Global Instability," *New York Times,* April 18, 2006, B6.

12 Thomas L. Friedman, *The Lexus and the Olive Tree: Understanding Globalization* (New York: Anchor Books, 2000), 9.

13 For a discussion of this flattening process, see Thomas L. Friedman, *The World Is Flat: A Brief History of the Twenty-First Century* (New York: Farrar, Strauss, and Giroux, 2005).

14 Friedman, *The Lexus and the Olive Tree.*

15 Friedman calls this process of reconciling the demands of modernization

with one's locality "glocalization." For a discussion of this, see Friedman, *The World Is Flat,* 324–329.

16 Kofi Annan, "Nobel Prize for Peace Address," December 10, 1991.

17 Carl von Clausewitz, *On War,* trans. Michael Howard and Peter Paret (Princeton, NJ: Princeton University Press, 1976), 87.

18 John L. Gaddis, *The Long Peace: Inquiries into the History of the Cold War* (New York: Oxford University Press, 1987), 245.

19 John Mueller, *Retreat from Doomsday: The Obsolescence of Major War* (New York: Basic Books, 1989). See also John Mueller, *The Remnants of War* (Ithaca, NY: Cornell University Press, 2004).

20 Mary Kaldor, *New and Old Wars: Organized Violence in a Global Era* (Palo Alto, CA: Stanford University Press, 1999). See also Kalevi J. Holsti, *The State, War, and the State of War* (Cambridge: Cambridge University Press, 1996).

21 For a discussion of these two concepts of power, see Joseph S. Nye Jr., *Bound to Lead: The Changing Nature of American Power* (New York: Basic Books, 1990), 31.

22 Commission on Global Governance, *Our Global Neighborhood: Report of the Commission on Global Governance* (Oxford: Oxford University Press, 1995), 2.

23 Anne-Marie Slaughter, *A New World Order* (Princeton, NJ: Princeton University Press, 2004), 5, 12.

24 Robert O. Keohane, *Power and Governance in a Partially Globalized World* (London: Routledge, 2002), 245.

25 Margaret P. Karns and Karen A. Mingst, *International Organizations: The Politics and Processes of Global Governance* (Boulder, CO: Lynne Rienner Publishers, 2004), 335.

NOTES TO CHAPTER THREE

1 Robert Cooper, *The Breaking of Nations: Order and Chaos in the Twenty-First Century* (New York: Atlantic Monthly Press, 2003), part I.

2 In his satire of the Soviet Union, Orwell observed: "All animals are equal, but some are more equal than others." See George Orwell, *Animal Farm* (New York: New American Library, 1956).

3 For a discussion of the impact of these ideas on the world, see Michael Mandelbaum, *The Ideas That Conquered the World: Peace, Democracy, and Free Markets in the Twenty-first Century* (New York: Public Affairs, 2002).

4 See Inis L. Claude Jr., *Swords into Plowshares: The Problems and Progress of International Organization,* 4th ed. (New York: Random House, 1971), 53.

5 Antonio Cassese argues that the right of self-determination applies only to racial groups and is "blind to the demands of ethnic groups and national, religious, cultural, or linguistic minorities." See Antonio Cassese, *International Law* (Oxford: Oxford University Press, 2001), 108.

6 John le Carré, "The Shame of the West," *New York Times,* December 14, 1994, 17.

7 Michael Mandelbaum, "The Reluctance to Intervene," *Foreign Policy* 95 (Summer 1994): 8.

8 K. J. Holsti, *Taming the Sovereigns: Institutional Change in International Politics* (Cambridge: Cambridge University Press, 2004), 114–115.

9 Holsti, *Taming the Sovereigns,* 99–100.

10 For a discussion of this topic, see Francis Fukuyama, *State-Building: Governance and World Order in the 21st Century* (Ithaca, NY: Cornell University Press, 2004).

11 Kalevi J. Holsti, *The State, War, and the State of War* (Cambridge: Cambridge University Press, 1996), 84–90.

NOTES TO CHAPTER FOUR

1 Arthur Schlesinger Jr., "The Necessary Amorality of Foreign Affairs," *Harper's Magazine* (August 1971): 76.

2 Robert Cooper, *The Breaking of Nations: Order and Chaos in the Twenty-First Century* (New York: Atlantic Monthly Press, 2003), 88.

3 Cooper, *The Breaking of Nations,* 124.

4 Graham T. Allison, *Essence of Decision: Explaining the Cuban Missile Crisis* (Boston: Little, Brown, 1971).

5 Schlesinger, "The Necessary Amorality," 74.

6 George F. Kennan, "Morality and Foreign Policy," *Foreign Affairs* 64 (Winter 1985/86): 206, 217.

7 Alexander L. George and Robert O. Keohane, "The Concepts of National Interests: Uses and Limitations," in Alexander L. George, ed., *Presidential Decisionmaking in Foreign Policy: The Effective Uses of Information and Advice* (Boulder, CO: Westview, 1980), 218.

8 Kenneth Waltz, *Theory of International Politics* (Reading, MA: Addison-Wesley, 1979), 92.

9 Paul Kennedy, *The Rise and Fall of the Great Powers* (New York: Random House, 1987).

10 Quoted in Schlesinger, "The Necessary Amorality," 74.

11 Garrett Hardin, "Living in a Lifeboat," *Bioscience* 24 (October 1974): 561–568; and "The Tragedy of the Commons," *Science* 162 (December 13, 1968): 1243–1248.

12 Waltz, *Theory of International Politics,* 194–195.

13 Karl W. Deutsch, *The Analysis of International Relations,* 3d ed. (Englewood Cliffs, NJ: Prentice-Hall, 1988), 20.

14 Kennedy, *The Rise and Fall of the Great Powers.*

15 Ivan Arreguín-Toft, *How the Weak Win Wars: A Theory of Asymmetric Conflict* (Cambridge: Cambridge University Press, 2005), 2–5. Some of the reasons why the powerful do not win asymmetric wars include: such conflicts do not involve vital interests, the citizenry get tired of supporting a distant political conflict, democratic regimes are unwilling to use the necessary violence to prevail, and weak states are not as weak as they seem because of their access to modern armaments.

16 G. John Ikenberry has argued that following major wars, victorious states contribute to global order by transforming their favorable postwar position through the creation of institutions that preserve their dominance while also creating norms that are favorable to weaker states. See G. John Ikenberry, *After Victory: Institutions, Strategic Restraint, and the Rebuilding of Order after Major Wars* (Princeton, NJ: Princeton University Press, 2001).

17 For an excellent overview of the role of democracy and free markets in postwar U.S. foreign policy, see Michael Mandelbaum, *The Ideas That Conquered the World: Peace, Democracy, and Free Markets in the Twenty-first Century* (New York: Public Affairs, 2002).

18 Joseph S. Nye Jr., *Bound to Lead: The Changing Nature of American Power* (New York: Basic Books, 1990), 30–32.

19 J. Anthony Lukas, "Class Reunion: Kennedy's Men Relive the Cuban Missile Crisis," *New York Times Magazine* (August 30, 1987): 58.

20 Quote in John G. Stoessinger, *Henry Kissinger: The Anguish of Power* (New York: W. W. Norton, 1976), 14.

21 To the extent that sanctions fail as an instrument of behavioral reformation, the cause of their ineffectiveness is no doubt due to the dubious validity of this assumption.

22 The level of economic hardship will depend on a number of factors, including: 1) whether the sanctions are collective; 2) whether the sanctioning state(s) is much stronger economically than the target state; 3) whether the target state is economically dependent and vulnerable to foreign economic pressures; and 4) whether the cost of imposing sanctions is significantly higher on the target state than on the punishing states.

23 Charles Kindleberger, *Power and Money: The Economics of International Politics and the Politics of International Economics* (New York: Basic Books, 1970), 97.

24 Margaret P. Doxey, *Economic Sanctions and International Enforcement* (New York: Oxford University Press, 1971), 139.

25 Gary C. Hufbauer, Jeffrey J. Schott, and Kimberly Ann Elliott, *Economic Sanctions Reconsidered: History and Current Policy*, 2nd ed. (Washington, DC: Institute for International Economics, 1990), 49–73.

26 John Keegan, *A History of Warfare* (New York: Vintage Books, 1993), 56.

27 Carl von Clausewitz, *On War*, trans. Michael Howard and Peter Paret (Princeton, NJ: Princeton University Press, 1976), 87.

NOTES TO CHAPTER FIVE

1 For a discussion of four varieties of realism, see Michael W. Doyle, *Ways of War and Peace: Realism, Liberalism, and Socialism* (New York: Norton, 1997), 418.

2 According to John Mearsheimer, the frailty of international cooperation is a result of two factors in particular: the concern with relative advantages and the problem of cheating. The first problem derives from the fact that states are not simply concerned with absolute gains but also with their relative standing in the international community. The second problem, which derives from deceit and lying, occurs when states commit to an agreement but secretly fail to fulfill the obligations that they have agreed to. See John J. Mearsheimer, "The False Promise of International Institutions," in *The Perils of Anarchy: Contemporary Realism and International Security*, ed. Michael E. Brown, Sean M. Lynn-Jones, and Steven E. Miller (Cambridge, MA: MIT Press, 1995), 339–340.

3 Kenneth Waltz, *Theory of International Politics* (Reading, PA: Addison-Wesley, 1979), 118.

4 Waltz, *Theory of International Politics*, 92.

5 Robert Cooper, *The Breaking of Nations: Order and Chaos in the Twenty-First Century* (New York: Atlantic Monthly Press, 2003), 151.

6 Hans J. Morgenthau, *Politics among Nations: The Struggle for Power and Peace*, 5th ed. (New York: Random House, 1978), 5.

7 E. H. Carr, *The Twenty Years' Crisis, 1919–1939: An Introduction to the Study of International Relations* (New York: Harper Torchbooks, 1964), 41–60.

8 For a discussion of Kant's theory, see Doyle, *Ways of War and Peace*, 252–258.

9 For a comparison of internationalism and globalism, see Marc F. Plattner, "Two Kinds of Internationalism," *National Interest* (Spring 2005): 84–92.

10 Robert Kagan, *Of Paradise and Power: America and Europe in the New World Order* (New York: Alfred A. Knopf, 2003), 3.

11 Although the ostensible purpose for maintaining armies has historically been to secure and protect territorial boundaries, armed forces have been used often to maintain political control domestically. Dictatorships, for example, are maintained by the use of a state's coercive power over its citizens.

12 Stockholm International Peace Research Institute, *SIPRI Yearbook 2005*, available at http://www.sipri.org. (Accessed May 30, 2007.)

13 Raymond Aron, *Peace and War: A Theory of International Relations* (New York: Praeger, 1968), 594–619.

14 Cooper, *The Breaking of Nations*, 40.

15 Mearsheimer, "The False Promise," 337.

16 International Commission on Intervention and State Sovereignty, *Responsibility to Protect: Report of the International Commission on Intervention and State Sovereignty*, available at http://www.iciss.ca/menu-en.asp. (Accessed May 30, 2007.)

17 This is Adam Smith's argument in the *The Wealth of Nations*, in which he argues that a free enterprise system would contribute to the general interest of society. According to Smith, the actions of individuals would lead to the general prosperity of society as if an "invisible hand" had guided production.

NOTES TO CHAPTER SIX

1 During the second half of the twentieth century, average longevity in many developing nations increased, on average, by ten to fifteen years, and per capita national income also rose significantly.

2 The challenge of improving living conditions to rapidly growing nations is captured by this fact: A country whose population is growing by 3 percent will double the size of its population in twenty-four years.

3 The HDI is a coefficient based on three criteria: longevity (measured by life expectancy), knowledge (based on adult literacy and mean years of schooling), and standard of living (measured by per capita income, using purchasing power parity).

4 For example, Zimbabwe's score declined from 0.626 in 1985 to 0.496 in 2001, and Ivory Coast's coefficient fell from 0.420 in 1990 to 0.396 in 2001.

5 To be sure, some resources are pivotal to modern economic life, such as petroleum, copper, and cobalt. Although oil-exporting countries have greatly benefited from the rising demand for petroleum, most wealth is not based on extraction but on increased productive efficiency of goods and services.

6 P. T. Bauer, "Western Guilt and Third World Poverty," *Commentary* (January 1976): 22.

7 "The New Titans: A Survey of the World Economy," *Economist* (September 16, 2006): 12.

8 Martin Wolf, *Why Globalization Works* (New Haven, CT: Yale University Press, 2004), 44.

9 Robert Heilbroner, "The Triumph of Capitalism," *New Yorker* (January 23, 1989): 98.

10 For a discussion of the strategic trade theory, see Robert Gilpin, *Global Political Economy: Understanding the International Economic Order* (Princeton, NJ: Princeton University Press, 2001), 122–127.

11 Wolf, *Why Globalization Works*, 45.

12 Robert Gilpin, *The Challenge of Global Capitalism: The World Economy in the 21st Century* (Princeton, NJ: Princeton University Press, 2000), 3.

13 Milton Friedman, *Capitalism and Freedom* (Chicago: University of Chicago Press, 1962), 25–27.

14 Wolf, *Why Globalization Works*, 316.

15 See Michael E. Porter, *The Competitive Advantage of Nations* (New York: Free Press, 1990).

16 Although the United States derived some financial advantages from serving as the reserve-currency country, it also imposed significant costs. The most important of these was the inability to correct an overvaluation of the dollar, which contributed to balance of payments deficits. In 1971, President Richard Nixon decided to solve this problem by unilaterally halting the dollar's convertibility to gold, thereby forcing appreciation of other currencies.

17 Gilpin, *Global Political Economy*, 6.

18 See, for example, David Dollar and Aart Kraay, "Growth Is Good for the Poor," World Bank, 2002, available at www.worldbank.org/research. (Accessed June 4, 2007.)

19 *New York Times*, October 25, 2006, C4.

20 Gilpin, *The Challenge of Global Capitalism*, 88.

21 Thomas L. Friedman, *The World Is Flat: A Brief History of the Twenty-First Century* (New York: Farrar, Straus, and Giroux, 2005). For a penetrating critique of this argument, see John Gray, "The World Is Round," *New York Review of Books*, August 11, 2005, 13–15.

22 Robert Gilpin argues that confidence in the liberal international economic order requires strong leadership by one or more states. In his view, the United States is the only country with the capacity to provide the necessary leadership to sustain the liberal order. See Gilpin, *The Challenge of Global Capitalism*, 346–357.

23 For a discussion of the nature and impact of the Asian crisis, see Wolf, *Why Globalization Works*, 278–304.

NOTES TO CHAPTER SEVEN

1 Robert H. Bork, "The Limits of International Law," *National Interest* (Winter 1989/90): 9.

2 Quoted in Gerhard von Glahn and James Larry Taulbee, *Law among Na-*

tions: An Introduction to Public International Law, 8th ed. (New York: Pearson Longman, 2007), 5.

3 Daniel Moynihan, *Loyalties* (New York: Harcourt Brace Jovanovich, 1984), 83.

4 James Larry Taulbee, "Preface to the Eighth Edition," in Glahn and Taulbee, *Law among Nations,* ix.

5 Michael Akehurst, *A Modern Introduction to International Law,* 6th ed. (London: Unwin, Hyman, 1987), 24.

6 The Third Law of the Sea Convention, adopted in 1982, provides for territorial waters of twelve nautical miles and an exclusive economic zone of two hundred nautical miles.

7 For a discussion of regimes, see Stephen D. Krasner, ed., *International Regimes* (Ithaca, NY: Cornell University Press, 1983), and Oran Young, *International Cooperation: Building Regimes and Natural Resources and the Environment* (Ithaca, NY: Cornell University Press, 1989).

8 Karl W. Deutsch, *Politics and Government: How People Decide Their Fate,* 3rd ed. (New York: Houghton Mifflin, 1980), 15–18.

9 Robert Kennedy, *Thirteen Days* (New York: Norton, 1968), 27.

10 J. L. Brierly, *The Law of Nations: An Introduction to the International Law of Peace,* 6th ed. (Oxford: Clarendon Press, 1954), 56.

11 Hedley Bull, *The Anarchical Society: A Study of Order in World Politics* (New York: Columbia University Press, 1977), 139.

12 Antonio Cassese, *International Law* (Oxford: Oxford University Press, 2001), 86.

13 At the end of World War I, the Allies established the League of Nations, the first major global international governmental organization, but this organization failed to inhibit aggression.

14 Cassese, *International Law,* 88.

15 Perhaps the most famous illustration of this was the yearlong London detention of Gen. Augusto Pinochet, the former Chilean president. The detention originated from a claim by a Spanish judge who requested Pinochet's extradition to Spain to stand trial for the torture and disappearance of Spanish subjects in Chile in the aftermath of the 1973 coup. Pinochet was released in March 2000, when medical authorities ruled that he was not medically fit to stand trial.

16 Stephen Krasner, *Sovereignty: Organized Hypocrisy* (Princeton, NJ: Princeton University Press, 1999).

17 Michael Mandelbaum, "The Reluctance to Intervene," *Foreign Policy* 95 (Summer 1994): 14.

18 See, for example, Michael Walzer, *Just and Unjust Wars: A Moral Argument with Historical Illustrations,* 4th ed. (New York: Basic Books, 2006), 74–108.

19 For a discussion of de Vattel's views on intervention, see Lloyd Cutler, "The Right to Intervene," *Foreign Affairs* 64 (Fall 1985): 96–112.

Notes to Chapter Eight

1 The genocide began after Rwandan president Juvenal Habyarimana was killed when his jet was downed by missiles as it was landing in Kigali.

2 David Rieff, "The Age of Genocide," *New Republic* (January 26, 1996): 31.

3 Thucydides, *History of the Peloponnesian War,* trans. Rex Warner (London: Penguin, 1971), 121.

4 George F. Kennan, "Morality and Foreign Policy," *Foreign Affairs* 64 (Winter 1985/1986): 206.

5 Arnold Wolfers, *Discord and Collaboration: Essays on International Politics* (Baltimore, MD: Johns Hopkins University Press, 1962), 58.

6 Lea Brilmayer, *American Hegemony: Political Morality in a One-Superpower World* (New Haven, CT: Yale University Press, 1994), 25.

7 Sir Harold Nicolson, *Diplomacy,* 3d ed. (New York: Oxford University Press, 1973), 147.

8 Dean Acheson, "Ethics in International Relations Today: Our Standard of Conduct," *Vital Speeches of the Day* 31 (February 1, 1965): 227.

9 Michael Walzer, *Thick and Thin* (Notre Dame, IN: University of Notre Dame Press, 1994), 1–19.

10 Walzer, *Thick and Thin,* 8.

11 Dorothy Jones, *Code of Peace: Ethics and Security in the World of Warlord States* (Chicago: University of Chicago Press, 1992).

12 Jones, *Code of Peace,* xii, 163–164. Jones argues that in addition to the nine basic principles, two supplementary norms began to emerge in the second half of the twentieth century. These two norms are regarded as auxiliary principles because they have not achieved the universal support that is found for the basic set. The two emerging principles are the creation of an equitable international economic order and the protection of the environment.

13 George Kennan, *Realities of American Foreign Policy* (New York: Norton, 1966), 48.

14 Arthur Schlesinger Jr., "The Amorality of Foreign Affairs," *Harper's* (April 1971): 72–74.

15 Schlesinger, "The Amorality of Foreign Affairs," 73.

16 The communitarian perspective is best represented by political theorists John Rawls and Michael Walzer. For an overview of their state-centered theories, see John Rawls, *The Law of Peoples* (Cambridge, MA: Harvard University Press, 1999) and Michael Walzer, *Just and Unjust Wars: A Moral Argument with Historical Illustrations,* 4th ed. (New York: Basic Books, 2006).

17 For a modern reprint of this classic, see Hugo Grotius, *On the Law of War and Peace* (Kila, MT: Kessinger Publishers, 2004).

18 For a strong defense of the cosmopolitan perspective, see Simon Caney, *Justice beyond Borders: A Global Political Theory* (New York: Oxford University Press, 2005).

19 Peter Singer, *One World: The Ethics of Globalization,* 2nd ed. (New Haven, CT: Yale University Press, 2004), 148.

20 Rawls, *Law of Peoples.*

21 John Rawls, *A Theory of Justice* (Cambridge, MA: Harvard University Press, 1971).

22 Rawls, *Law of Peoples,* 83.

23 Rawls, *Law of Peoples,* 35.

24 Rawls, *Law of Peoples,* 37.

25 International Commission on Intervention and State Sovereignty, *Responsibility to Protect: Report of International Commission on Intervention and State*

Sovereignty, December 2001, available at http://www.iciss.ca/report-en.asp. (Accessed May 30, 2007.)

26 ICISS, *Responsibility to Protect,* xi.

27 Peter Berger, "Moral Judgment and Political Action," *Vital Speeches of the Day* 54 (December 1, 1987): 179.

28 Stanley Hoffmann, *Duties beyond Borders: On the Limits and Possibilities of Ethical International Relations* (Syracuse, NY: Syracuse University Press, 1981), 143–144.

29 Michael Walzer, *Just and Unjust Wars: A Moral Argument with Historical Illustrations,* 4th ed. (New York: Basic Books, 2006), 62–63.

30 Walzer, *Just and Unjust Wars,* 81.

31 "National Security Strategy of the United States," September 2002, Section V. The 2002 NSS was updated in 2006. The new version is available at www.whitehouse.gov/nsc/nss/2006. (Accessed May 30, 2007.)

32 Kofi A. Annan, "Two Concepts of Sovereignty," *Economist* (September 18, 1999). The article is available at http://www.un.org/News/ossg/sg/stories/kaecon.html. (Accessed May 30, 2006.)

33 Rawls, *Law of Peoples,* 118.

34 Rawls, *Law of Peoples,* 106.

35 The HDI is an index based on three criteria: longevity (measured by life expectancy), knowledge (based on adult literacy and mean years of schooling), and standard of living (measured by per capita income adjusted for purchasing power parity). For the 2006 rankings, see United Nations Development Programme, *Human Development Report, 2006* (New York: Palgrave Macmillan, 2006), 283–286.

36 It is estimated that 80–90 percent of the world's energy comes from fossil fuels and that electrical power plants, cars and trucks, and households and business enterprises each produce roughly one-third of the total greenhouse gases.

37 The Kyoto Protocol established the following cuts in pollution: 8 percent for the European Union, 7 percent for the United States, and 6 percent for Japan. Significantly, no binding targets were established for China and India.

38 Jack L. Goldsmith and Eric A. Posner, *The Limits of International Law* (New York: Oxford University Press, 2005), 201.

NOTES TO CHAPTER NINE

1 Thomas L. Friedman, *The Lexus and the Olive Tree* (New York: Anchor Books, 2000).

2 Friedman, *The Lexus and the Olive Tree,* 31.

3 Friedman, *The Lexus and the Olive Tree,* 42.

4 Benjamin R. Barber, "Jihad vs. McWorld," *Atlantic Monthly* (March 1992): 53. Using this article as a foundation, Barber authored the book *Jihad versus McWorld: How Globalism and Tribalism Are Reshaping the World* (New York: Ballantine Books, 1996).

5 Barber, *Jihad versus McWorld,* 6.

6 Barber, *Jihad versus McWorld,* 8.

7 A modern container vessel can carry thousands of containers that can be

loaded and unloaded with great efficiency. Similarly, once a container is un-loaded, it is easily transported by truck or train to its final destination.

8 Thomas L. Friedman, *The World Is Flat: A Brief History of the Twenty-First Century* (New York: Farrar, Straus, and Giroux, 2005).

9 Samuel P. Huntington, "The Clash of Civilizations," *Foreign Affairs* 72 (Summer 1993): 22. For a more complete development of this argument, see Samuel P. Huntington, *The Clash of Civilizations and the Remaking of World Order* (New York: Simon and Schuster, 1996). For a critique of Huntington's thesis, see "Comments," *Foreign Affairs* 72 (September/October 1993): 2–26, and S. Huntington, "If Not Civilizations, What?" *Foreign Affairs* 72 (November/December 1993): 186–194.

10 Rather than viewing civilizations as coherent, established, and inflexible human groupings, it is best to view a civilization as a dynamic, ever-changing human movement as it adapts to changing economic, political, and social conditions. Just as Joseph Schumpeter viewed capitalism as a process of "creative destruction," so a civilization must be viewed as a continuously reforming human movement.

11 James M. Rosenau, *Distant Proximities: Dynamics beyond Globalization* (Princeton, NJ: Princeton University Press, 2003).

12 James M. Rosenau, "Globalization and Governance: Bleak Prospects for Sustainability," *International Politics and Society* (Internationale Politik und Gesellschaft) 3 (2003): 12.

13 K. J. Holsti, *Taming the Sovereigns: Institutional Change in International Politics* (Cambridge: Cambridge University Press, 2004), 318.

14 Maryann Cusimano Love, *Beyond Sovereignty: Issues for a Global Agenda*, 3d ed. (Belmont, CA: Wadsworth, 2007), 333.

15 Because democratic structures do not exist in the world, some scholars argue that global governance need not meet the domestic standards of democratic consent. For a proposal on how global governance can be reconciled with democratic legitimacy, see Allen Buchanan and Robert O. Keohane, "The Legitimacy of Global Governance Institutions," *Ethics and International Affairs* 20 (2006): 405–437.

16 For a discussion of this concept, see Robert D. Putnam, *Making Democracy Work: Civic Tradition in Modern Italy* (Princeton, NJ: Princeton University Press, 1993), Chapter 6; see also Robert D. Putnam, "Bowling Alone: America's Declining Social Capital," *Journal of Democracy* 6 (1995): 65–78.

17 The European Union is of course the boldest experiment in history to create a regional political order from twenty-seven member states. It is still too soon to determine whether sovereignty will remain in each of the member states or be centralized in an EU federal state.

18 Francis Fukuyama, *State-Building: Governance and World Order in the 21st Century* (Ithaca, NY: Cornell University Press, 2004).

19 Amartya Sen, *Development as Freedom* (New York: Knopf, 1999), 160–188.

20 Michael Mandelbaum, *The Case for Goliath: How America Acts as the World's Government in the Twenty-first Century* (New York: Public Affairs, 2005).

21 "The New Titans: A Survey of the World Economy," *Economist* (September 14, 2006): 12.

22 For a discussion of the obsolescence of major war, see John Mueller, *Retreat from Doomsday: The Obsolescence of Major War* (New York: Basic Books, 1989), and John Mueller, *The Remnants of War* (Ithaca, NY: Cornell University Press, 2004).

23 The notion of two global zones is taken from Max Singer and Aaron Wildavsky, *The Real World Order: Zones of Peace, Zones of Turmoil* (Chatham. NJ: Chatham House, 1993).

24 Rawi Abdelal and Adam Segal, "Has Globalization Passed Its Peak?" *Foreign Affairs* (January/February 2007): 107.

25 The Tour is a three-week race covering a circuit of most areas around France and often neighboring countries. Normally, the race involves twenty to twenty-two teams of nine riders each. The race is divided into some twenty stages from one town to another, each of which is an individual race. The overall winner of the race is the one with the lowest cumulative time.

26 The quadrennial Olympics are divided into summer and winter events and are held every two years. The most recent Summer Olympics were in 2004 in Athens, Greece; the most recent Winter Olympics were held in 2006 in Turin, Italy.

Index